Alex

The Authorised Biography of
SIR ALEXANDER GIBSON

Conrad Wilson

MAINSTREAM
PUBLISHING

EDINBURGH AND LONDON

First published in Great Britain in 1993 by
MAINSTREAM PUBLISHING COMPANY (EDINBURGH) LTD
7 Albany Street
Edinburgh EH1 3UG

ISBN 1 85158 574 5

A catalogue record for this book is available from the British Library

Typeset in 11/12 Lasercomp Palatino by Servis Filmsetting Ltd, Manchester

Printed in Great Britain by Bookcraft, Avon

Contents

Preface

In deference to Philip Larkin – who preferred to start reading biographies halfway through, 'when the chap's grown up and it becomes interesting' – this book about Sir Alexander Gibson begins in the present, describing him at work on a new American production of *Madama Butterfly*, one of the operas he has known longest and loves best. Yet how a Motherwell boy 'with a good ear' and an affection for Gilbert and Sullivan grew up to become Scotland's leading conductor is not something a biographer would want to ignore. The facts are worth chronicling. The trouble, I found, was that his modesty about them – as about later episodes in his life – meant that I had to prise the information out of him. Happily, there were other people's memories, as well as my own, with which to flesh out his self-effacement. Together, I hope, they form a picture, which I have entitled *Alex*, because that is what most of us call him.

Though this book is an 'authorised biography', it is also a personal memoir which is roughly, but by no means rigorously, chronological. As in my recent history of the Royal SNO, which was the orchestra he conducted for twenty-five years, I have employed a method of contemporary comparison in order to contrast, or give extra bite to, different periods in his career. Though I like to think I know Alex quite well, I have not found him a simple subject. The main events of his life are easy enough to list, the personality behind them is harder to probe. So my account is laced with comments from people he has worked with, as well as with my own thoughts on what he is like as a man and musician.

As acknowledgments these days have a way of unrolling endlessly, I shall mention just a few. People who have been particularly helpful, either in talking or writing to me, have included singers, players, friends, advisers, and colleagues old and new; most of them are mentioned by name in the course of the book. I am grateful for their help. I have tried to avoid quoting too many old reviews, preferring where possible my own recollections. But there are events – some of them occurring abroad, others early in his career – about which I do not have first-hand knowledge, and which are placed in sometimes amusing perspective by quotes from the period. His many volumes of cuttings and souvenirs, scrupulously compiled and annotated by Richard Telfer and Helen Brebner, have helped to trigger my memory, but my main source of information, all the same, has been Alex himself.

Though he does not always talk willingly, and is often away, I have spent many hours with him in recent months, most of them in his Glasgow home, where he and his wife Veronica (or 'V', as she is usually known) have been hospitality personified. Sometimes, when I have not been in touch with him for a week or two, he has phoned me to say, 'About our next meeting . . .' So maybe he has enjoyed the experience more than has sometimes seemed the case. I have tried to respect his sense of privacy yet at the same time to avoid what Robert Louis Stevenson once called 'genteel Edinburgh evasion'. He has always struck me as an admirable, if sometimes exasperating, conductor, but from either point of view he is still the best thing that has happened to music in Scotland.

The setbacks he has suffered – one or two of which must have wounded him deeply, however bravely he handled them at the time – are facts a biographer must face. His two greatest triumphs – the founding of Scottish Opera and the international expansion of the SNO – became eventually his two greatest heartbreaks. But today all this is behind him. At the age of sixty-seven, he has revitalised his career and is demonstrating, as somebody puts it in the following pages, that 'a large part of his reservoir remains untapped'.

Conrad Wilson
Edinburgh, Scotland, and Introbio, Italy, 1993

CHAPTER ONE

A Clutch of Butterflies

The scene is Louisville, Kentucky; the date October 1992. Sir Alexander Gibson has arrived in town, not to watch the Kentucky Derby (wrong time of year), not to eat Kentucky Fried Chicken (Colonel Sanders is dead and gone, though a museum, complete with his original battered cooking pot, commemorates him), not to see Blue Grass or sail down the River Ohio to the strains of Aaron Copland's Boatman's Song, but to conduct a new production of *Madama Butterfly* – the latest of many in his life – at the city's handsome modern Arts Centre.

Thanks to the internationally acclaimed Kentucky Opera, to an excellent resident symphony orchestra and ballet company, to the notable Actors' Theatre, to the visionary renovation of some of the old riverside office blocks, and to a serene art gallery dominated by a magnificent Henry Moore sculpture, Louisville has been hailed in recent years as the cultural capital of the American South. It is a good place to walk around. By American standards there is little crime.

On a mild mid-October evening, upstairs in one of the Arts Centre's large and windowless studio rooms, the Louisville Symphony Orchestra fills most of the floor. The players wear regulation rehearsal gear, mostly T-shirts, jeans, and trainers. Sir Alexander, in cream lightweight jacket and black polo neck, has been in the United States since September, first for preliminary *Butterfly* rehearsals, then for concerts featuring Nielsen's *Inextinguishable* Symphony at San José on the Pacific coast, and now back in Louisville where he is deep into his favourite Puccini opera.

Positioned around the walls of the room are some of the principal singers who will be taking part in the production, the first night of which is still a few days off. Like the orchestra, they are dressed in casual gear. Act One is already over when I creep into a seat at the side, out of view of most of the performers. The American tenor who is singing Pinkerton has mouthed the love scene silently. His voice, I am told, disappeared the previous week, and he has asked if he can remain mute until the opening night. It is a problem, but at least he is there, and he has learnt his moves in a production, by Jonathan Eaton, which is said to be blessedly straightforward. The following day the action is to shift to the main auditorium, so we shall see.

Meanwhile, the orchestra, under Gibson's direction, begins to intone the sweet music of Act Two which tells us that the abandoned Cio-Cio-San continues to live in hope. The Greek–American soprano, Marianna Christos, who is singing the role, has a voice reminiscent of Maria Callas's — expressive, slightly curdled, perceptibly below the note, though not in a disagreeable way. 'She knows she's singing flat,' Gibson says later, 'and she knows how to deal with it.'

For the moment he is not harassing her. But he is watchful. After a silent Pinkerton in Act One, he cannot make much headway with rehearsals if he has a silent Butterfly in Act Two. In the end, when the show opens, that is exactly what he is going to have, but he does not know it yet. It will not be the first Puccini crisis he has survived. For someone who had recently lost a Butterfly at short notice in Aberdeen during a run of Scottish Opera performances, it is simply business as usual. (On that occasion Act One had begun without mishap and the stand-in, Anne Williams King, had gone out for a meal, assuming that the Cio-Cio-San had recovered from the virus from which she had been suffering. But the singer's voice deteriorated and five restaurants had to be phoned before the young deputy could be found. She had been in the middle of a pizza when she was summoned back to the theatre and a few minutes later walked on to the stage to sing Act Two.) Gibson has been conducting *Madama Butterfly* for most of his professional career, and there is not much that can happen in a performance that can take him by surprise.

In any case, during this rehearsal, he is concentrating more on the youthful Louisville Symphony Orchestra than on the singers. As its name implies, it is not a full-time opera orchestra but a concert one which plays for the Kentucky Opera several times a year, just as the Scottish National Orchestra once did for Scottish Opera. Few of the players have performed *Madama Butterfly* before – Harrison Birtwistle,

10

Krzysztof Penderecki, and the fashionable John Corigliano's Symphony No 1, a ferocious American memorial to those who have died of AIDS, are more this enterprising orchestra's sort of fare – so Gibson is painstakingly teaching Puccini to them phrase by phrase. One of the nice things about the Kentucky Opera is that (as happens in all but the biggest American cities) it is a company that operates on lines very similar to Scottish Opera in the old days: seasons of four or five operas, thoughtfully chosen, scrupulously rehearsed, and imaginatively cast, make every performance a festival event, skilfully blending local and international talent, and encouraging in the process a great deal of civic pride and support.

Another nice thing is that the company is run by Thomson Smillie, a Glaswegian who served his apprenticeship as Scottish Opera's head of public relations when Gibson was artistic director and Peter Hemmings was general manager. Later, for five successful years, he ran the Wexford Festival in Ireland, which helped him to gain his first American appointment as manager of Sarah Caldwell's Boston Opera, a short but traumatic experience for him, but one which taught him a lot about how things are run in the United States.

In Louisville for the past ten years, Smillie's position has been secure. He has three theatres, of different sizes, at his disposal. He can choose his own conductors (the company has no official musical director) and he directs some of the productions himself, including a recent *Traviata* with Gibson. Indeed, since 1986 he has taken advantage of Gibson's long-established American links by inviting him to conduct a substantial Verdi cycle (five operas, including *Aida*, *Otello*, and *Falstaff*, the cream of the composer's achievement). The new *Butterfly* marks the start of a similar Puccini survey that is expected to continue with a *Bohème*, a *Girl of the Golden West*, and a *Trittico*, in the course of the 1990s, again with Gibson as conductor.

In the meantime, Sir Alex, as the players cautiously address him, is perched on a stool talking them through Act Two of *Butterfly*. Though a little wary of him on earlier visits, they have grown, says Smillie, to like their British knight, to look forward to his annual appearance, and to understand his idiosyncratic stick technique, which has long been one of his most controversial features as a conductor, in the United States as elsewhere. 'He has an elusive beat,' Smillie warned them before his first Louisville date, in 1984. And they soon found out that Gibson meant what he said when he told them that beating time was, in his opinion, strictly for bandmasters.

Yet, on this particular day, time takes its place prominently among his demands. 'Oboes, come off on the third beat, one, two, off,'

11

is a typical request. Points are sometimes emphasised in two or more languages – 'Ein, zwei, I do it in quattro' – an old Gibson ploy, which Scottish Opera players must know well. Then, to another player, he says abruptly: 'No, you must stay on, this opera is full of people having to stay on after everyone else.'

The demands grow sharper: 'C'mon, c'mon, it's pianissimo.' ('He seems a bit grumpy tonight,' Smillie whispers in my ear.) But gradually the orchestra is discovering how, Gibson style, it should shape a Puccini line. 'A tiny pause on the fourth beat, then back into tempo,' he requests, and what previously sounded square sounds suddenly eloquent. The orchestra's all-women cello section makes a fuzzy entry. 'There,' says Gibson with amusement, 'you see. That's what comes of my giving you a clear downbeat. I would like to hear more solo clarinet. That's lovely.'

The mood is relaxed. In spite of its vocal troubles, the rehearsal is going well. Though no acting is called for – it is a conductor's, not a producer's, rehearsal – the striking Greek Butterfly shows that she has the dramatic potential to give a true and touching portrayal. 'One Fine Day', Act Two's great soprano hurdle, is reached. 'Would you like to leave this? We've done it before,' asks Gibson considerately. He omits the bulk of the aria, jumps to its climax, then imitates the cheers of the audience. Now the first violins hit an awkward passage. 'Let's do it slowly, without the other instruments,' he proposes. Then, after working on it: 'Shall we do it once up to tempo or shall we leave it?' 'Once up to tempo,' says the leader. A few bars later everybody is playing too loudly. 'Piano, piano and legato' is now the command. 'At the moment it's as Brahmsian as it can possibly be. You've got to make it very soft and light.'

Now comes one of the opera's most magically lilting orchestral passages, which Gibson refers to as the Wiener Walzer. 'If I beat it clearly, it'll sound mechanical,' he says, significantly. An immense amount of time is spent over the little pauses, hesitations, and accelerations that Gibson wants here. It has to be played again and again, until finally: 'We've reached the easy bit now. We're through all the danger. But please, dolce, dolce and again dolce.'

Few people, other than performers, ever have the opportunity to see a conductor rehearse behind the closed doors of an empty theatre or concert hall. Occasional glimpses are given on television, but it is often a false picture, carefully edited, devoted to visual 'highlights' and explosive confrontations (such as Bernstein's famous one with José Carreras in the filming of West Side Story), seldom the hours of drudgery that go into making a performance.

How conductors achieve their results remains one of the mysteries of music. Some do so through arduous rehearsals of the most mechanical kind. Some say almost nothing to the players; others talk endlessly. Some use their eyes more than their hands and arms; others seem to have no eyes at all or, like Herbert von Karajan, keep them soulfully closed. Some speak in nothing but technical terms; others use imaginative figures of speech. Some are ponderously serious, others flippantly amusing. Fascinating talkers are capable of producing lifeless performances; boring ones can obtain playing that bursts with life.

What an orchestral player says about a conductor may bear no relation to what an audience hears. Players, unwillingly, will admit that sometimes it sounds different 'out front'. Some conductors work hard to gain very little. Others are said to be 'lazy' at rehearsal, to be insufficiently versed in the fine detail of the score, yet achieve miraculous playing on the night. The only rule of thumb is that there is no rule of thumb. Memorable performances seem sometimes simply to happen. All conductors, like all players, have their faults and – with luck – their virtues. Most conductors are finally disliked by their players, or even despised by them, in the way husbands and wives may feel about each other in long and no longer rewarding marriages. Yet sheer hatred has been known to bring about remarkable performances. Fritz Reiner, it is said, dealt with the Chicago Symphony Orchestra's sometimes rebellious relationship with him by reducing his beat until it became almost invisible. At the point when the players could no longer see it, he considered that he had them in his power.

Gibson has never been a tyrant of the rostrum. His principal virtues, which even his opponents are unable to deny, are that he is supremely and naturally 'musical', and that he is essentially a nice man and, by conductors' standards, uncommonly modest. Again and again, in researching this book, I have heard the word 'musical' used of him, always admiringly, sometimes grudgingly – for players detest praising conductors and, when they do, it is usually qualified.

Respect, if that is the word, is hard for a conductor to win and easy to lose. 'Oh him,' they will say of someone they have not encountered for some years. 'Is he still around? What a pity. He just gets in the way.' What he gets in the way of is seldom clear. Players who make such remarks are often the ones who object to conductors in general, to their high salaries and positions of strength, and yet who are incapable of playing interestingly on their own. Only a few conductors – Beecham being the best known example in Britain, though foreign orchestras often deemed him eccentric – successfully evade that sort of opposition.

As a critic, I have seen Alexander Gibson rehearse many times and I know he can be some of the things that conductors are accused of being. I have attended rehearsals in which nothing much seems to have happened, yet the performance has taken fire on the night. This chapter describes a not untroubled series of rehearsals of an opera he adores. It was the first opera he ever heard and it has never lost its effect on him. Yet on this occasion it was, for reasons I shall come to, an event that only partly took fire. Nevertheless his handling of the situation shows a practical and gifted musician doing what he can against difficult odds.

Gibson has never claimed to be a 'musicological' conductor. He is not specially interested in resuscitating first versions of a score, or researching a composer's original metronome markings, or opening out long-established cuts, or employing ancient instruments, unless there is a very good reason to do so. To know that there is an original version of *Butterfly*, to know what it contained, and to know why it failed, is sufficient for him. He has never had any special desire to conduct it that way, but he would not say no if an opportunity arose. After all, it is a piece that has always held him in thrall, the first version of Act One does contain some illuminating material that Puccini subsequently deleted, and he does not possess a closed mind.

But long before reaching Louisville, Gibson had insisted on one thing. He wanted to do the theatrically tighter two-act version of *Butterfly*, with no break after the Humming Chorus. It is, as most Puccini experts agree, the best way to do it, providing a real sense of continuity, but it does mean that the principal soprano's role is more arduous than in performances that incorporate an interval between the second act's two scenes.

Just how arduous it is going to be on this occasion, however, is not discovered until the day after the studio rehearsal. For the moment, with the Humming Chorus to his liking, Gibson is satisfied and the rehearsal soon ends. Cio-Cio-San rushes round to the rostrum to thank him for his help and attentiveness. 'I just love him,' she says to Lady Gibson, who has arrived that day. 'These are going to be great performances.'

Veronica Gibson, the conductor's beloved spouse, and I have reached Louisville two days apart, and by different routes – she from Glasgow via Chicago (where she has had a long wait), I ahead of her by USAir from Gatwick via Baltimore and Pittsburgh. By the time she arrives, I have heard all about her husband's visits to Louisville, and have had two late-night chats – a time, I have discovered, when he is specially communicative – with him at his hotel. He is staying, as I am, at the Seelbach, the stately downtown pile where, in *The Great Gatsby*,

14

Daisy's wedding reception was held, and where Dickens resided during his American lecture tour.

The previous evening, with a spot of freedom between rehearsals, Gibson and I had decided to hear the Louisville Symphony Orchestra give one of its first concerts that season under its own conductor, Lawrence Leighton Smith. Bizet's Symphony in C, an old Gibson favourite (he once recorded it with the Orchestre de la Suisse Romande) was in the programme, along with Strauss's *Don Quixote*, featuring a good young German cellist. Unlike some conductors, Gibson enjoys concert-going; and although, sitting beside him, you sense that he reacts a bit like a motorist when someone else's hands are on the steering wheel, he tends to be a generous listener and, in the company of a critic, tactfully keeps his thoughts to himself.

Interviewing the orchestra's administrator later, I learn that Gibson is popular with the Louisville Symphony, that the players look forward to his annual visit, that they respect his operatic know-how and would also like to give a concert with him before long. 'It's a good and long-lasting connection, and they have enormous respect for him,' I am informed.

Louisville's arts administrators are aware, however, that he is expensive – Smillie has to do some painstaking budgeting when inviting him to conduct an opera – but it is plain that he has become part of the Louisville scene. It is a long way from home, but the proud aspirations of the place must remind him of how things were in Scotland in the 1960s and '70s, before things began to go wrong with Scottish Opera, the company he founded.

To provide a further reminder, Peter Hemmings, his old colleague and administrator, drops in for a night, en route from California, where he is now in charge of the Los Angeles Opera, to New York, where he is going to see David Pountney's production of a new Philip Glass opera at the Met. Pountney, Scottish Opera's one-time director of productions and creator with Gibson of a sensational Verdi *Macbeth*, as well as of fascinatingly eccentric productions of *The Rake's Progress* and *Die Fledermaus*, has said that he, too, would like to make it to Louisville. But, in the end, Glass gets in the way.

Tendrils of Scottish Opera, as it used to be, nowadays spread right across the United States. When Hemmings took charge at Los Angeles, one of the first things he did was to invite Gibson to conduct *Madama Butterfly* there. Then he invited Roderick Brydon to conduct *A Midsummer Night's Dream*. But not everybody finds California to his taste. John Currie, after five years in charge of a Los Angeles chorus, was recently relieved to return to Scotland and run Perth Festival Opera.

15

Tuesday afternoon, in the main Louisville auditorium, reveals the *Butterfly* decor to be standard stuff, the usual flimsy Japanese summer-house with sliding panels, trees, flowers, and a view of distant mountains – a slightly larger and glossier version of what Scottish Opera offered its audiences in its very first season, back in 1962. This is not a *Butterfly* in a dilapidated tenement, as Scottish Opera now does it, nor is it an updated *Butterfly*, with an atom bomb exploding over Nagasaki, as has been favoured more than once elsewhere. It is the sort of *Butterfly* in which any singer, acting as a last-moment deputy, would feel at home, a fact that will prove invaluable a few days later when a new Cio-Cio-San has to be recruited in a hurry.

That is not to say, however, that Jonathan Eaton's production is short of fresh ideas. Each role is thoughtfully characterised, there is some deft social observation, and Kate Pinkerton, in the final scene, is very sharply portrayed. Headmistressy in demeanour, and wielding a menacing walking stick, she is obviously, in Eaton's eyes, the power behind her feckless husband's decision to return to Japan to retrieve his half-Japanese child, even at the cost of Butterfly's life.

When I arrive, after attending a witty 'lunch-and-listen' discourse on the background of Puccini's opera delivered by Thomson Smillie in a local Italian restaurant, I find that Gibson's rehearsals have backtracked to 'One Fine Day'. There is a brief hold-up. 'I'm sorry,' says a voice from the pit, 'but we have a second trumpet missing.' The music picks up again. Then, Gibson to Butterfly: 'Are you marking or singing?' ('Marking', in operatic rehearsal parlance, means doing little more than murmur the words, in order to preserve the voice). Butterfly replies: 'I was marking.' A diversion occurs when suddenly all the lights in the pit go out, provoking an outburst from the conductor. 'For God's sake,' he expostulates. 'First of all we've been told there are no dimmers in operation. Now the lights have gone off altogether and the players can't see. What is going on here?' There is a hushed silence. The lights go back on.

During a break, Gibson drinks Diet Coke from a can and asks for the bird-calls to be checked for the end of Butterfly's all-night vigil. 'Too loud,' he shouts. 'Can it be softer?' The voice of a cuckoo comes robustly in answer. There is laughter but the mood is not yet wholly relaxed. The surtitles are next to arouse concern. 'There are far too many of them,' observes Smillie. 'They make the place look like Times Square.'

The rehearsal resumes. Butterfly and Suzuki, who are too far back on the stage, say they cannot hear the orchestra when it is playing quietly. Gibson replies: 'We've got to find a happy medium. It's what we're here to rehearse for.' Jonathan Eaton proposes placing a sub-conductor in the wings. Gibson grimaces: 'No, I don't like that.' The distant voices of the Humming Chorus are also causing balance problems. 'Is it audible?' someone calls from offstage. 'No,' says Gibson, 'it's completely inaudible.' A second try provokes the comment: 'Too much, too much. It's known as the Humming Chorus, not the ooh-ing and ah-ing chorus.' A singer grumbles: 'We couldn't hear the string chord.' Gibson responds: 'Can't you just try to imagine it?'

By seven o'clock, in spite of interruptions, Gibson brings the opera to its harrowing climax. Now Act One is to be rehearsed again, but tension is noticeably growing. Butterfly steps forward and asks if she can merely mark her entrance music. Gibson says no, he wants her to sing out, because her voice is first heard off-stage and requires careful balancing. In response, she starts to walk off, eyes downcast.

'Marianna,' calls Gibson to her receding figure, 'it's really very difficult when some people are marking and some are not singing at all.' Without acknowledgment, she disappears from view. It turns out later that she has overheard an orchestral player making rude remarks about her tendency to sing flat, and it is this, combined with Gibson's demand, that has prompted her show of temperament. When she reappears she is in tears, and her servant Suzuki – now acting in earnest – tries to console her.

Word reaches Smillie, who has been attending to business elsewhere in the building, that all is not well. He enters in haste, and takes up a position at the side of the stage, ready to intervene if necessary. The crisis passes. The rehearsal flows on, with Gibson lightening the atmosphere with the odd quip or bit of praise. Cio-Cio-San seems back to normal. Everything else is going well. Finally, Gibson lays down his baton, looking pleased.

'Our troubles are over,' he says to the orchestra. 'Thank you, you've been very patient.' The players applaud him. Later Smillie says Gibson's professionalism is a godsend on such occasions. 'I have never had any doubt whom I wanted to conduct this *Butterfly*,' he adds. 'Each season, before Alex leaves, I tell him I have five more operas coming up and ask him which one he would like to do next time.' But the visits are not all solid work. There are meals *en famille* with the Smillies – who, like the Gibsons, have four offspring, all but one of them now away from home – and suppers in one or another of Louisville's good restaurants. In October the trees are as gorgeously red and gold as those of New England. A local horse-breeder called Dinwiddie, with

Dumfriesshire origins, provides rides along the banks of the River Ohio in his coach-and-four (he played a bit part, in charge of a chariot, in the *Aida* that Gibson conducted a few years ago). And art galleries are a constant lure.

With question-marks over the voices of two of the principal singers, however, there can be no respite this time until after the first performance has safely taken place. Inevitably the various 'what if' situations must be seriously discussed. Smillie receives a phone-call at home from Gibson saying that Marianna Christos remains the best option 'so long as the position does not deteriorate' (by which, one assumes, he means the state of her voice).

Gibson suggests it will be best to keep going with her and try not to damage her confidence. She gets through the first night, but it is clearly a struggle. Smillie, as a safeguard, phones another soprano to ask if she can stand by. She is Edith Davis, who fortunately lives in Louisville, has sung regularly with the company, has already worked with Gibson, and knows the role. While such delicate negotiations are in progress, Smillie wants to keep his phone line clear for urgent calls, but one of the company's financial donors manages to break through. He has attended the first night and, unaware of the vocal problems, has been so excited by it that he promises $12,000 towards the cost of the next production, which is to be Britten's *The Turn of the Screw*.

By the evening before the second performance, the crisis is not yet resolved. Gibson's long experience continues to prove invaluable. Edith Davis has been back in touch, saying that the last time she sang Butterfly was three years ago at New York City Opera and she may have a problem re-memorising it in time. 'But,' says Smillie, 'she is such a trouper that she has promised that she will sing if necessary.' Phone-calls are now flying backwards and forwards between Smillie, Gibson, and Davis. Smillie arranges a private stage and piano rehearsal for Davis for the following morning, a few hours before the performance, so that she can be coached in the role. 'Alex,' he tells me, 'will now call Edie and discuss it with her.'

For the moment, no more can be done. So with the Gibsons and Smillies I go off to a matinée of *Brief Lives*, a lengthy monologue after John Aubrey's seventeenth-century collection of vignettes, which the Actors' Theatre is staging. It is a sleep-inducing event in a stuffy theatre, but undoubtedly a calming interlude in the developing drama of the Louisville *Butterfly*. Dinner at Le Relais, a beautiful art deco restaurant built out of an aerodrome from which light aircraft still fly, inevitably involves a close analysis of the *Butterfly* situation.

Early on the morning of the Sunday matinée, Smillie phones

Marianna Christos to check on the state of her voice, and on what has now developed into a throat complaint, but finds her phone engaged. At last, by ten o'clock, he gets through and is told she is warming up, 'getting her middle register slowly into place', but is delighted to hear that Edith Davis is standing by. She says she would be happy, should she lose her voice, for Edie to sing the role from the wings, while she herself mimes it on stage. It is not an ideal solution, but worse things than this have happened in opera.

And it is what happens this time. After Act One, Smillie goes in front of the curtain to explain the situation to the audience. Edith Davis, her score on a music stand, sings from the side of the stage. Wearing a discreet dress, she is not distracting. Marianna Christos mouths the role. Yet inevitably one finds oneself turning increasingly to the actual source of the singing. The audience, as American audiences do, rises to the occasion and cheers both sopranos along with Gibson for saving the situation.

With the third and last performance looming, Christos asks for the same arrangements as before. She will again mime the long Act Two if necessary, while Davis sings from the side. But this time neither Smillie nor Gibson is prepared to go along with her. The third performance must be a proper one. Smillie consults Christos's doctor, and is told that her voice is unlikely to be back in shape. With Gibson's agreement, he decides to replace her with Davis, who will now both sing and act the role. Christos is flown out. Smillie alerts the newspapers, radio, and television to an operatic crisis resolved. 'The company has had a very narrow escape,' he informs them. The critics are invited to attend a second time. The performance takes wing. For Gibson, it may be just one more *Butterfly* for his collection, but for me it has been an enlightening example of how a truly professional opera conductor functions under conditions of stress.

CHAPTER TWO

Youth

Puccini's *Madama Butterfly* has been a running theme of Alexander Gibson's life, and one that has recurred, like a Berliozian *idée fixe*, at several crucial turning points in his operatic career. It was the first opera he ever attended, at the age of twelve, when his parents took him to Glasgow as a treat to hear Joan Hammond and Parry Jones in the leading roles. Little did he know that one day he would himself conduct the illustrious Hammond, whose recording of 'O mio babbino caro' sold more than a million copies, in the part, and that he would be instrumental in transforming the Theatre Royal into Scotland's first opera house.

Butterfly was one of the first operas he tackled as a novice conductor at Sadler's Wells in the 1950s. It was the first he conducted for the newly-formed Scottish Opera in 1962, and the last he conducted as that company's music director a quarter of a century later. When his one-time colleague, Peter Hemmings, became manager of the Los Angeles Opera in 1986, one of his first decisions was to invite his friend Alexander Gibson to conduct *Butterfly* there.

Gibson was a Motherwell boy, a pupil of Dalziel High School, when he saw *Butterfly* for the first time. But those who would like to trace the *fons et origo* of his whole career back to that early event would be frustrated in their hopes. Gibson himself does not see it that way. Yes, it was his first major operatic experience, but in terms of its long-term effect on him it could just as easily – perhaps more easily – have been one of the Gilbert and Sullivan operettas in which he took part at school, or else Smetana's *Bartered Bride*, which was the first opera he was given to conduct at Sadler's Wells. That his first childhood experience of opera happened to be *Butterfly*, rather than some other work, was something he now considers entirely fortuitous, and nobody should entertain romantic notions to the contrary.

But that, of course, is the opinion of Gibson the practical, objective musician and matter-of-fact Scot. What effect his first *Butterfly* really had on him is impossible to say, and something which, if he remembers it at all, he would not dream of disclosing. Again and again, in interviewing him for this book, I have come up against this sort of impasse. He is, as I have discovered, a man who detests any sort of false sentiment, any attempt to 'interpret' his life and find a pretty pattern in it. He would be delighted to let his career speak for itself, without frills, or psychological probing, or any attempt to link one event in it significantly with another. He would really rather not be interviewed at all, but puts up with it as a necessary evil.

It is something I learnt about him when, as a newly-appointed music critic of *The Scotsman*, I first met him in 1963. I had, as it happened, just given him two sour reviews in succession – one for Debussy's *La Mer*, the other for Beethoven's *Eroica* – and, as Kenneth Tynan used to say on meeting actors or directors he had recently savaged, 'I was prepared to flinch'. But he was friendly, not at all aloof, nor in any way 'the great conductor'. Others have given me a much harder time in such circumstances.

He never, then or later, talked down to me, though there were times, as I discovered, when he could be abrupt, and there was a reserve about him that I immediately detected, respected, and never tried to penetrate, however impatient it sometimes made me. If ever, in my questioning, I steered too close to him, he would immediately say 'I can't answer that'; or, if I pressed him too hard on some aspect of Scottish Opera or the SNO, he would rebuff me with the words, 'That's too political', by which I assumed he meant that he did not wish to be seen to be taking sides.

Partly, no doubt, this was because, for a large part of his career, he held two major appointments simultaneously in the same city, and there were rival (and increasingly sensitive) factions to be considered whenever he ventured a statement. Had his work been divided equally between Glasgow and, say, Detroit – a conductorship he once seriously considered going for – the problem would never have arisen.

There are times, indeed, when he seems unable to bear being questioned at all, when being probed by a journalist is positively painful to him, though he has always remained polite, at least to me. In

1972 for instance, on the tenth anniversary of the founding of Scottish Opera, I decided it would be nice to write a topical profile of him in *The Scotsman*. Dinner seemed a good idea, especially as the newspaper, in one of its rare moments of largesse, was willing to pay. So we met in Poachers, one of Glasgow's fashionable (but now defunct) restaurants off the Byres Road. And we got nowhere. Every question I asked was batted back at me like a cricket ball I could not catch.

Eventually Gibson said, 'This isn't working, is it?' I could not fail to agree. So we arranged to meet on the same evening the following week. By then he had had time to think about the sort of questions I had been asking, and it all went conspicuously better. I was happy because I thought I had got the article I wanted. He was happy because he thought he had retained enough, but not too much, of his privacy.

So when, twenty years later, I proposed the idea of a book – not necessarily a formal biography but certainly a detailed tribute to his achievement and a description of him as conductor and friend – I feared there would be some lack of enthusiasm on his part. The idea had come to me after one of the occasional interviews – this time about a performance of Britten's *War Requiem* he was soon to conduct at the 1991 Edinburgh Festival – with which I have continued to chronicle his career.

Our talk about Britten went exceptionally well. It was the first time for many years that I had visited him at home. He was relaxed, and so was I. On a sunny Glasgow afternoon our conversation had shifted from the drawing-room to a seat in the front garden. I had seen part of his fine collection of Scottish paintings, browsed briefly among his books, and inspected a few of the musical souvenirs that decorate the house – among them, in a silver frame on a small side-table, the photograph of a *Madama Butterfly* curtain-call at the Theatre Royal featured on the cover of this book. And I had suddenly thought it was time somebody wrote something more substantial and permanent about him than a mere newspaper article.

Gibson himself had been, on this occasion, in his most outgoing and funny form, mimicking (one of his special offstage attributes) such things as the stick technique of his old mentor, Ian Whyte, and (more pertinently) the sound of Peter Pears's tenor voice. Gradually, and without difficulty, a picture began to emerge of his long experience of the *War Requiem*, a work he had first conducted more than a quarter of a century before, laced with some fascinating anecdotes.

He talked of how he had given it its Scottish première in Edinburgh and Glasgow in the 1960s, soon after its baptism in the new Coventry Cathedral; how he had done it in Aberdeen Cathedral with the Haddo House Choral Society; how he had given it its South American première in the famous Teatro Colon, Buenos Aires, and then conducted it with the Royal Philharmonic Orchestra in the great Herod Atticus amphitheatre on the slopes of the Acropolis in Athens and, after that, in East Berlin.

Because he has never employed the sort of publicity machine favoured by other, more demonstrative, conductors, some of these episodes were ones that few people in Britain knew about. And now, with his old orchestra and with the Edinburgh Festival Chorus (which, in 1965, had been formed to take part in his performance – the Scottish première – of Mahler's Eighth Symphony) he was to conduct the *War Requiem* yet again. I wanted to know more. I wrote my article. I reviewed the performance. And in the normal way of a busy music critic's life, I went on to attend to other things.

But memories of that Glasgow afternoon persisted. I dropped him a letter, saying I had a book in mind. Would he be interested? I promised certain safeguards. Sensationalism, I reminded him, was not my line. I would not be seeking salacious detail, even if it was there to be sought. But it would be an honest book, critical as well as admiring, which would attempt to explore the personality of a conductor I liked, as well as his problems and achievements.

His response – 'I can't imagine a book about me' – was characteristic. But something had been tacitly agreed. I drafted an outline. In the end he said yes and, having done so, offered me, with typical generosity, all the time I needed to talk to him in his home surroundings, to have meals with him and his wife in their L-shaped kitchen, and to become, for sometimes eight or nine hours at a time, part of his household.

His vast volumes of press cuttings and souvenirs, over twenty of them in all, were put at my disposal, though we had agreed that the book was not to be merely an adulatory scissors-and-paste job of the sort with which the careers of other conductors are too often commemorated. Inevitably, there were times when our talks had to be temporarily abandoned, when one or other of us was away. On one occasion Gibson was conducting a series of concerts in and around Paris with a young French orchestra. On another he was in Madrid. He was surprisingly often in England, either with Scottish Opera – with which, in his role as Conductor Laureate, he had what seemed an interminable series of performances of Puccini's *Tosca* – or with a variety of English orchestras, large and small.

Guest appearances in Scotland, with the SNO during its winter season and at its summer proms, with the BBC Scottish Symphony

Orchestra in Glasgow and Stirling, and with the Scottish Chamber Orchestra at the Edinburgh Festival, were less of an interruption. Yet I did at times feel a little like the Edinburgh artist, John Houston, who in the 1980s painted a series of portraits of Gibson for the Scottish National Portrait Gallery and, through lack of continuity, gradually found his approach to the subject changing.

'The trouble,' Houston told me, 'was pinning him down. We went on for one and a half years, much too long. That's how it developed into a group of portraits, because every time I saw him he seemed slightly different. Sometimes I'd go to his house; more often he'd come to mine. I found that he liked sitting with his arms crossed. It seemed a typical pose. Or else standing with his hands in his pockets. He would come in a dark blue suit, pale blue shirt, blue tie. Sometimes I'd get a phone call to say that his rehearsal schedule had changed and he'd have to call off. He enjoyed talking and would sometimes ask, "Have you got my Chinese eyes in?". The easy bits were his hands and body – long hands, quite a strong body. I felt him to be physically quite sturdy, though he sometimes complained about his back. But his head changed dozens of times, and especially his hair. He has strong eyes, a strong jaw, but his nose is tricky [he had broken it some years before in a car accident].

'Painting him was all very enjoyable from my point of view. Occasionally he would say he didn't want to talk – he would have a score to study. People tell me he can be moody, but I never encountered it. I usually listen to music while I'm working. I'm mad about Bartók, Schubert, jazz piano. But when I was painting Alex there was no music. I didn't even suggest it. He seemed to prefer thinking about things, chatting, or working. I've known him quite a while. We first met in the early 1960s when he bought a painting of mine. A bit later he bought another. But I never really knew whether he liked the portraits or not.'

My view of Gibson, being less intensely visual than Houston's, did not change much while I was trying to capture him in words. I knew, after all, a good deal about him already, and what I did not know – including his many, often surprising and sometimes (in my opinion at least) undeserved acts of kindness to a variety of people – I discovered simply through being in his company more often than usual, or else learnt from friends of his who were willing to talk to me.

Yet just as Houston's portraits of him grew richer and more complex as they progressed – the first was a standard 'sitter's portrait', with a window in the background and the subject looking somewhat uneasy, while others were more powerful, emotional, expressionistic, thickly painted – so I too began to recognise the complexity of the man. Trying to glean his views on some of the music he conducts was inevitably difficult. His performances, he would be inclined to say, speak for themselves, for better or worse. But if you caught him at the right moment there would be sudden *aperçus*.

His memory, as is true of most conductors, is phenomenal. An off-chance chat about *The Merry Widow*, a work he has not conducted for years, revealed that his knowledge of its fine detail is as precise as ever. And he can catch you out, though never cuttingly, on any slipshod remark you may make to him about music. He remembers the contents of concerts he conducted forty years ago, and why he assembled them the way he did. Critics, too, remember such things, or should do. But whenever he and I have found ourselves in disagreement over a question of fact, such as whether I once saw him conduct in army uniform (a long-term fantasy of mine), he is usually right.

Gibson's army days I shall describe later. My false memory of a uniformed Gibson, I realise now, dates back to a time when musicians (usually Polish pianists with comprehensive repertoires of Chopin) periodically appeared in Edinburgh thus dressed. Denis Matthews, a dapper RAF officer, once played Beethoven's Fourth Piano Concerto in uniform at the Usher Hall. But on the occasion in question Gibson, who was conducting the BBC Scottish Orchestra (as it then was) in a lunchtime concert at the Music Hall, George Street, at the age of twenty-five, wore a very formal morning suit, and it was probably the incongruity of his striped trousers and tails, making him look as if he was en route to a wedding, that had stuck in my memory and transformed itself into army uniform.

That performance was his first Edinburgh appearance, and my first sight of him, though as Ian Whyte's assistant he had already made many a broadcast which, as an avid radio listener, I had heard. It was also one of my first outings as a junior critic, for at the time I was receiving my journalistic training on the old Edinburgh *Evening Dispatch*, which, before its merger with the *News*, was a serious paper with aspirations akin to London's *Evening Standard*. It gave lavish space to critics, and I seized my opportunities, even being permitted to go to Covent Garden for the Munich Opera's great Richard Strauss season in 1953 – something that would be unthinkable under that newspaper's present policy.

But if I forgot what Gibson wore that day, I do remember what he conducted. I shall be honest and say that I had gone hoping to hear Ian Whyte, whose work on behalf of music in Scotland I had admired from my early schooldays. But Whyte, as was so often the case in the years before his untimely death, had backed out through illness, and Gibson had replaced him. The concert was poorly attended, because the BBC, as usual, had been weak on publicity. In any case, even with Mendelssohn's *Hebrides* overture to launch it, the programme was not quite to Edinburgh's polite lunchtime taste (the Music Hall had served since 1947 as the Edinburgh Festival Club, where Morningside ladies sipped afternoon tea).

The works that succeeded the Mendelssohn were Busoni's *Tanzwalzer*, David Stephen's *Coronach*, and – in tribute to Edinburgh's most influential musical figure – excerpts from Donald Francis Tovey's opera, *The Bride of Dionysus*. Gibson's programming has always been bold whenever practicable, even when, as here, the gaunt Scottish presence of Ian Whyte could be detected behind it. But whether initially influenced by Whyte or not, he has always been prepared to put Scotland first, something no other musical director of the SNO, either before or since Gibson's time, has been prepared to do.

And what, in 1952, did the prentice music critic say in his first review of the prentice conductor? 'Clear-minded and logical,' I wrote the next day in a half-column review. 'One hopes to hear more of Mr Gibson.'

But if Whyte, as senior conductor of the BBC Scottish Orchestra, was Gibson's boss, he was not entirely Gibson's mentor. Though each had a passion for the music of Sibelius, and each brought an identifiably 'Nordic' personality to symphonic music in general, they otherwise had little in common.

Whyte naturally creamed off the works he himself wanted to do, and left the residue to Gibson. Yet the atmosphere of the BBC's Glasgow studios at that time must have been inspirational in its way. Whyte, even if he kept himself to himself, bred a remarkable stable of youthful talent. Colin Davis was another young conductor who, having been Whyte's assistant, went on to bigger and better things; and Bryden Thomson, Andrew Davis, and Simon Rattle were three more who were later to hold the assistant conductor's post.

Whyte himself had an imposing repertoire and a fine sense of symphonic structure that must have rubbed off in some way on all who worked with him. Yet those who suggest that Gibson learnt about Sibelius through Whyte have got it wrong. Gibson recalls borrowing Sibelius scores from Motherwell Public Library long before he came under Whyte's aegis, and listening enthralled to Warwick Braithwaite conduct Sibelius performances with the SNO in St Andrew's Hall during the Second World War.

He remembers his first encounter with the Seventh Symphony, via a pale-blue Hansen pocket score, as one of the milestones of his adolescence. Later, as a student, he borrowed Sibelius discs from the Royal Scottish Academy of Music's library. But once he was working with the BBC Scottish, it was soon made clear to him, he says, that 'Sibelius was something for Whyte to handle'. Whyte, during Gibson's period, conducted all but the Fourth and Seventh Symphonies, and I myself recall that, during my schooldays, he was forever broadcasting the symphonic poem, *En Saga*, a work with which he seemed to have some mystical identification.

But if all this must have frustrated, or at least tantalised, a young conductor eager to conduct Sibelius himself, Gibson soon got his chance. When, in 1959, he became musical director of the SNO, his first act was to programme all seven symphonies. Today, his Sibelius is internationally esteemed. He has been awarded Scandinavia's prestigious Sibelius Medal, and when he was invited to become principal guest conductor of the Houston Symphony Orchestra it was for his Sibelius performances that his services were specially sought.

From Whyte, he says, he learnt more about Dvořák and Brahms. 'I remember going out to see him at Milngavie, when he was very ill, and going over Dvořák's D minor Symphony with him. He was very good, discussing the score with me, much more helpful than when I was his assistant. He tended to be more confrontational when I was actually working with him, and was apt to bring up pointless little arguments, for instance about Rossini's overture to *The Barber of Seville* in the days before there were so many ur-texts available.'

Imitating Whyte's craggy Scottish voice, Gibson has given me an idea of one of their Rossini conversations:

Whyte: 'That is how you should conduct it because that is how the greatest Italian conductor, Toscanini, conducted it.'

Gibson: 'On his recording?'

Whyte: 'Yes, irrefutable evidence of how he conducted it.'

Gibson: 'But surely it depends on which of his two recordings? Even Toscanini was known to change his mind.'

So risky a remark must have taken courage. Whyte, as Gibson admits, could be intimidating. Once, when he had been given the opportunity to conduct Brahms's Second Symphony (today a pillar of the Gibson repertoire) he was quizzed beforehand, with rolling r's, by the senior conductor.

Whyte: 'Do you know your score? How do you describe the first bar on the cellos and basses?'

Gibson: 'Do you mean by that question that the first bar is not the first bar but really the fourth bar if you think in four-bar phrases – in other words an anacrusis?'

Whyte: 'Precisely. It is an anacrusis [an unstressed note at the start of a musical phrase], though it does not sound like one when Barbirolli conducts it. Paa-ra-ra – utterly banal, boy.'

In this way they went through the music together, note by note, until in the end Whyte said darkly: 'Well, you seem to have the technicalities right. But do you know what it means in the face of God, laddie?'

There was, as Gibson knew, no answer to that. But today he remembers above all the precision of Whyte's ear. 'He was a very honest musician, almost too honest, obsessed by intonational accuracy which he couldn't always achieve.'

This would sometimes lead to another dialogue:

Whyte: 'You know, boy, I could teach you to have absolute pitch in a few weeks, because, when you sing a phrase to me, it is always in the right key.'

Gibson: 'Yes, but if I'm asked to sing an "A" I have to think about it, and I'm not always right.'

Whyte: 'You could do it if you wanted to.'

Gibson: 'But sometimes it can be more a drawback than a blessing, as when a choir starts to sink in pitch.'

Whyte: 'Aye, on reflection I think you're better off with a keen sense of relative pitch, which, thank God, you've got.'

Gibson's musical apprenticeship began when, at Dalziel High School, it was discovered that he, too, had 'a good ear'. Like most aspects of his childhood, Gibson's schooldays are a subject about which he is reticent, but he appears to have both enjoyed and to have benefited from them. Recalling as I did a conversation with Peter Susskind, Walter Susskind's son, who once disclosed to me that his only memories of his period at a Glasgow school were the beatings he had witnessed, and of a similar talk with Donald Runnicles, who endured what he described as a 'reign of terror' at one long-established Edinburgh school before he was sent to another, I must have visibly raised a sceptical eyebrow at Gibson's words. At any rate, he returned to the subject the following day. He said he had thought seriously about what I had asked him, but felt bound to reiterate that his schooldays were unclouded. He was encouraged from the start in the subjects he was good at, English and German as well as music. And when music became dominant in his life, no barriers were placed in his way, as they might easily have been in a country that continues to regard music as peripheral (John Ogdon once told me that Manchester

Grammar School – hardly, you would think, an inartistic establishment – did its utmost to stop him becoming a pianist).

Since Gibson does not come of specially musical parentage, and was an only child, there was nobody to steer him, Tortelier-fashion, into fanatical family music-making, or to plan a musical career for him, or to plead with a perhaps unmusical headmaster on his behalf. Nevertheless, he says that his mother, Wilhelmina Williams, the daughter of a Welsh miner who moved north to the steelworks of Motherwell when there was no work to be had in North Wales, had a natural ability to sing, and encouraged her son to take up music. She was a contralto and possessed a good enough voice to be a chorister and to take part in church concerts.

His father, James McClure Gibson, was a Lanarkshire man who possessed a lifelong devotion to music. He was, says Gibson, 'very sensitive', even though – 'like Dvořák's father' – he was a butcher by trade, working in the 'fleshing' department of the Dalziel Co-op. James Gibson would have liked to become 'a small businessman', but his hopes were frustrated by high blood pressure and recurrent malaria after serving with the Highland Light Infantry in India in the First World War.

At home young Alexander was usually addressed as Alec, and sometimes, in the Scottish way, as 'Son'. On the lid of his piano, I have noticed, there are pieces of music with the name Alec Gibson signed, obviously many years ago, in ink. When he moved to England, first as a soldier and then to study at the Royal College of Music in London, he became Alex, and that is the abbreviation that has stuck. He was seldom called Sandy, and those who today refer to him in that way can be assumed not to be close friends.

Though his mother was the more musical of his parents, he recalls that his father loved to hear him singing and playing the piano, especially Schubert's G flat Impromptu and the B flat variations – his father's favourite pieces. He recalls, too, that there was a clarinettist on his father's side of the family, and that his Uncle Eddy, a merchant seaman who lived across the street, had a pedal organ which his father sometimes played by ear (he never learned to read music).

On his mother's side, the stock was sturdy. His grandfather would walk ten miles from Tollcross in Glasgow to Stewart's and Lloyd's steelworks in Motherwell – a journey that entailed rising at three in the morning to be in time for the six o'clock shift. But his father died while still in his fifties. Later, when he was a student at the Royal College of Music, his mother moved to London to be nearer him, taking a job in the dress department of Barkers in Kensington, and remaining there, proud and independent, into her grand old age. When Gibson received his knighthood, in 1977, she joined him and his wife at the Buckingham Palace ceremony.

The Gibsons, it is obvious, were a close-knit family; and though the young conductor's meteoric career soon took him into exciting new pastures – to classes in Salzburg and Siena as well as in London and Glasgow – he now regrets that he saw much less of his father than he would have liked. 'Around the age of fifteen and sixteen, in particular, I was spending so much time at school and elsewhere playing the organ in churches of practically every denomination that I didn't seem to spend much time at home.'

He was, clearly, a much appreciated son. When his earliest music teacher, Miss Isobel Taggart of New Stevenston Primary School, realised that at the age of seven he could sing in tune, she went immediately to his parents and informed them he was talented. Was there, she asked, a piano in the house? She thought it would be a good idea if he could have lessons. So a piano was acquired, and young Alec was sent to study under Miss Lilian Wright in Motherwell. Miss Taggart, who had picked him out of a class of thirty, must have been delighted that her diagnosis of his potential was to prove so accurate. Soon, thoroughly grounded in Mozart Allan's *Catechism of Music*, he was playing in Miss Wright's pupils' concerts and passing Associated Board examinations with distinction. Miss Wright, he says, was a 'big influence' on his early development.

But in school activities, too, he seems to have been an asset. True, sport was not his scene, and journalists who write from time to time of his 'mean' game of tennis could be said to be indulging in wishful thinking. He has never had Colin Davis's enthusiasm for cricket, nor Claudio Abbado's for football, and he was fifty years old before he learned to swim (when, taking advantage of the honorary doctorate he received from Glasgow University, he began to make use of the university pool).

His flair was quite simply for music. His ability to keep time and sing in tune made him popular with the school's Gilbert and Sullivan society, which staged an annual production with a children's cast. Gibson, at the age of fourteen, played the Major General in *The Pirates of Penzance* and later, more ambitiously, he sang baritone to Duncan Robertson's tenor in *The Gondoliers*. The fact that his fellow gondolier went on to become a distinguished professional singer speaks well for Dalziel High School's musical education. When, years later, Gibson formed Scottish Opera, Robertson was regularly invited to take part, most memorably and touchingly as the simpleton in *Boris Godunov*.

But his uncle's pedal organ was a special inspiration, and with encouragement from another of his school teachers, 'Taffy' Johnson – so nicknamed because of his reliance on the musical nomenclature that depends on rhythmic expressions like 'taffetiffy' – he became an adept performer. Johnson was organist at Brandon United Free Church in Motherwell and Gibson soon became his deputy. During his wartime boyhood he used to cycle the two miles from New Stevenston in the blackout to practise in the darkened church before school. 'At that time,' he says, 'I was anxious to get somewhere, anywhere, that had an organ,' and he collected and annotated organ specifications the way other boys collected stamps.

By his third year at Dalziel, he had to make a firm decision about where his education was going. Though he was winning plenty of prizes (including one, surprisingly, for woodwork) his desire to take Higher Music governed everything else. This meant sacrificing German, which he regretted, in order to continue with Latin for Glasgow University entry. Music, however, seemed by now to be occupying almost his every thought.

On Saturdays, with a group of friends from Motherwell, he would go to hear the Scottish Orchestra (as it was then known) in Glasgow. Aylmer Buesst and Warwick Braithwaite were his boyhood conductors; and though he was too late to benefit from George Szell's disciplined readings of the classics (he was only thirteen years old when Szell left for America in 1939), perhaps something of Buesst's devotion to Wagner may have communicated itself to him.

Buesst, an Australian who had become an authority on *The Ring* with the by then defunct British National Opera Company, must have found it hard during the war years to indulge in his Teutonic passion, but his Scottish Orchestra programmes nevertheless continued to be littered with Wagnerian titbits, even while the Wehrmacht was advancing on Leningrad. His successor Braithwaite, however, was the one who found the young Gibson in his most responsive frame of mind, especially if Sibelius or Walton was being performed. But even Boccherini's Minuet – played on muted strings, the way people like Yuri Temirkanov now do it as an encore piece – still sticks in his mind.

His most special memory, however, was of being taken by his uncle to hear Solomon play Schumann's Piano Concerto, a work he himself was to play at a time when his career might have made him a concert pianist. A little later he was to attend Walter Susskind's opening concert, with that special favourite of Gibson's, Brahms's Second Symphony, in the second half. Some of these events he heard from the North Gallery of St Andrew's Hall – the auditorium in which,

31

twenty years later, he would be one of the three conductors in the British premiere of Stockhausen's *Gruppen* – and others in the vast reaches of Green's Playhouse, which the orchestra rented for its more popular programmes.

At school he had always wanted to form a musical society, but the closest he got to this was organising concerts in the gymnasium with the encouragement of his teachers, and getting the four 'houses' – Avon, Brandon, Clyde, and Douglas – to compete with each other chorally. Gibson himself conducted choruses from *Carmen* and Sibelius's *Valse Triste* in the form of a ballet.

The piano was by now looming large in the teenager's life, and he was lucky enough to be taken on as a pupil of Wight Henderson, who taught at the Royal Scottish Academy of Music and who, as an exemplary recitalist, convinced many another would-be pianist (myself included) that the leathery tone he brought to Beethoven and Schubert was something worth trying to emulate. Gibson says Henderson was more than a piano professor: 'He was really interested in the wider aspects of music and conveyed them to me in his lessons.'

Henderson used to speculate on why Gibson was almost obsessively anxious to gain diplomas. In fact, at this time, he was determined to prove to his father, before being conscripted into the army, that music was worth taking up as a career, and obtaining qualifications seemed the best, as well as a very Scottish, way of doing so. If the worst came to the worst, he could always fall back on teaching, as so many others have done.

Did he ever, I asked him, think of becoming a professional pianist rather than a conductor? Gibson admits that, while still in his teens, that was where his ambitions lay. The thought of playing concertos attracted him enormously. And practical piano playing – accompanying at all sorts of concerts, playing the piano for choirs – occupied much of his time. 'I thought that one day I might get interested in conducting, but I believed that I had to prove myself as a practical all-round musician first, and then see what might happen.'

Nor, at this time, did he forget about the organ. This was something that meant enough to him to persuade him to acquire practice pedals to place beneath his piano, and he managed to become a pupil of Wilfred Emery at Glasgow Cathedral. At the age of seventeen he applied to be organist at Hillhead Congregational Church, whose minister, Vera Kenmure, was the first woman to be ordained in Scotland. There he gave the first performance of a sonata by Derek Lisney, one of the Scottish Orchestra's hornists, and his Saturday trips to Glasgow to hear the orchestra perform at St Andrew's Hall were now extended to Sunday duties at Hillhead.

But by now, in 1944, Gibson's army service was approaching, and he became even more eager to 'get some kind of qualification' before being called up. So, as a pianist, he sat and passed his performers' LRAM. For an organ qualification as well, he headed to Euston by train and thence to the Royal College of Music, 'which had a replica organ on its top floor, where you could book a session in order to practise the right registrations but were at your own risk if an air-raid warning went off. In fact, if you were playing the organ, you couldn't possibly hear the sirens, but I took the risk.' In the course of the paperwork examination the next day in the Royal College of Organists, two flying bombs landed, one on each side of the college. In that perilous way, Alexander Gibson became an Associate of the Royal College of Organists.

CHAPTER THREE

Army Days

You can always identify army bandsmen, it is said, by their air of untidiness and inability to march properly. Malcolm Rayment, when he was music critic of *The Herald*, once confirmed this for me, to his own deep satisfaction, on a trip to the Warsaw Autumn Festival, at which Alexander Gibson and the Scottish National Orchestra were performing. Rayment, an ex-bandsman himself, drew my attention to some Polish troops on parade near the opera house. Those carrying rifles marched immaculately. Those playing wind instruments had their caps at odd angles and were incapable of keeping a straight line. 'There,' remarked Rayment, 'you see, just like everywhere else.'

Alexander Gibson's army years, from 1944 until 1948, had a vein of comedy running through them, reminiscent of episodes in one of Kingsley Amis's early comic novels. On the principle that the armed forces put people into the jobs least fitted for them, Gibson might have ended up mending boots in Middle Wallop. But if, at one point, he did very nearly become a marine, it was pure musical expediency that attracted him in that direction. He had his eyes and ears not so much on potential overseas heroism as on membership of the Royal Marines Band.

At one time this was the British band of all bands. Kenneth J. Alford, composer of *Colonel Bogey* and *On the Quarterdeck*, had been its director of music from 1930 onwards under his real name, Frederick Joseph Ricketts. But Britain's great bandmaster, hailed by the *New Grove* as superior to Sousa, had retired just as Gibson was called up (he subsequently died one week after VE Day). Yet the Marines Band remained a glorious institution, and was perceived by Gibson to be the best possible substitute for the RAF Central Band, to which Britain's musical élite had begun to gravitate during the war. That was where the likes of Dennis Brain, Norman Del Mar, and Denis Matthews could be found.

Yet wherever they end up, musicians in the forces usually manage to preserve something of their own individuality. The story goes that Harry Blech, future conductor of the London Mozart Players, arrived on parade by taxi. Gibson, certainly, found his own musical Eldorado, though not immediately, and not until he was wisely advised that his destiny lay in the Royal Signals Band (over which Frederick Ricketts's brother, composer of *The Contemptibles*, had presided).

Being a pianist, however, Gibson was faced with a problem. Brain and Del Mar were both hornists, but pianos can hardly be taken on parade. Happily for Gibson, military bands do more than march, and one of their frequent functions during and after the war was playing in bandstands. There is a story of how Ivor Newton, the distinguished British accompanist who had been on many a pre-war recital tour with Gigli and Casals, was sauntering along the Eastbourne seafront one afternoon in the 1940s when he heard the strains of Beethoven's Third Piano Concerto wafting from the bandstand. He paused in surprise. The string parts, disconcertingly, were being played by wind instruments, but at least there was a solo piano, and what sounded like an able performer. The pianist was Alexander Gibson.

Since to be accepted as a bandsman you had also to be adept on a more mobile instrument, Gibson astutely developed a flair for the clarinet. His other orchestral instrument was the cello, which he studied at the Scottish National Academy of Music with Grace Dick. After a variety of false trails and unmusical postings, he ultimately became a member of the Royal Signals Band at Catterick, in the North of England, which was filled with Hallé players at the time. It was a busy band. There were not only bandstand assignments but also troop entertainments and broadcasts to occupy its time. Its status, moreover, was sufficiently high that when the war ended it was shipped to Germany to play for the forces of occupation.

During Gibson's period as a bandsman, Lance-Corporal Clifford Knowles, a peacetime leader of the Liverpool Philharmonic Orchestra, provided invaluable help. It was he who made the arrangements of Beethoven's Third and Fourth Piano Concertos, the Mozart D minor Piano Concerto, the Grieg and Schumann concertos, the Rakhmaninov Second and the ubiquitous *Warsaw Concerto* by Richard Addinsell that together were soon to form the bulk of Gibson's repertoire. In seaside resorts, he says, he would play the slow movements in the afternoon 'when all the old ladies were asleep' and save the more spirited movements for the evening. The finale of Mozart's D minor, accompanied 'mostly by clarinets', must have sounded more like a wind serenade than the concerto we all know. Scarborough, Southport, and Weymouth were on the sunny itinerary, in addition to Eastbourne. The only cloud over this idyllic existence was the sudden illness and death of his father; Gibson was temporarily released to take an overnight train to Motherwell but arrived home just too late to see him alive.

Even before becoming a bandsman, however, Signalman Gibson had led a charmed army career, which had incorporated a radio mechanics' course in Huddersfield. Today he remains fascinated by electronic gadgets; he travels with the most up-to-date cassette players, drives a SAAB not only for its qualities as a car but for its acoustical potential, and pours music into his study through the best and most up-to-date Quad electrostatic speakers.

While in Huddersfield he watched Sir Malcolm Sargent record *The Dream of Gerontius* — later to be a pillar of Gibson's own substantial Elgar repertoire — with Heddle Nash and Gladys Ripley as soloists with the Liverpool Philharmonic and the Huddersfield Choral Society in the Town Hall. A carpet firm had lent rolls of carpet to soak up the sound ('the opposite of now, when they're looking for resonance') and the music had all to be divided up beforehand, with markings indicating where to stop, so as to fit the four-minute sides of the old black shellac 78 r.p.m. discs (*Gerontius*, when completed, required a dozen such discs and weighed as much as a few volumes of *Grove's Dictionary*).

Sargent, as always, was meticulous in matters of timing and, says Gibson, 'he tore a strip off Nash, who had become very emotional during the *Sanctus Fortis*, clutching his score to his chest and forgetting to stop singing at the four-minute side change'. Gibson's memory of the episode inspires one of his most wicked acts of mimickry, with Sargent's clipped, impatient voice being brought back to life as he says: 'It's absolutely ruined, ruined. Everyone, get your pencils out.' Nevertheless, Nash's recording of the passage was subsequently praised for its 'beseeching passion'.

From Huddersfield, where he had found time to play the organ for services in Huddersfield Parish Church, Gibson returned to Catterick but had yet to find his proper *métier* in the army. It was now thought that he might be suitable Intelligence Corps material, thanks to his knowledge of French and German and the fact that the musical diplomas he had gained in Scotland demonstrated an ability to apply himself. So he signed to do an officer's training course on Anglesey, where pistol shooting and motor-bike riding turned out to be higher priorities than intellectual pursuits.

After losing the bolt from his rifle, and having a day's pay stopped, a post in the Seaforth Highlanders Band seemed a happier prospect ('just say your father was in the Seaforths and you'll get in', he was advised), with the Royal Marines Band as an alternative. So he consulted some of his contacts to see if there were any vacancies. On hearing that the Marines needed a pianist, he applied to see the commanding officer who, though ill in bed, was prepared to interview him. A transfer was possible, he was told, as he stood to attention at the invalid's bedside. The snag was that he would have to be ready to go on active service at any time, and would have to possess musical versatility. 'In this outfit,' he was informed, 'a viola player plays the saxophone, a pianist plays the flute, so you would have to be prepared to double.'

Noting that Gibson was in the Signals, the officer said he would surely be far better applying to join his own band. So back he went to Catterick, only to find that the Royal Signals Band was away on a tour of the bandstands of England. Nevertheless, he was again granted an interview. 'Signalman Gibson,' he was asked, 'do you know the standard concertos from memory? If you don't, you've got two months in which to learn them, plenty of time in which to do so.'

He soon found out that he would also have to learn the bizarre amendments that had been made to some of them. The ending of the first movement of Schumann's Piano Concerto, for instance, was considered too abrupt in army circles, so a more acceptable alternative had been devised. If Signalman Gibson was not prepared to learn it, he would be put on a charge. Once, in Eastbourne, Gibson says he genuinely forgot to incorporate it, and left a huge gap at the point where it was normally included. Fortunately the conductor – 'wearing spurs and black trousers with red stripes' – thought that he himself had caused the mishap, so Gibson escaped retribution.

But on one occasion he did find himself on a charge for blatant insubordination. It was a day when the rest of the band had gone off to play *Music While You Work*, the BBC's regular morning radio programme of popular favourites, for which the players had to be driven to Leeds. Gibson's services not being required in the broadcast, he stayed behind to practise his concertos. But no sooner had he started to play than a formidable ex-trumpeter, a regular soldier called Sergeant Skinner, immediately thundered into the room and told him to scrub the floor.

'I've got music to do,' Gibson retorted. He was instantly charged. 'I ordered him to scrub,' Skinner later reported to the commanding officer, 'and he replied that he had no intention of scrubbing.' When the rest of the bandsmen returned from Leeds, they were dumbfounded to learn that Signalman Gibson had been sentenced to a week's jankers.

The next day Gibson told his bandmaster that he would rather resume officer training if he was going to be treated that way just for practising the piano. As a result he was taken off jankers and returned to his role as solo pianist with the Royal Signals Band for the remainder of his military service.

His subsequent studies at the Royal College of Music in London seem in some respects to have been not so very different. Armed with the Caird Scholarship he had won during his year at the Royal Scottish Academy of Music immediately before call-up, he applied to join the college's conducting class, only to be told (in the classic manner of Joseph Heller's *Catch-22*, a novel not yet written) that because he was a pianist he was not eligible to conduct. In 1948, it seemed, everybody wanted to be a conductor, an ambition the authorities seemed determined to thwart.

On learning that there was no space available in the conducting class, Gibson decided it was time to take the initiative. So he formed his own student orchestra, rehearsing it in premises outside the college. When, ultimately, he was appointed conductor of the official Student Association Orchestra, he succeeded in joining the conducting class under the tuition of Richard Austin, founder of the New Era Concert Society and conductor of the first British performance of Mahler's Tenth Symphony in its incomplete version. But though Gibson prudently continued his piano studies with Lance Dossor, accompaniment with Eric Gritton, and worked on composition and orchestration under Gordon Jacob, it was as conductor of the Student Association Orchestra that he felt the greatest pride, especially as the students themselves had voted him into his role. 'It was no bad thing to be chosen,' he says today. 'My biggest critics were my fellow students.'

His conducting of a student performance of *Così fan tutte*, his most ambitious effort so far, made history because he employed his own orchestra rather than the two-piano accompaniment traditionally used by the college for such events. This revolutionary act put him into temporary disgrace, but undoubtedly strengthened his operatic ambitions, which were now steadily growing. In any case he possessed what he recognised to be 'the temperamental qualities of leadership which have to be there in the first place'. There was a world of difference, he was becoming aware, between conducting and playing the piano. 'I could see that conducting, apart from the purely technical side of stick technique or beating time, is very much a question of developing your own personality or, as a novice, watching and comparing notes with your fellow students who are not actually your mentors.'

As evidence of this, he cites his period as a pupil of Igor Markevitch at the Salzburg Mozarteum, which was his reward in 1950 for winning the Tagore Gold Medal as the college's best student of his year (the *Hamilton Advertiser*, getting wind of this, reported to its readers that the young musician had been presented with his award by Princess Elizabeth and 'had the honour of having tea with her and the college professors in a private room').

At Salzburg he studied alongside Wolfgang Sawallisch, today one of Germany's leading conductors, and this, he says, was in its way just as important as having Markevitch as his teacher. 'With Sawallisch and one or two others, I found myself discussing conducting methods, appraising Markevitch himself, and learning that what suits one pupil may not suit another pupil of entirely different mental make-up or physical build.'

During his last years at the Royal College of Music, much of Gibson's experience was of chamber music, just as Sawallisch's also was in Germany (the young Duo Seitz Sawallisch, with Sawallisch as pianist, came more than once to Tertia Liebenthal's pioneering lunchtime concerts at the National Gallery, Edinburgh, in the 1950s). At college recitals in London, Gibson played the piano in performances of violin sonatas by Brahms, Walton, and Malcolm Arnold, with Tessa Robbins among his partners, and accompanied Britten's folk-song arrangements, which at the time were regarded as rather racy.

England's music clubs, gaining momentum after the war, proved another useful source of experience. A clarinet recital by Gervase de Peyer at Leicester Museum and Art Gallery, with 'Alec Gibson' as pianist, featured music by Brahms, Mendelssohn, Finzi, and Shostakovich; and at Keble College, Oxford, he shared with George Stratton (a former leader of the LSO and founder of the Stratton String Quartet) a programme entitled 'The Development of the Violin', again with Brahms and Mendelssohn prominently featured.

In London he played piano trios, with Hugh Bean as violinist and Dorothy Browning as cellist, at Overseas House, St James's. Saffron Walden Music Club heard him accompany the baritone Gordon Clinton, future principal of the Birmingham School of Music, in Mozart arias interwoven with solo piano pieces by Debussy and Shostakovich.

But the fact that he won the college's senior conducting prize for the year 1949–50 showed where his aspirations really lay. And a concert with the Student Association Orchestra in aid of the Lord Mayor of London's National Thanksgiving Fund – in gratitude for the £80 million of food parcels that had been sent from the Commonwealth and the United States during and immediately after the war – gave him his first, but certainly not his last, opportunity to conduct Elgar's *Enigma Variations* and *Sea Pictures*, with the warm-voiced Nancy Evans, who had been the first to sing the role of Nancy in Britten's *Albert Herring*, as contralto soloist. The pianist in Brahms's Second Piano Concerto, which completed the programme, was Lance Dossor, Gibson's professor from the Royal College of Music. The event prompted John Amis, *The Scotsman*'s London music critic, to declare that 'Alexander Gibson, though still a student, has a thorough grasp of the art of conducting'.

Other concerts he conducted featured interesting contemporaries. Lamar Crowson, later to play with the Melos Ensemble, was pianist in Turina's *Rapsodia Sinfonica*, an attractive snapshot of Spain long since dropped from the repertoire, and John Warrack, who would later become an outstanding music critic with the *Sunday Telegraph* and author of a fine book on Weber, was cor anglais soloist in Gordon Jacob's *Rhapsody*.

But Salzburg was not the only opportunity for a spot of foreign training that Gibson's success as a student provided. He also had the perhaps more dubious, and certainly briefer, benefit of tuition from Paul van Kempen, the Dutch conductor and Nazi sympathiser who had been Herbert von Karajan's successor at the Aachen Opera during the Second World War.

Finding himself understandably unpopular when he returned to his homeland, Van Kempen was running a conducting class at the Accademia Chigiana in Siena when Gibson came under his aegis in 1952. By the time the opportunity presented itself, Gibson had served as a *répetiteur* at Sadler's Wells and was already Ian Whyte's assistant conductor in Glasgow. A Caird Travelling Scholarship still seemed a feasibility and Gibson duly applied for one to cover his fees and fares. Since Whyte was a trustee at the time, Gibson sought his master's advice. He has reconstructed their dialogue as follows:

Gibson: 'I'd like to go to Siena for six weeks this summer to study under Paul van Kempen. I've applied to the Accademia Chigiana and been accepted. Could I take my holiday at that time, and also have some extra time off?'

Whyte: 'Laddie, I want to explain about the Caird Scholarship. I'm sympathetic to the idea, but because you're in work, earning good money, I have to say that there are more deserving cases.'

Gibson: 'It's not a question of money. For me it's really a question of time. Can I delay my return from holiday in order to do this?'

Whyte: 'What about your Glasgow dates? Dates are things you have to do. You can't get round them.'

Gibson: 'But supposing it's possible to fit Siena in?'

Whyte: 'If the Caird grant isn't possible, will you still go? Will you drive there?'

Gibson: 'Oh no.'

Whyte: 'What will you do, then, boy? How will you get there?'
Gibson: 'I'll fly. I'll get the money from somewhere.'

Whyte's final questions, as the fledgling conductor discovered, were the ones that really mattered. Always a car enthusiast, Gibson was the proud possessor of what was known as a 'honeymoon' car, a stunning cream-coloured two-seater Morris Isis with – a financial consideration at the time – an Irish registration number IN 3120. 'With a British number, an eighteen-horsepower car such as this would have cost me the earth to register.' The dour Whyte, it turned out, coveted his assistant conductor's flamboyant car. As soon as he ascertained that Gibson might not be using it during the summer, conducting lessons in Siena became more feasible.

'So,' Whyte mused, 'you won't be using your car. Can I borrow it?' Whyte had his mind on a congenial tour of the Highlands. Gibson said yes and set off for Siena, but the hassle of getting there proved too much for him. On arrival he went down with a tummy bug, which Van Kempen sought to cure with glasses of grappa, the lethal Italian fire-water which, to quote Henry McNulty's book on liqueurs and spirits, needs 'a fairly hardy constitution to take as a regular beverage'.

Recovering from both the bug and the cure, Gibson was taught how to start Beethoven's Fifth Symphony – whose four opening notes are a notorious hurdle for conductors even of Karajan's expertise – but not, he recalls, very much else. 'One technical thing I learnt from Van Kempen was how to deal with recitative, which admittedly is not unimportant. But I never really took to him.' After just three weeks of tuition, enhanced by a wine-tasting in Orvieto and a *Tosca* in the square at San Gimignano, he returned to Glasgow. 'Gibson,' said Van Kempen in gruff farewell 'remember grappa.' They were among the few words the Dutchman ever uttered to him.

Back in Scotland, he found that Whyte, too, had been having problems. At the wheel of the honeymoon car, he had got no further than Bridge of Orchy when the big end went. Abandoning it at a local garage for Gibson to retrieve, he had continued his journey in a different vehicle.

Whyte, who was born in Dunfermline, seldom stirred from his homeland. Gibson, being twenty-five years his junior, enjoyed travel, and another foreign sortie of the period proved more rewarding than Siena. The lure this time came from France in the form of the 1951 Besançon Conducting Competition, in which he was one of the ten finalists and ultimately the winner of the Georges Enescu prize.

In this pleasant spa near the Swiss border he found himself in stimulating company of the sort he had already encountered in Salzburg. Now, instead of Sawallisch, it was another German, Reinhard Peters, with whom he shared the podium, and who, twenty years later, would bring the Deutsche Oper, Berlin, to the Edinburgh Festival to perform Alban Berg's *Lulu* and the British première of Aribert Reimann's *Melusine*, each with the glorious Catherine Gayer in the title-role.

Besançon's competition programme, in addition to such nasty little test pieces as Mozart's *Magic Flute* overture and (even nastier) Johann Strauss's *Tales from the Vienna Woods*, included the sight-reading of a new work by the French composer Florent Schmit, the score of which was booby-trapped with five deliberate errors. Summing up the result, a leading French critic later reported:

> The struggle was a close one between Gibson and Peters. For our part we preferred the conducting of the Englishman [*sic*] which was elegant and precise. The German, however, was able to discover one of the five faults in the parts (a matter of wrong harmonies in a score abounding with dissonances) and it was this, no doubt, that decided the jury, presided over by Florent Schmit himself, to give the first prize to Peters. A second prize of 50,000 francs will compensate the Englishman, whom we would like to see again in Besançon.

It was plain where the critic's sympathies lay, and France has always remained high on the list of countries where Gibson regularly appears as guest conductor.

His student years behind him, Gibson had already started his professional career. But professional conductors in Britain do not always get the jobs they desire, and are forced to fall back, all too often, on the routine of teaching. For Gibson this was never a likelihood. While still at college he was snapped up by Sadler's Wells Opera as a *répétiteur* – a lowly enough appointment, and often a frustrating one, but the traditional European (though not entirely the British) way of reaching the first rung on the climb to stardom. Gibson climbed sensationally fast, quicker than his rival and near-contemporary, Colin Davis, quicker even than Simon Rattle, who is usually reckoned the fastest of them all.

Even as a pianist *répétiteur*, whose principal tasks were to coach singers and accompany rehearsals for forthcoming productions, he was given conducting opportunities such as the six performances of *The Bartered Bride* that marked his debut in the pit of the much-loved Islington theatre that was the company's home until it moved to bigger premises in the West End and changed its name to English National Opera.

Another Scot might have turned his back on his homeland at this point. At the age of twenty-five, Gibson had every prospect of a successful London career ahead of him. But the Motherwell boy who had cycled to church to play the organ still cared about music in Scotland. Motherwell and Glasgow had bred him and he wanted to give something back. In an open competition he won the two-year assistant conductorship of the BBC Scottish Orchestra under Ian Whyte, and the duality in his ambitions – first between Scotland and England, then between opera and symphonic music – began to assert itself. It was something which, even at the height of his future career, was to remain not wholly resolved.

Gibson's apprenticeship with Whyte has already been mentioned. It gave him an invaluable practical training, enabling him to conduct 361 works (sixty-six of them by modern British composers) and helping him begin to make his name in Scotland. It was the sort of appointment any young conductor in what was then a not particularly musical country would have dreamed of. But it was important to him in other ways also. It showed him at first hand where Scotland's musical deficiencies lay, and it gave him the desire – soon to grow – to do something about them.

This was the period when, spurred by Walter Susskind, the old Scottish Orchestra had at last become a full-time orchestra and proudly added the word 'National' to its name. But, in a country of five million people, there was no other full-size symphony orchestra. Nor was there a professional chamber orchestra. Opera was a sporadic affair, dependent mostly on an annual visit from the hard-pressed Carl Rosa company, the presence of Glyndebourne at the Edinburgh Festival, and chance encounters with one or another of the touring Italian companies that burgeoned briefly after the war, sometimes sporting fine if by then ageing singers (I once heard Carlo Tagliabue sing Rigoletto, his most famous role, at the King's Theatre, Edinburgh), sometimes with a promising young conductor at the helm (the gifted Giuseppe Patanè, taut as a wire, seemed at that time Italy's white hope). The stagings were invariably crude and hastily executed, yet the flavour of Italy was powerful.

Like every other Scot who grew to love opera at that time, I found myself utterly dependent on the vicissitudes of these travelling companies. Sometimes the music took fire. If Maurits Sillem was the conductor, Carl Rosa could produce a potent *La Bohème*; and Arthur Hammond, likewise, had the measure of *Tosca*. Middle-period Verdi, in the hands of Fritz Busch and Carl Ebert at the Edinburgh Festival, was a revelation. And in the days when Covent Garden toured Scotland, the Barbirolli *Aida* and *Tristan*, in particular, were events to treasure.

On one occasion, Barbirolli dropped in on one of Gibson's live broadcasts from Glasgow – an all-Elgar programme including the *Enigma Variations* and the *Sea Pictures* with Constance Shacklock as soloist – and invited him out for a late lunch at Guy's Restaurant and to attend one of the Covent Garden performances.

Gibson remembers it as one of the most memorable days of his life. Over a leisurely meal, Barbirolli spoke encouragingly to his young colleague. As for the invitation to the King's Theatre, 'If it's *Tristan*,' said Barbirolli, 'it's compulsory. If it's *Bohème* you're excused.' It was indeed *Tristan*, and Gibson found himself in the front row of the stalls, immediately behind Barbirolli himself.

But as the young conductor realised, sporadic opera performances in Scotland were not enough. The boy who had seen *Madama Butterfly* at the age of twelve had matured into a man who was prepared to treat opera as a personal crusade. His first act, while still Whyte's deputy, was to accept Glasgow Grand Opera's invitation to conduct Gounod's *Faust* and Wolf-Ferrari's *Jewels of the Madonna* at the Theatre Royal. Professional conductors who associate themselves with amateur companies in performances of Gounod's *Faust* do so at their own risk. At the time Gibson accepted the assignment, the work's credibility in Britain was at its lowest ebb. Readers of *Opera* magazine had voted it the piece they least wanted to see at Covent Garden. The Garden Scene, the Jewel Song, the Soldiers' Chorus and, above all, the aria known in Victorian times as 'Even Bravest Heart' had all combined to make *Faust* seem the summation of all that was bad about nineteenth-century opera. Yet Gibson, risking his youthful reputation, conducted it because he believed in it, and his belief was what made the performance the successful event it was.

It was an act he was to perform again on behalf of other ailing or underrated operas in the years ahead. But what made Glasgow Grand's *Faust* prophetic was the fact that the Scottish National Orchestra was in the pit. Investing in the services of a professional orchestra made Glasgow's long-established company a cut above its rivals. But then, this was the company which, in the 1930s, had staged the British premières of not only Mozart's *Idomeneo* but also Berlioz's *Benvenuto Cellini* and *The Trojans*, with Erik Chisholm (who on one occasion successfully invited Bartók to Glasgow, and himself conducted the Scottish premiere of *Bluebeard's Castle*) as their visionary conductor. Championing Gounod's *Faust* was not perhaps so bold an act, but the thinking behind it was of long-term significance. For it was this experience, along with his first chance to conduct the SNO, which gave Gibson the first inkling of an idea that one day he would form a Scottish national opera company.

Championing Wolf-Ferrari, the hybrid German–Italian composer famed for his overture to *Susanna's Secret*, was another brilliant Gibson ploy of the period. The grace, deftness, and wit of the music suited one aspect of his own personality to perfection. He possessed what has been called the 'Beecham touch', which Beecham's detractors dismissed as an affection for the second rate at the expense of the masterpieces he should have been devoting his time to. Nevertheless, it resulted in a number of neglected pieces being made to shine like new.

Beecham, of course, had been peerless in his ability to transform what some saw as paste into pearl; but Gibson also, more than most of his contemporaries, had a way with what could be described as the fringes of the repertoire – dances, intermezzi, suites, preludes and other titbits, as well as longer works – which an ambitious young conductor might easily have disdained. After his success with *The Jewels of the Madonna*, he proceeded to tackle two other operas by Wolf-Ferrari: *I quattro rusteghi*, known in Britain as *School for Fathers*, at Sadler's Wells in 1956 and, the following year, *Susanna's Secret* in a concert performance at the Pavilion in Hastings with the London Philharmonic Orchestra. It is sad that in recent years he has never found an opportunity to return to these delicious operatic trifles he conducts so well, though his flair for the style was briefly revealed when he chose the intermezzo from *School for Fathers* as a contribution to a celebratory concert given by the Scottish Opera Orchestra at the Theatre Royal, Glasgow, in 1992.

But that is to anticipate a later chapter of this book. In 1954, Gibson had other things on his mind, the most important of which was what to do after his two-year contract with the BBC Scottish had ended. The ailing Whyte had aided him obliquely by being ill for much of his time there. Nevertheless, it was plain that Gibson needed a new challenge. It soon arrived in the offer of a conductor's post at Sadler's Wells Opera, which led in due course to the company's musical directorship. It would be no exaggeration to say that Gibson's acceptance of this marked a turning point not only for himself but for the fortunes of British opera in general.

CHAPTER FOUR

The London Years

As assistant conductor of the BBC Scottish Orchestra, Alexander Gibson showed talent and promise but, for me, not yet much more than that. He lacked, I thought at the time, Ian Whyte's craggy authority on the one hand and Walter Susskind's romantic sophistication on the other. But then, he was only twenty-six years old, and I was even younger. The Edinburgh Festival had opened my eyes and ears to Bruno Walter's high-minded Beethoven, Charles Münch's galvanic Berlioz, and Fritz Busch's fierce Verdi. I was deeply intolerant of budding Scottish talent. And when, at the end of his two-year contract, Gibson disappeared to England, I thought no more about him. For me, like many other Scots who read mainly Scottish newspapers, he had simply ceased to exist.

That this was far from the truth subsequently became apparent, but for the time being Scotland's musical life dribbled on in a claustrophobic and unprogressive way. Karl Rankl, who succeeded Walter Susskind as conductor of the SNO, reduced that orchestra's repertoire to a shadow – and a Germanic shadow at that – of its former self. Touring recitalists like Pouishnoff, Kendall Taylor, and Waldo Channon came and went. In Edinburgh a sparse winter season of chamber music at the Freemasons' Hall, featuring performers of the calibre of Wilhelm Kempff and the Amadeus Quartet, struggled to survive. Tertia Liebenthal's lunchtime concerts, which brought Peter Pears, Benjamin Britten, and the young John Ogdon to Scotland, were almost the only oasis. The Scottish Committee of the Arts Council (as it then was called) considered it had had a successful year if there was money left in the till that could be returned to its head office in London at the end of the season. An air of stagnation spread across the country, with the Edinburgh Festival bringing the only gleam of light and hope. Things, as the Festival eloquently demonstrated, were better elsewhere.

The best musicians got out fast, Iain Hamilton and Thea Musgrave to England and then the United States, Susskind to Canada (having, after numerous attempts by his predecessors, established the SNO as a full-time orchestra), and Gibson, of course, to London. Even I managed to disappear for much of the 1950s, first compulsorily – if such a word can be used in the circumstances – to Paris, where I spent two years listening to French music while doing my National Service in the RAF, and later voluntarily, when I moved to Amsterdam to work for Philips Records.

To escape from the dead hand of Karl Rankl's programming, yet returning each year for the Edinburgh Festival, may suggest a lack of loyalty, but it was the only way to gain the experience a would-be critic needed. Gibson, as a conductor, had similar thoughts. So why, after seven years in London, he decided to return to Scotland must be something which he still asks himself in moments of self-appraisal. Scotland is not a country strong on gratitude – not that it should be expected to be – and Gibson's stupendous efforts in the 1960s and '70s to make it as musically self-sufficient as any other small European country, and a lot more musically exciting than some, have been too often grudgingly received.

If he had remained in Scotland after completing his stint with the BBC Scottish Orchestra, he could have drifted into insignificance. Rankl was solidly in charge of the SNO, and guest conductors – Paul Kletzki and Fernando Previtali were the regulars in those days – came mostly from abroad. William Fell, the orchestra's rigid-minded administrator, saw no scope in nurturing local talent, apart from tossing a few crumbs (such as Beethoven's Fifth Symphony or the harpsichord part in Bach's Fifth Brandenburg Concerto) to Herrick Bunney, who was conductor of the Edinburgh Royal Choral Union at the time.

To encourage a Gibson, or a James Loughran, or a Bryden Thomson would have struck him as dangerously subversive and a recipe for disaster. Even after Rankl had been replaced in 1957 by Hans Swarowsky, and Swarowsky had turned out to be just another Rankl, there still seemed little awareness in the SNO offices that a change of policy was needed. How Gibson came to be appointed in 1959 remains one of the miracles of Scottish music. It could easily have been Willem van Otterloo from the Hague Philharmonic, whom one influential member of the board of directors had lined up as Swarowsky's successor.

But if, after his interlude with the BBC Scottish Orchestra, Gibson was unwanted in Scotland, he was certainly desired in London. Having begun in 1950 to work his way up at Sadler's Wells from the bottom rung, having put his piano playing to good use as a *répétiteur*, and having accepted an appointment as staff conductor, in 1957 he rose to the post of musical director, the youngest in the company's history at that time.

For an inexperienced and little-known Scot, it was an extraordinary achievement. In the 1950s, after all, London was just as devoted as Scotland to giving positions of rank to senior foreigners (and things today have not changed much). The Royal Opera House, Covent Garden, having sent Rankl packing to Scotland in 1952, was now on the brink of appointing the ill-fated Rafael Kubelik in his place; he, in turn, would be succeeded by Georg Solti. The London Symphony Orchestra was dominated by the unpleasant Viennese, Josef Krips. The Philharmonia Orchestra had not yet lost the services of the even more dominating Herbert von Karajan, and the London Philharmonic and Royal Philharmonic had two English *eminences grises*, Sir Adrian Boult and Sir Thomas Beecham, as their figureheads. For young British talent there was little scope.

Although Sadler's Wells Opera was a homelier outfit then than it has since become under the grander title of English National Opera, it played no less important a role in London's burgeoning operatic life. In the 1950s it was a genuine *Volksoper*, complementing rather than competing with Covent Garden. Founded in 1931, it had reopened in 1945 with the premiere of *Peter Grimes*, and had built up a post-war repertoire ranging from operetta to Verdi's *Simon Boccanegra* and Lennox Berkeley's *Nelson*, along with old faithfuls like *Carmen, The Barber of Seville* and *The Bartered Bride*. It was, above all, an ensemble company, with its own house style, and all works were sung in English – as they still are – just as most of its singers were of British origin.

Here, then, was one organisation that saw nothing wrong with having a young British conductor at the helm. And Gibson blossomed. As staff conductor in 1954 he scored an immediate hit with *Madama Butterfly*, the first opera he had seen as a child, and the one which, more than any other, would exert an almost mystical force upon his musical destiny. 'The test of a performance of *Madama Butterfly*,' pontificated the music critic of *The Times*, 'is whether it makes the listener think that

Puccini's music is good or revolting.' The 28-year-old Gibson passed the test. 'This performance,' the review continued, 'persuaded everyone that it is a good and not deplorable opera.'

Amy Shuard, just turned thirty and not yet the great Janáček singer she would become, was the first of the many Cio-Cio-Sans with whom Gibson has worked in the course of his long career. Recognising his flair for Puccini, Sadler's Wells allowed its new staff conductor to open the 1954–55 season with a *Tosca* in which, again according to *The Times*, he phrased with shape and point and 'showed himself an aptly flexible conductor for this elastic kind of music'. He was hailed as a 'valuable acquisition' who, the critic hoped, had come to stay.

From *Butterfly* to Menotti's still-new melodrama *The Consul* two months later was a leap Gibson made with ease. Though the music displeased Eric Blom of *The Observer* ('unbelievable cheapness'), he had nothing but praise for Gibson's conducting of it. Blom, having just re-emerged from editing the ten volumes of the 1954 edition of *Grove*, was by then in the twilight of his journalistic career, and it was his successor, the usually abrasive Peter Heyworth, who reviewed Gibson's next Sadler's Wells project for the Sunday paper, a performance of *La traviata* which he praised for its impetus. It was infinitely superior, he claimed, to the 'emaciated' performances of the same work that another British conductor was at that time presenting at Covent Garden.

For a staff conductor who had not yet reached the status of musical director, Gibson was being given the opportunities he needed, and performances of *Eugene Onegin* (Desmond Shawe-Taylor: 'natural and sincere') and *The Bartered Bride* (*The Times*: 'irresistible youthful verve') the following season continued them. Back in Scotland, moreover, the SNO registered his progress by inviting him to make a guest appearance in Glasgow and Edinburgh with a programme including Sibelius's still neglected Symphony No 3, music that was much more pared down than the big romantic pronouncements of the first two symphonies, but soon to become a Gibson speciality.

Christopher Grier, *The Scotsman*'s music critic at the time, recognised the portents. Extolling Gibson's masterly control, he said 'one rarely hears the composer's wholly individual type of scoring reproduced with such clarity'. Though Gibson's success with Sibelius, which was to win him the Sibelius Medal in the 1970s, still lay in the future, its roots were already apparent.

His desire to spend as much time on the concert platform as in the orchestra pit was already growing. It was not that he saw the opera house merely as a means to an end – opera, whether he admitted it or not, would always be his first love — but simply that he did not wish to spend all his life down in Nibelheim when there was a Valhalla up there glinting in the sunshine. Each, of course, could be treacherously alluring to a young conductor as yet uncertain of his sense of direction. Would Gibson's reputation be the greater if he had stuck exclusively to the opera house? (There are those who still claim that Wilhelm Furtwängler was a great opera conductor but a butcher in the concert hall.) Gibson's splitting of his talents was questioned more than once at this time, but his performances of Mahler's Eighth Symphony, Berlioz's Te Deum, and Elgar's *Falstaff* at the Edinburgh Festival would later provide an answer.

His period as Ian Whyte's assistant in Glasgow had shown that concert work was undoubtedly an ambition. And in London, too, he was proving himself to be at home on the concert platform. Moreover, he was willing to face challenges of a sort that many another conductor, intent on easy success, traditionally sidesteps. One of these was a BBC concert in 1956 featuring the British première of Luigi Nono's *Liebeslieder* for chorus and orchestra. Nono, a thorny modernist if ever there was one, was regarded in the 1950s as the kiss of death in Britain. Though his Brechtian opera, *Intolleranza*, still lay in the future, his reputation – or notoriety – had already been founded on a variety of shorter works, most of them as uncompromisingly mathematical in inspiration as they were leftist in politics. From time to time, as one authority put it, an Italian lyricism managed to break through all Nono's constraints, but not everybody could hear it.

Peter Heyworth, who sat in on one of Gibson's Nono rehearsals, admitted that his 'immediate reaction was one of puzzled revulsion from what seemed an arid, inhuman landscape'. As the rehearsal wore on, however, he discovered that his first impression was not only wrong but the very reverse of the truth. Though the work was an austere affair that may not have been everyone's idea of a love song – Nono wrote it for his wife-to-be, the daughter of the avant-garde conductor Hermann Scherchen – Heyworth recognised that beneath the surface there ran 'hot, red blood and profound passion'.

Clearly, then, Gibson's performance was no mere statement of – or, worse, approximation of – the notes, such as modern works often received from uncommitted British conductors during the 1950s. And the rest of the programme, which could easily have been propped up by a Beethoven symphony as bait for the audience, was equally uncompromising in its attention to modern music.

In this concert, surely, lay the germ of the pioneering performance of Stockhausen's *Gruppen* that Gibson would give in

Glasgow six years later (with Norman Del Mar and John Carewe as fellow conductors of this circling music for three orchestras). Indeed, the roots of Musica Nova, the festival of modern music he would establish in the 1970s with the support of the SNO and Glasgow University, were equally discernible here.

Between performances of Wolf-Ferrari's *School for Fathers* and Bizet's *Pearl Fishers* at Sadler's Wells, Nono's *Liebeslieder* must have given Gibson a taste for risk. At any rate, by June 1956, he was conducting a late-night performance of Stravinsky's anti-opera, *The Soldier's Tale*, in the Royal Festival Hall, which, even in its early days, was not the sort of auditorium that lent itself readily to anything audacious.

Again, Peter Heyworth of *The Observer* was quick to identify a ripple in the stagnant pool of London music-making. In an article headed 'Bridging the Chasm' he declared that 'it seemed as though London had finally decided that the music of our own time might not, after all, be so unappealing as is generally supposed'. Pointing out that the hall was packed for Stravinsky's astringent little music drama, he nevertheless admitted that the size of the audience may have had more to do with the presence of Ralph Richardson and Peter Ustinov as speakers than with the composer's genius.

A programme containing Bartók's Second Piano Concerto two nights later proved less of an attraction, yet Gibson's success was not to be gainsaid: as the *Sunday Times* remarked, he 'conducted with the suave, unruffled accuracy of an Ansermet or Desormière'. A subsequent performance, this time at the 1967 Edinburgh Festival, confirmed Gibson's flair for the Stravinsky. Though Wendy Toye's clever production was a late addition to the Festival's special survey of Stravinsky that year – at which Gibson also conducted *The Rake's Progress, Petrushka, Fireworks,* the *Capriccio* for piano and orchestra, and the *Ode* – it was in no way ill-prepared. Perched on a stool at the base of the apron stage of the Assembly Hall of the Church of Scotland, and wearing sweater and slacks, Gibson savoured the bracing air of incongruity that hung over this performance of a work in which, at the end, the Devil emerges triumphant.

But at Sadler's Wells in London it was a very different cautionary tale, Humperdinck's *Hansel and Gretel*, which along with *The Moon and Sixpence*, a new opera by John Gardner, paved the way for Gibson's appointment as musical director in 1957. It was the first peak of his career, achieved with the quietness, musicianship, and absence of hype that have stamped all his achievements before or since. Sometimes, at least for a Scottish-based critic keen to keep tabs on his progress, the veil Gibson seems deliberately to draw over his own activities can be frustrating. Information has to be dragged from him. His dates in recent years with leading American orchestras, a *Tristan* in Austria, a *Damnation of Faust* in Spain, a *Lobgesang* and a *Don Giovanni* in France, *War Requiems* in Germany and Greece, have come and gone without a drop of publicity in his homeland, whereas more egoistical conductors would employ high-powered marketing consultants to further their fame.

But then, it is the nature of the man that this is so. And in his quiet way at Sadler's Wells he won respect. When Toscanini made his sensational final visit to London in January 1957, Peter Heyworth took pains to include alongside his eulogy for those unforgettable Brahms concerts the news that Gibson, who had what might have seemed the misfortune to be conducting *Eugene Onegin* that same week in Rosebery Avenue, showed 'impressive ease and authority'. Gibson's conducting, he added, 'has never lacked vitality and dramatic sense, but he is now adding to these qualities an ability to secure refinement of detail that promises well for the future'. Another critic, carried away by the impact of Toscanini, might have failed to mention Gibson at all. Similarly, it was Heyworth who, when Gibson conducted Puccini's *Gianni Schicchi* the following month, praised his 'unflustered assurance that results in lively orchestral playing and smooth ensemble on the stage'.

If I have tended in this chapter to quote Heyworth's reviews, it is because he was the critic I myself esteemed more than any other. Right up until his recent death at the age of seventy, his outlook was invariably progressive; his last major article was a thorough, admiring, and beautifully written appraisal of Harrison Birtwistle's *Gawain*, a long and difficult opera that carried by no means universal appeal; and whenever Gibson fell below what Heyworth perceived to be the standards expected of him, *The Observer's* critic did not conceal his disappointment.

Happily, in 1957, Scottish audiences were in a position to confirm Heyworth's enthusiasm for Gibson's conducting of *Onegin* and *Schicchi*, because both these productions were brought to the King's Theatre, Glasgow, as part of the first major Sadler's Wells tour with its new musical director in charge. It was the first time I had heard him since his Edinburgh lunchtime concert with the BBC Scottish Orchestra, and I was astounded by the change in him. Here, it seemed to me, were performances that rose far above the category of 'local boy makes good'. Their vibrancy and élan suggested that a born opera conductor was at the helm. They could be compared with what I was becoming accustomed to hearing at the Edinburgh Festival, and not be found wanting. Though still learning my trade as critic with the *Evening Dispatch*, I sought my editor's permission to write a special article declaring that this was what Scotland needed, not just from time to time by courtesy of London, but on a regular basis. Little did I know that the same thoughts were already in Gibson's mind, and were to be realised five years later when he founded Scottish Opera.

Meanwhile, he was relishing the chance to direct his own company, even if it was not the Scottish one that his keen sense of patriotism might have preferred. But his intention to maintain the links with his homeland was demonstrated by another of his occasional appearances as guest conductor of the SNO. Even if there was nothing startling about his choice of music – Brahms's Second Symphony was the main work – it prompted Christopher Grier of *The Scotsman* to speculate on whether, as the 'white hope of British opera', he would one day become 'Generalmusikdirektor' of Covent Garden.

Grier was not the only person in Scotland with an eye on Gibson's future. So, too, had W. Borland, a senior Edinburgh lawyer and music-lover, who wrote a letter to *The Herald*, signed by himself and four others, proposing that Gibson be appointed forthwith as Karl Rankl's successor as conductor of the SNO. They were aware, they said, that his reputation in Scotland rested mostly on his flair for modern music, and that canny Scots might have doubts about how well he would deal with the classics. But they themselves had no such uncertainty. 'We venture the view,' they declared, 'that Gibson has everything which could be desired in a conductor of an orchestra of the standing and calibre of the SNO.'

But it was not to be – not yet at any rate. With a canny Englishman as administrator, the SNO was unlikely to replace a venerable Viennese with a young Scot who might lead the players into the treacherous waters of modern music. Soon Rankl was replaced by the faded charms of Hans Swarowsky, who conducted hardly any modern music at all, unless it was by 'safe' Germans such as Hindemith or Blacher. But while the SNO in Glasgow marked time, Gibson in London strode forward.

His first opportunity to conduct an orchestral concert at the Royal Festival Hall came to him the way it also came to Colin Davis: he deputised for someone else and won instant acclaim for his efforts. The *Daily Express* spelt it out for its readers. 'Yes,' declared its arts page in big letters, 'fame beckoned this man last night.' Below the banner headline, Noël Goodwin, the paper's music critic, proclaimed that: 'A British conductor who I believe is destined to reach the top seized his chance with both hands . . . and remained master of the situation despite a distressing soloist.'

Being invited to appear with the Royal Philharmonic in the days when it was still Sir Thomas Beecham's orchestra meant a great deal to Gibson. Whatever the shortcomings of the Yugoslav soloist in Brahms's Violin Concerto, he had no difficulty in establishing his authority as conductor. According to Goodwin, 'it was entirely through Gibson's watchful care that the performance held together'. In Tchaikovsky's Sixth Symphony he 'employed an expressive left hand that almost spoke'. Or, as Peter Heyworth put it later that week, Gibson's Tchaikovsky had 'all the brilliance and excitement of a cavalry charge'.

Gibson's watchful care was something that became one of his special assets later in his career, particularly in the opera house, where so much can go wrong, but also in many other rescues of wayward soloists. It was not, as he discovered, something that wins a conductor any medals. A soloist saved from public disaster is not necessarily a soloist who later bursts with public or even private gratitude. Only in Thurber's *Walter Mitty* would a distinguished pianist leap to his feet at the end of Beethoven's *Emperor* concerto and thank the conductor for concealing the memory lapse that had resulted in the omission of five pages of the first movement.

What is more likely to happen, as Gibson discovered when he conducted Lili Kraus in what could have been a catastrophic account of a Mozart piano concerto, is that the soloist will find some way of conveying to the audience – it may be with no more than a smile and a gesture – that the fault is someone else's. It takes a particularly brutal sort of conductor to bellow 'Go on!' when, at an Edinburgh concert I once attended, a nervous young woman pianist got hopelessly lost and ground to a halt in the middle of the treacherously cyclic finale of the Schumann concerto. That particular conductor is still conducting, but the pianist has vanished without trace.

It is generally singers rather than instrumentalists who are prepared to admit, sometimes years after the event, that Gibson once saved them. It is a flair he possesses even at rehearsal, when he can build up a novice's confidence at a point of crisis where another conductor might destroy it. Patricia Hay, the Scottish soprano whom Gibson groomed during Scottish Opera's formative years, recalls how he nursed her through one of her earliest roles, that of the Second Niece in Britten's *Peter Grimes* at the 1968 Edinburgh Festival.

'Though I'd done Kate Pinkerton in *Madama Butterfly*, Woglinde in *Götterdämmerung*, and Cherubino in *Figaro*, I didn't really get to know him until that first *Grimes* rehearsal. I had a particular entrance, away up at the back of the stage, with Ann Baird as the First Niece singing in canon, if you please. It was a rotten entrance with nothing to help us beforehand but the somewhat approximate voice of John Shaw as Captain Balstrode and an orchestral pizzicato.

'Well, we missed it. Alex looked up at us. We missed it again, and then a third time. Alex asked what was wrong, and we told him we couldn't hear the orchestra. He replied that there was nothing for the orchestra to play at that point. So we said we couldn't hear the nothing. Alex looked severe, then gave us a big grin and said he would make the nothing sound a bit clearer. And that was what I learned from him that day. If anything begins to go wrong, Alex can gauge it – he picks things up. When something happens, in a performance but also in a rehearsal where tensions rise, he can defuse it.'

It was a knack of which I had become intuitively aware when he brought Sadler's Wells to Scotland in 1957, conducting no fewer than three of the productions himself (in addition to *Onegin* and *Schicchi* there was a real ensemble performance of *The Marriage of Figaro*), which was more than many musical directors would bother to do under touring conditions in those days, when the effort of mounting opera in primitive theatres often seemed more trouble than it was worth. If some of these performances hovered on the brink of mishap, the audience never knew it. And when, in the same year, Gibson was invited by an Edinburgh schoolteacher to conduct an amateur performance of Verdi's *Nabucco* at the Usher Hall, he accepted the challenge instead of replying that he did not do that sort of thing.

The teacher was Richard Telfer, a tiny man who henceforward would play a quiet but curiously Svengali-like role in Gibson's life. As conductor of the ambitiously named Edinburgh Grand Opera Society, Telfer had presented the odd *Faust* and *Martha* in the Music Hall, George Street, and had first contacted Gibson three years earlier when he wanted advice on how to tackle *La traviata*. In a formal letter of introduction he told the London-based conductor that he had 'benefited greatly' in the past from having consultations with two of the SNO's former conductors, Aylmer Buesst and Warwick Braithwaite. Would Gibson, too, be prepared to help him? As it happened Telfer was coming south to stay with an old friend in Brighton, and if, by chance, Gibson had any free time he would be grateful to be able to pause in London and have a lesson, for whatever fee the conductor proposed.

Since Gibson had only just begun to learn the opera himself, for a series of performances he was giving at Sadler's Wells in 1958, he wrote back to say that he was hardly in a position to give someone a lesson on the piece, let alone charge a fee, but maybe it would be mutually beneficial if they spent an hour or so together going through the score. Telfer accepted, and in due course arrived at Gibson's Chelsea flat carrying a full score and a large bag containing a chicken and champagne lunch which, to save them going out to eat, he proposed that they share while poring over Verdi.

Telfer, it turned out, had ambitions that rose above his own personal attainments, and it was in Gibson that he perceived the future of opera in Scotland. Would he be prepared to come and conduct *Nabucco* in Edinburgh? Telfer's instincts were soon proved accurate. Not content with transforming the Usher Hall into an opera house for a few nights, or with recruiting singers of the calibre of David Ward and William Dickie to give the production a professional vocal topping, Gibson conducted Verdi's early masterpiece with the raw passion one would have expected to find in Parma or Palermo.

Having reviewed the opening night for the *Evening Dispatch*, I went back and reviewed it a second time. If I failed to recognise that the roots of Scottish Opera had been planted, I at least perceived that a new dimension had been brought to opera in Scotland, and that Gibson was the man of the moment.

CHAPTER FIVE

The Turning Point

In London, Gibson continued to be in demand. True, a Tchaikovsky concert at the Festival Hall, with Eileen Joyce as soloist in the B flat minor Piano Concerto, was unlikely to further his career or attract the attention of the critics, but the première of John Gardner's opera, *The Moon and Sixpence*, at Sadler's Wells was a different matter. The 83-year-old Somerset Maugham, on whose book the opera was based, sent a telegram from Salzburg, where he was staying at the time, conveying his good wishes. And when, on reaching London, he saw what had been done to his Gauguinesque novel — about a prosperous stockbroker who put art before duty and finally died of leprosy in Tahiti — he appeared much less disheartened by it than by the fact that the literary award bearing his name had recently been won by the upstart Kingsley Amis's *Lucky Jim*.

'I enjoyed *The Moon and Sixpence* very much,' he was quoted as saying, 'and should like to hear it again. I haven't read my book now for thirty-five years, nor am I a musician. But this splendid company brought it vividly back to me.'

Not all the London critics were so enthusiastic. 'Alexander Gibson,' declared *The Times*, 'secures a smooth reading of a very rough score.' Peter Heyworth went further. 'It is often difficult,' he said, 'to put your finger on what precisely is wrong with an unsuccessful new opera, but in the case of John Gardner's *The Moon and Sixpence* it is all too easy. The music is very poor indeed.' By the time Paul Griffiths compiled his *Encyclopedia of Twentieth-Century Music* in 1986, Gardner was one of

yesterday's men; neither he nor his opera earned a mention. But Sir
John Barbirolli, whose advice Gibson valued, had clearly admired the
Manchester-born composer, and indeed it was Barbirolli's espousal of
Gardner's Second Symphony at the 1951 Cheltenham Festival that led
to *The Moon and Sixpence* being commissioned by Sadler's Wells.

Though Andrew Porter valiantly defended it in the *Financial
Times*, the work was plainly a lost cause. But Gibson, conducting – as
Opera magazine put it – with 'cool, efficient detachment', demonstrated
an aspect of his personality that was to serve him in good stead as his
career progressed. He was willing to take on duties that were unlikely
to bring him personal glamour. He would do this again many times
when he returned to Scotland, accepting that a resident conductor has a
responsibility to champion the works of local composers, even when
the works sometimes seem scarcely worth championing. And though
Gardner's opera was performed just seven times before it finally bit the
dust, its failure had two happy outcomes: it launched the operatic
career of a young director called Peter Hall, whose contribution to the
evening passed almost unnoticed; and it led a month later to the
announcement that the thirty-year-old Alexander Gibson – 'already
being hailed as the new Barbirolli' – had been appointed the first
musical director of Sadler's Wells.

Gibson promptly celebrated his promotion by conducting *Tosca*
at Covent Garden, the rival house. It was his first appearance there and,
with a fading star to contend with – Zinka Milanov sang the title-role,
with Franco Corelli as Cavaradossi – it was not without its stressful
moments. For a start, the distinguished Croatian diva, long famed for
her remarkable command of *pianissimo* tone, did not deign to attend the
early rehearsals, even though she had already arrived in London. 'She
was,' Gibson recalls, 'down at the Savoy Hotel, supposedly ailing, and
David Webster [the company's haughty Dundee-born administrator]
asked me if I could persuade Amy Shuard to come in from Sadler's
Wells to do it instead.'

Shuard had already sung *Tosca* several times with Gibson at the
Wells. But as Webster notoriously disliked slumming it, and had a high
disdain for the Wells's resident singers, who invariably sang opera in
English translation, his aim on this occasion may merely have been to
galvanise the temperamental Milanov into action. At any rate, says
Gibson, their conversation continued thus:

Webster: 'Would she know the role in Italian?'
Gibson: 'Probably.'
Webster: 'Would you mind if I asked her?'
Gibson: 'I can't stop you, and I certainly wouldn't mind.'

The sub-text, never actually stated, was that as soon as Milanov heard that she was about to be replaced by a much younger singer she would be bound to turn up for the dress rehearsal. Bearing this in mind, Gibson began Act One with Shuard sitting in readiness in the stalls. The bait worked. 'My introduction to Milanov,' says Gibson, 'was the sound of her voice singing "Mario, Mario" [*Tosca*'s marvellous entrance music, which occurs some distance into Act One] offstage. She then swept down to the front and addressed me, saying "Ciao, Maestro, sempre in due." The implication seemed to be that she was not as young as she was, so I agreed to beat it in two.'

This was Milanov's farewell to Covent Garden, and it coincided with Corelli's debut there. 'Everybody was curious to know what this reputedly enormous voice sounded like. I'd rehearsed him beforehand at the piano, when he was apt to say to me "Per favore, una piccola corona" [please, a little pause], and would simply mark instead of singing out. By the time of the dress rehearsal, there were lots of staff sitting expectantly in the stalls, and the orchestral players were hoping they would hear his voice at some point. We were approaching the moment when, in Act Two, Cavaradossi learns that Napoleon has won the Battle of Marengo and cries "Vittoria". Corelli was lying on the floor at this point but got up and suddenly let it rip, flinging himself into the trio that followed. The whole thing took off. The orchestra jumped out of their seats.'

Yet whatever the allure of the two star names – the Scarpia, Gian Giacomo Guelfi, was less well known – it was Gibson himself who stole the show. According to *The Times*, he 'revealed a treasure-trove of incidental beauties in the score, drawing a wealth of emotion from each little descriptive phrase'. And Martin Cooper of the *Daily Telegraph* said: 'his knowledge of the score, sense of style, and ability to coax extremes of violence and sweetness from the orchestra revealed him as already unquestionably the finest of our younger opera conductors.'

It was an assessment of him with which the Scottish critic and broadcaster, Neville Garden, would agree. On the evidence of a pirate recording of one of the Covent Garden performances, Garden has told me that, for him, in terms of electric energy, only one other performance has ever come close to it, and that was the one Maria Callas did with Victor de Sabata as conductor. It put, he said, the hair on his neck on end from first note to last, and 'considering that it was recorded live, it was very together, real knife-edge stuff'. But more than that, it was a considerate performance: 'He supported Milanov all the way, and made her sound wonderful even when she was getting old.'

When, in 1958, the production was revived with a different cast, it was again Gibson who got the praise. This time *The Times* said he 'showed all the opera conductor's virtues and one more: strength of mind in refusing to stop for the audience's unmannerly applause'.

Today, *Tosca* remains one of Gibson's best pieces. Though it is among the works he has conducted more often than any other – at Sadler's Wells alone he notched up thirty-six performances of it – its incidental beauties have never grown stale for him, and he still exults in its violence and sweetness. Whenever Scottish Opera revives its fine Anthony Besch production, first staged in the 1970s, it is Gibson whom the company invariably invites to conduct it. On one recent occasion, Sian Edwards – the latest of his successors with what is now the English National Opera – came to listen to him at work. She was preparing to conduct it herself in London, and wanted to learn from Gibson's expertise. But when the ENO next stages *Tosca* – a minimum of twelve performances of a new production are planned, with Rosalind Plowright in the title-role – the conductor will be Gibson again.

Though there are times, inevitably, when he wishes people would invite him to conduct something else, his Puccini is undoubtedly very special. Few other conductors rival his feeling for a Puccini phrase, for the delicacy of instrumental timbre, the ebb and flow of the music's lyrical lines, or the pauses that make all the difference between a performance that breathes and one that is hustled. When I asked Patricia Hay if she could explain this to me, she cited Musetta in *La Bohème*, a role she has sung many times for Gibson, as well as for other good Puccini conductors.

'I never did it better than with him. He simply gave me space. He could always hear what I was trying to do. It was his amazing gift for timing. If I was up there on the stage, and he sensed that I was having difficulties, he had this incredible capacity for moving the orchestra on, in order to help me through whatever the problem phrase happened to be. It's such a rare virtue, especially in a conductor who is a non-singer, like Alex. Puccini is *so* difficult, nobody understands how difficult. If it's rigid, if you're counting the crotchets, it does not work.

'Alex's little pauses were always perfectly judged, as at the start of Musetta's Waltz Song. First there would be the soft, beautifully spaced "ting-ting-ting" from the orchestra, then a big beat, a simply enormous beat, a great sense of anticipation, and in I'd come on the word "Quando". But it was he who created the atmosphere, not me. How does he do it? People joke about his downbeat, saying he doesn't have one, but it never bothered me – I always felt what he was doing, and never needed it. And it wasn't just me. Recently I sat out front when one of my students was doing *Butterfly* with him. He was sensational, she said. She was replacing someone else in the title-role, and they had a half-day talk-through together, after which she felt capable of singing anything for him.'

Neville Garden, a conductor himself as well as a critic, shares Patricia Hay's appreciation of the finesse of Gibson's Puccini. 'He once brought out a flute obbligato in Pinkerton's aria and made me realise that I'd never noticed it before. Alex does these things. There are times when he's conducting that I find myself listening to the orchestra more than to the singers.'

And Garden, like Hay, is aware of the power of the pauses. 'There's that moment in Act Two of *Butterfly* when Sharpless asks Cio-Cio-San what she will do if Pinkerton never comes back. The orchestra underlines her reaction with a bang and a pause. Once, when Gibson was conducting, he held that pause for fully ten seconds. In London I've heard another conductor hold it for no more than a couple of seconds, and it went for nothing. Puccini's pauses, as Gibson treats them, are as eloquent as the music itself.'

Yet to suggest that his success as an opera conductor revolves round Puccini would be wholly misleading. At Sadler's Wells, as the list of works he conducted testifies, his tastes were wide. Unlike his successor, Colin Davis, he revealed no obvious phobias. Davis, in his Wells days, did not conceal his contempt for Puccini and Richard Strauss (though he was to change his mind, or at any rate his attitude, later).

Gibson, on the other hand, seized his opportunities. He did not despise the popular repertoire, as his fifty-two Sadler's Wells performances of *The Merry Widow*, his thirty-five of *La Bohème*, his thirty of *Madama Butterfly*, his eighteen of Gounod's *Faust*, and his seventeen of *Schicchi* confirm. But he also, during those years, conducted nineteen performances of *The Marriage of Figaro*, eighteen of *Così fan tutte*, fifteen of *Don Giovanni*, fifteen of *The Consul*, fifteen of *Eugene Onegin*, and fourteen of *The Bartered Bride*. Add to these the odd *Carmen*, *Pearl Fishers*, and *Samson and Delilah*, a few *Seraglios* and *Falstaffs*, a *Flying Dutchman* and even some *Bluebeard's Castles* and *Riders to the Sea*, and the wealth of Gibson's operatic repertoire becomes clear. The only glaring gaps were Britten and Richard Strauss, and these he filled later, as soon as Scottish Opera gave him the opportunity.

Yet if he remembers *The Merry Widow* as well as any of the slightly superior masterpieces on the above list, it is not simply because he has conducted it more often. It is also because, on the opening night in January 1958, something memorable happened. On a backstage staircase at Sadler's Wells he encountered a 21-year-old ballerina called Veronica Waggett, who was one of the dancers in the production. The daughter of a Calcutta-based businessman, she had been born in the Home Counties, had been sent back from India to boarding school, and had been dancing since she was twelve. Though she now says that her future husband took an incredible time to pop the question – 'when he suddenly invited me out to dinner, ordered champagne, and asked me to dance, I knew that something must be coming because I was a ballet dancer and normally he never danced with me' – they were eventually married in Chelsea Old Church, near Gibson's London flat. And, unusually among conductors and their spouses, they have remained married.

Today they travel the world together. While he rehearses, she explores cities and art galleries, meets friends, and searches out promising places to eat, telling him later what he should see and do before they depart for their next destination. While some conductors live solely for music, the Gibsons have a wide range of cultural interests. Their home in Cleveden Gardens, which they bought from the artist David Donaldson, is mentioned in Glasgow architectural guides. Their astutely gathered collection of (mostly) Scottish paintings – there are seven marvellous specimens in the drawing-room alone – could fill a small art gallery.

The house is instantly recognisable, not just because it is beautiful but because it is conspicuously different from anything else in the gardens. An elegant example of the Glasgow style, designed by A. N. Prentice and dating from 1903, just before *Pelléas et Mélisande* was first performed in Paris, it stands in one of those peaceful sloping byways of the Great Western Road where the city's arts community traditionally chooses to live. The recent Penguin guide to Glasgow calls it a 'small and unusual Wrenaissance villa, built of finely-dressed ashlar with boldly arched ground-floor windows, understated pilasters defining the front elevation and a glazed cupola on the ridge'. But that is to analyse it like the chords of a Bach chorale. What matters is its appealing symmetry, and the pleasure it gives you just to step inside and see how the Gibsons live in it.

The drawing-room is dominated by two glowing Robin Philipson altar pieces and, less restfully, by the flurry of John Houston's *Man Feeding Birds*. Philipson was a personal friend. Many of the Gibsons' friends, indeed, are artists, and their gleaming Steinway grand, which would form the focal point of any other room, is upstaged by what hangs on the walls surrounding it. When, in 1974, Marc Chagall and Henry Moore were elected to the Royal Scottish Academy, Gibson was simultaneously honoured.

Nor are the lofty bookcases in the drawing-room confined to music books. True, the expected items, methodically arranged, are all there: Ernest Newman on opera, Norman Del Mar on Richard Strauss, Eric Walter White on Stravinsky, Joseph Kerman on the Beethoven quartets, Hugh Macdonald on Berlioz, Mosco Carner on Puccini, William Mann on Mozart. But there are also books on art, architecture, philosophy, drama, and literature. Peter Hall's *Diaries* catch the eye, along with Richard Buckle's biography of Diaghilev, Norman MacCaig's *Collected Poems*, Sir Robin Day's *Grand Inquisitor*, Lord Boothby's *Recollections of a Rebel* and Alastair Dunnett's *Among Friends*.

And, though Gibson no longer smokes and his wife is a non-smoker, the presence of La Scala ashtrays, with Toscanini's name in big type, shows that the room is not a puritanical no-smoking zone. Like the rest of the house, it is immaculately tidy. Their four grown-up children – James, Philip, John, and Claire – live elsewhere in Britain (none has become a conductor or dancer, though all have cultural leanings). Gibson confines his scores, discs, hi-fi equipment, and vast collection of tapes and records to his study across the hall, where he and his secretary Helen Brebner (a former member of the SNO Chorus) do their administrative work.

Now that he no longer has his own office at the Theatre Royal, a fair amount of business – interviews, discussions, coaching sessions, and forward planning – takes place at home. During busy periods, other rooms are brought into play. In a single day, in my experience, he may coach a novice conductor in one room, and discuss the strategy for a forthcoming charity concert in another, while all the time I am in the drawing-room sifting through documents he has placed at my disposal.

Near the kitchen, a small cloakroom contains a shelf of travel books, one of them explaining how to cope with Japan, where Gibson enjoys conducting. Working lunches and suppers tend to be kitchen meals, cooked by Veronica Gibson, or, if she is out, by the conductor himself. Because musicians live on their nerves, and because they must watch their weight, the fare tends to be simple, quickly digestible, good quality stuff – smoked salmon, smoked venison, home-made vegetable soups, plates of asparagus, chicken, steak, salad, a selection of cheese, preceded if it has been a hard day by a vintage champagne or Mumm's brilliant new Napa Valley fizz, and accompanied by one of the flowery Sancerres or fat Pouilly-Fuissés the Gibsons favour.

If he is modest about his musical attainments, Veronica is even more so about her culinary ones. 'I'm sorry,' she will say as she produces a sequence of delicious courses served on delicate Villeroy &

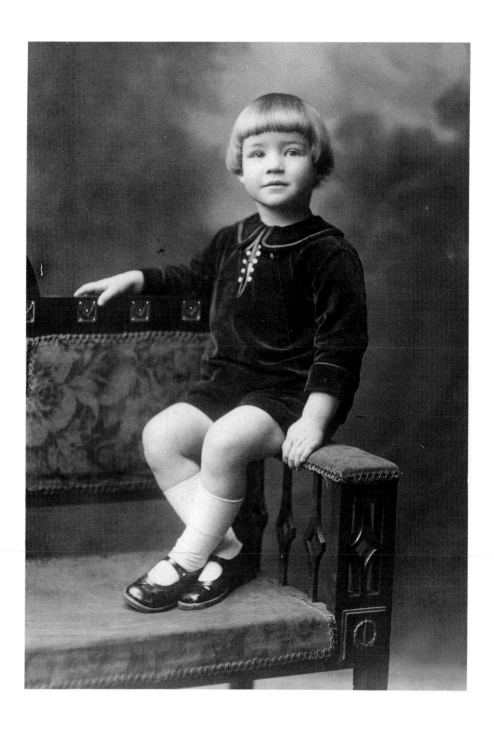

Alexander Gibson – an early photograph (1929)

*Young Alex – winner of the Holmes Gold
Medal at Stevenson Public School (1937)*

*The fourteen-year-old Gibson (back row, left) as the very model of a Modern Major-
General in Dalziel High School's production of* The Pirates of Penzance *(1940)*

Army days (1944–48)

Gibson at rehearsal with the Royal Philharmonic in London in the 1950s

Gibson and Wolfgang Sawallisch (side by side, rear left) at Igor Markevitch's conducting class at the Salzburg Mozarteum in 1950 (Picture by courtesy of Boosey & Hawkes)

Alex and Veronica's wedding in Chelsea Old Church (1959)

Gibson in dialogue with (left) Erik Knussen, orchestral manager of the SNO, and (right) Robert Ponsonby, the orchestra's administrator, and Sam Bor, the leader (1960s)

An early rehearsal: Gibson with Sam Bor (1963)

The Edinburgh Festival Chorus makes its début on the first night of the 1965 Edinburgh Festival, singing Mahler's Eighth Symphony with the Scottish National Orchestra under Alexander Gibson at the Usher Hall

Gibson and Janet Baker at the Salzburg Festspielhaus during the SNO's first European tour in 1967

Gibson, accompanied by his wife and mother, receives the CBE at Buckingham Palace (1967)

Gibson, between Dame Joan Sutherland and June Gordon, Marchioness of Aberdeen, becomes an Honorary Doctor of Laws at Aberdeen University (1968)

to alex Gibson in gratitude [signature] Edinburgh 1969

Gibson with Sir John Barbirolli (1969)

Early days with the SNO (1960s)

Boch plates of the sort employed by French three-star restaurants, 'I'm sorry this is all there is. I'm sorry, but this is the best I can do.'

A meal with the magisterial George Szell, who perfected his own secret recipe for goulash, and who could have been a great Hungarian chef had he not become a great American conductor, would doubtless have been more ostentatious. Deprived of his own kitchen during his period as conductor of the Scottish Orchestra in the impoverished 1930s – he resided in Glasgow in the now defunct More's Hotel near St Andrew's Hall – he famously feasted in his private first-class compartment on the train between Waverley and Queen Street after his Edinburgh concerts at the Usher Hall. Henri Temianka, who served for a year as Szell's leader, seems also to have acted as his butler, buyer, and major-domo, spending hours, as he once related, shopping with Szell and 'going over every item on the menu in great detail'. The orchestra's factotum, he said, would almost collapse under the weight of 'huge buckets filled with finest wines, caviar, *foie gras*, and lobster, all carefully packed in ice, and deposited in our dressing-room'. These, after the concerts, were transported to the train and, said Temianka, 'no banquet at the Ritz could have equalled it'.

But Szell, who got married in the SNO's Glasgow office (the ceremony was presided over by Joseph Barnes, the lawyer who was the orchestra's administrator at the time) and who subsequently taught the Cleveland Orchestra to play better than its more famous rivals in New York, Boston, Chicago, and Philadelphia, did everything on a grand scale, though nobody seems to have loved him for it. A meal at Cleveden Gardens, with Gibson doing imitations of people like Szell, would be bound to be a better experience than sharing a railway compartment with the sardonic martinet himself. Though Gibson can be brusque, he has never been a martinet. He is renowned for the help and advice he gives, the countless favours he bestows, without expecting anything in return. And as a conductor he is considerate, rarely showing impatience with a wayward soloist, or breaking a young singer's nerve. To quote Patricia Hay again:

'I did more than fifteen operas with him, and he gave me such help. My first role was Kate Pinkerton in *Butterfly* and I was scared stiff. Because she doesn't appear until the end of the opera, you have time to get seriously worked up, especially as she has a difficult entrance. Alex used to go round every dressing-room each night before the performance. Some conductors don't bother. On that particular occasion, I was there far too early, and up to high doh. He came to see me. I said I was in a state about my entrance. He said, "Don't worry, I'll give it to you," and he never failed. When I walked on to the stage to sing that dodgy little opening line, he always gave it to me.

'He is immensely practical. Even though mine was just a tiny part, he always said "well done". And he allowed a lot of us to build on these little roles. Later I sang Cherubino in *Figaro* and Zerlina in *Don Giovanni*. By then I'd been abroad, studying in Italy, and Alex was quick to pick up that I'd been working hard and had done my homework. Together we worked out extra decorations for "Voi che sapete", which most conductors don't bother about. Then I sang Despina in *Così fan tutte* alongside Elizabeth Harwood and Janet Baker and was totally bowled over. He always knew what was happening on the stage. There was complete contact.

'Liz, at the time, was singing Fiordiligi in Italian in Germany and in English here, and was going back and forward between the two countries. In Act Two, in our version, she had to sing the words "Bring me a helmet, cloak, and sword from the closet". Now, in Italian, the word for sword is *"spada"*, and one night in Scotland she accidentally asked for a spade. I looked down into the orchestra pit and saw that Alex was nearly off the podium with laughter. Yet Liz was quite unaware what she had said. These were wonderful times.'

From the very start of his career, Gibson has shown this responsive side of himself. And critics, though unaware of it, have sometimes been able to sense it. In a review of one of his concert appearances in London in 1958, with Louis Kentner playing Brahms's Second Piano Concerto, *The Times* wrote that 'he treated his players as intelligent colleagues, controlling or encouraging them with a minimum of gesturing, sometimes when the rhythm was clear hardly moving his stick but moulding the music unobtrusively with his left hand'. The London music critic of *The Scotsman* also paid tribute around that time to Gibson's 'elegant and markedly stylish baton technique', though adding that 'curiously enough, he is sometimes reproached for that'.

Later in his career, indeed, he would be increasingly reproached for it, mostly by players who failed, or were unwilling, to comprehend it. But Gibson has remained unrepentant, continuing to claim that he has never been, and will never be, a bandmaster, and jokingly saying that he is 'growing more and more Furtwänglerish'. Furtwängler's beat was certainly famously quivery, but the Berlin Philharmonic knew through instinct and experience how to interpret it and when to come in (halfway down the baton's descent, it used to be said). Had he wished to clarify it, he could doubtless have done so, but an essential feature of his conducting style – in his case more philosophical than, say, rhythmic – would have been lost. With Klaus Tennstedt it is the same.

Conducting Beethoven's Seventh Symphony at the 1992 Edinburgh Festival, he did little more than shudder. But if his movements looked palsied, the London Philharmonic coped with them and produced a spacious, if somewhat rough-edged, performance in the big-scale German tradition.

Similarly, it is the quality of Gibson's beat — in his case often more horizontal than vertical — that brings the special flow to his performances, and enables him to escape from the tyranny of the bar-line. And though members of the SNO came increasingly to resent it, or be exasperated by it, they also increasingly understood it. On certain nights, when things are not at their best, the result might sometimes be what Michael Tumelty, the present music critic of *The Herald*, has referred to as 'terraced chording'. On others the sound is cohesive, long-spanning, and shapely — the full realisation, one would say, of the conductor's intentions. It is in a performance of, say, Rakhmaninov's Second Symphony that the Gibson style can generally be heard to advantage, but there are no rules about this. Stravinsky, a composer in almost every way the obverse of Rakhmaninov, can also bring out the best in him, as his recorded set of the Stravinsky symphonies luminously demonstrates.

Since Gibson's beat has become one of the most controversial aspects of his musical persona, it is a subject I shall return to. But in 1958, though it was both admired and criticised, it was not an issue. As musical director of Sadler's Wells, he was continuing to establish himself in London's operatic life, whilst conducting the odd concert to prove that he had other predilections. He had friends and he had a fiancée who soon became his wife. He could keep an eye on his widowed mother. And he was one of a Scottish ex-patriate musical mafia, whose members included four opera singers — William McAlpine, Harold Blackburn, Ian Wallace, and David Ward — whom he would later lure back to Scotland from time to time. Old Scottish acquaintances like Robin Richardson of the BBC came down to visit, sometimes camping for a few nights in his flat.

Yet he was not wholly happy. People who live in London and love it frequently seem baffled that not everybody shares their belief in the place. Metropolitan critics, claiming it to be the musical capital of the world, cannot help being patronising about events north of Watford (I myself, as an Edinburgh-based critic, must admit to having been sniffy at times about Arbroath or Galashiels). Those who ungratefully escape from London are accused of wanting to be big fish in a small pool.

But Benjamin Britten disliked London, and successfully created his own musical environment in Aldeburgh. Peter Maxwell Davies, in recent years, has not concealed his growing preference for Edinburgh and Orkney. Gibson's feelings, however, appear to have been more complex. He was doing well. He had conducted György Cziffra, the sensational Hungarian pianist, in his British debut after his escape from his homeland in 1956. He had appeared with Artur Rubinstein in performances of Mozart and Saint-Saëns (and would do so again, in Scotland, when Rubinstein was eighty-seven years old). His first major recording, of Sibelius's Fifth Symphony with the London Symphony Orchestra, had been released by Decca. His first Wagner performances – of *The Flying Dutchman* – were shortly to take place at Sadler's Wells.

Nevertheless, he appears to have experienced around this time a deep longing for home. He was aware that, under its succession of Viennese conductors, the SNO was heading nowhere. He knew, as a touring opera conductor, that Scotland had no real operatic life of its own. Late-night discussions with the musical mafia increasingly turned towards Scotland and what could be done for it. Friends from the north pleaded with him to come back and do something. His occasional guest appearances with the SNO whetted his appetite. The Scottish critics were encouraging. After one glowing Edinburgh performance of Rakhmaninov's Second Symphony (even though at that time he still made the standard cuts in it) I remember writing that that was where the future lay.

All these factors played their part, but more important than any of them was Gibson's belief – as he puts it himself, whenever he is questioned on the matter – that it was not necessarily good for a young conductor to give most of his performances in the glare of metropolitan critical opinion. What he wanted, or thought he wanted, was a more private atmosphere in which to work out his musical ideas. This, he hoped, was what he might find in Glasgow.

Was he right in his instincts? Were they merely a rationalisation of inner conflicts and insecurities? Did he feel that his London luck – for he had certainly been lucky – might run out? Or was it simply that the SNO made him an offer he felt unable to refuse?

I have scanned his press cuttings of the period for evidence that the 'glare of metropolitan critical opinion' might have a secondary meaning. But, though the reviews he received were not invariably good, they were seldom bad. When he conducted his first *Falstaff* at Sadler's Wells in 1958, *The Times* declared that 'Alexander Gibson goes from strength to strength'. When the ill-fated Carl Rosa opera company went bust and was merged with Sadler's Wells at the cost of

170 jobs, Gibson was invited to make sense out of the plans. He was young, but was obviously admired and respected. If any British conductor could call himself a success, and in demand, at the age of thirty-two, it was he.

So the lure had to be the SNO, and with it the development of opera in Scotland. The SNO had never before sought the services of a native conductor in any sort of permanent way. Indeed, it had only recently accepted the notion that a Scot was fit to appear in guest capacity. Its earliest conductor, a century ago, had been a German, George Henschel. Next came a Dutchman, Willem Kes. Thereafter, sprinkled among the vast array of Germans, Austrians, Russians, Hungarians, Poles, and Czechs, the odd Englishman could be discerned – most notably Barbirolli in the 1930s (he was not only a fine conductor, but lucky enough to possess a foreign name), along with Frederic Hymen Cowen, Landon Ronald, and Adrian Boult.

But when Bryden Thomson returned from Hamburg with a testimonial from Hans Schmidt-Isserstedt, he made no headway with the SNO's then administrator, William Fell, who disliked him on sight. James Loughran, during the same period, had been given office duties of a menial nature, but never allowed to conduct. Yet the tide was turning. By 1958, Scotland was gaining a new awareness of its own identity, and people – not only W. Borland in his letter to *The Herald* – were beginning to ask why the SNO could not have a Scottish conductor when there was an obvious candidate available.

Yet, even with a boring Austrian such as Hans Swarowsky on the podium, the SNO management clung to its belief that foreign conductors were automatically better. When it ultimately became plain, even to Fell, that Swarowsky would have to go, a Dutchman seemed his likeliest successor. Well, there was nothing wrong with Willem van Otterloo. He had been the respectable conductor of the Hague Philharmonic since 1949, and would remain so until 1973, when at the age of sixty-six he moved to Australia (and was killed in a car accident five years later). But in Holland, Amsterdam was where the action was; and it seemed all too typical of the SNO's thinking at the time that, if it seriously wanted a Dutchman, the sedate Van Otterloo seemed preferable to a promising young tyro called Bernard Haitink, who had no orchestra of his own and who – if the SNO's management had even heard of him – would undoubtedly have been up for grabs.

But at least it had heard of the almost equally young Alexander Gibson and – whatever Lady Rosebery, Van Otterloo's champion, thought of the matter – several of the Glasgow members of the board of directors favoured approaching him to find out if he would like to come back from London and be Swarowsky's successor. Others thought him too young and inexperienced, even though his operatic training was exactly what would have steered him into a desirable appointment had he been a German working in Germany.

Meanwhile, Swarowsky's contract still had a season to run. Since it was unlikely to be renewed, a decision was urgent. Gradually, Gibson became aware that he was being headhunted, but this in itself was not enough. He would need a genuine offer before he resigned from Sadler's Wells for the second time in his career and quit London.

He had already expressed doubt about his readiness to take on an appointment as important to Scotland as the conductorship of the SNO to Lord Cameron, a senior Scottish law lord and strong Edinburgh member of the orchestra's board of directors. Cameron, giving him a lift in his Rolls Royce round Charlotte Square after a chance encounter in the Scottish Arts Club, had replied that Gibson's modesty would serve him in good stead. Having been in his time a hanging judge, he was not a man given to making casual remarks. Before long, while on tour with Sadler's Wells in Dundee, Gibson received word from Ibbs and Tillett, the London agents, that the SNO was his if he wanted it.

Gibson accepted. A dumbfounded Swarowsky was told that his contract was not being renewed. Happily, the two conductors did not know each other, Gibson never having been one of Swarowsky's vast assembly of pupils at the Vienna Academy of Music. His only feeling of awkwardness, he admits, came when he was conducting the Student Orchestra of Great Britain at the Brussels Expo in 1958. Exploring the exhibition site, he suddenly spotted, through the fish-eye windows of the Austrian pavilion, Swarowsky coaching a line-up of novice conductors in the art of accompanying operatic recitative. It was a faintly surrealist moment, which has stuck in Gibson's memory. But then, deposing another conductor was not something he had done before or would do again, and it came less naturally to him than to other, more sly and egoistic members of his profession. As for Swarowsky, he was treated with tact. Told that it was time to let a young Scotsman have a chance, the distinguished Viennese trainer of conductors graciously – or so it is said – accepted defeat.

The young Scotsman was warily accepted by the orchestra. Sensibly, he did nothing to agitate the players to start with. When Thomas Matthews, who had been the leader under Rankl and Swarowsky, decided to resign, he recruited the immensely experienced Sam Bor (who had played under Toscanini) as his replacement.

True, for a while, he changed their platform layout, and –

Karajan-style – placed the violas, rather than the cellos, on his right, and the cellos in the middle to give their tone a chance to sing outwards. But he never insisted, as Sir Adrian Boult did on his guest appearances, on a purely classical setting, with first and second violins divided to the left and right of the podium in order to differentiate their parts, and a body of bass tone providing ballast in the middle.

After the viola experiment, he reverted to the established modern positions preferred by Swarowsky, with all the violins on the left, violas in the middle, and cellos and basses on the right. And when Scottish Opera was formed, with the SNO in the pit, he quite radically placed the players in their symphonic positions, rather than adopted the operatic convention whereby the strings played on one side, the wind on the other.

In this as in other matters, he saw himself as a 'caring' conductor. But above all he was a Scot, the first in the orchestra's history, and in that capacity he made his presence felt in the office as well as on the podium. His predecessors, even if they rented rooms, had always been visitors. Swarowsky may have conducted and shopped in Scotland – he had a passion for clothes and art books – but he headed back to Vienna whenever he could. Rankl, after his Glasgow concerts, had to be whisked to Central Station to catch his sleeper to London, where he lived and composed his music. But Gibson was always there. For Jean Mearns, the concert administrator, he instantly became 'an integral part of the organisation, very articulate and humorous, which made office meetings a pleasure'.

Since in those days you ascended to the office via a sombre, rather squalid staircase in Hope Street, a bit of humour must have been welcome. Yet Jean Mearns, who became Jean Caldow after she married, thought it the happiest of all the SNO offices. Though Rankl had been volatile and strict, and always called her 'Mearns', he was 'delightful to work with and would calm down if you let him explode'.

The sophisticated Swarowsky gave everybody Christmas lunch (Rankl never noticed it was Christmas). As for Gibson: 'He held pleasant social gatherings, was not awkward to work with, and never minded if you rang him up. He was the only one with a feeling of permanence about him. From the beginning it was his orchestra. Yet if the opera company hadn't got off the ground, he might have gone much sooner. Scottish Opera really changed his whole attitude.'

CHAPTER SIX

The Return of the Native

Long before his homecoming in 1959 became a reality, Gibson had been planning what he might do if it ever happened. As the first conductor of the SNO who would actually live in Scotland – as opposed to renting rooms or residing in a hotel – he wanted to establish a closer relationship with both the players and audiences than someone who merely came and went. He had pored over all Rankl's and Swarowsky's programmes and been shocked by the narrowness of the orchestra's repertoire in the 1950s. Rankl, who was defiantly Teutonic in his tastes, had notoriously rejected Sibelius and Nielsen as 'the scrapings of the Viennese masters', and had refused to conduct them, even though he was fully aware that Scottish audiences had a natural affinity for Nordic symphonies, especially those of Sibelius. Swarowsky, too, had stuck doggedly to the German mainstream, to the extent that when he found himself in difficulties accompanying a soloist in Rakhmaninov's Second Piano Concerto he had to confess that he had never conducted it before.

What astounded Gibson even more, however, was the fact that vast areas of British music – English as well as Scottish – had been almost wholly neglected. True, Rankl had found Vaughan Williams bearable, and had conducted the Scottish premiere of the *Sinfonia Antarctica*. He had even, to a limited degree, tolerated Britten, but most of his other permitted composers were safe traditional figures whose works were easy to conduct and which he could accept as necessary chores. With Swarowsky it was more or less the same, only marginally

72

worse. By planting a performance of Iain Hamilton's *Bartholomew Fair* overture – one of the very few Scottish pieces he ever conducted – in an Edinburgh Festival concert otherwise devoted to Brahms, Schumann, and Respighi, he thought he had done his duty.

Though Rankl at least accepted the odd Viennese challenge – in the form of Mahler's Fifth Symphony or Schoenberg's *Gurrelieder* – to his somewhat frayed abilities, Swarowsky was lazier and seldom trod beyond Brahms or the shorter works of Richard Strauss. A glance at what either of these conductors (but Swarowsky in particular) regarded as a suitable concert for the SNO to give at the Edinburgh Festival now makes dispiriting reading.

So Gibson's first decision, even before his arrival, was to enliven the repertoire, both during the winter season and at the Edinburgh Festival. Since Sibelius had been banned for seven years, he would conduct all seven symphonies in chronological order in a single season. They were works he knew and loved, and they would provide his introductory concert series with something that would never have occurred to Rankl or Swarowsky: a running theme.

Today the idea would possess less novelty value than it did then. Thematic programme planning has become an established musical strategy, and one which, unless it has constructive thinking behind it, can even seem tired and contrived. But in Britain in 1959 it was still quite fresh. Lord Harewood had not yet galvanised the Edinburgh Festival with his famous surveys of single composers or groups of composers. William Glock had not yet revitalised the London Proms. The Royal Festival Hall was as far as ever from achieving anything resembling a unified concert policy, and Birmingham – a generation before the revolutionary Simon Rattle arrived there – was equally unadventurous.

Only in Liverpool, where John Pritchard had recently become conductor of the Philharmonic, were there signs of progress. His Musica Viva concerts, in which performances of difficult modern works were preceded by spoken introductions with musical illustrations by the orchestra, were events that at the time were deemed suicidally daring in Britain; but they succeeded, at least for a while, and Gibson was quick to develop his own version of them in Scotland, paving the way for the more ambitious Musica Nova concerts that would be a later feature of his concert philosophy.

So, spotlighting Sibelius, a great composer of the first half of the twentieth century, was not simply a device for concealing a lack of enthusiasm for more recent music, as it might have been with another conductor; nor was it merely a way of currying favour with a

Sibelius-starved audience. In Gibson's case the interest in contemporary music was genuine, as it had always been, and he demonstrated it afresh, even before launching his pilot SNO season, by conducting his new orchestra in the première of Iain Hamilton's Sinfonia for Two Orchestras at the 1959 Edinburgh Festival.

In sound and effect, this was something very different from the token Hamilton overture that Swarowsky had conducted the previous year. The Sinfonia was a major work, a milestone in Hamilton's output, marking a turning-point in his style. The outcome of a close study of Webern, it displayed a terser, grittier, less ingratiating side of a composer whose previous works had included a set of *Scottish Dances* (1956) and a concerto for jazz trumpet (1957). Along with Thea Musgrave, Hamilton had begun to bring a more international, less specially 'Scottish' accent to Scottish music, but he was paying the penalty for it by being dismissed by retrogressive compatriots as one of fashion's victims. Finding the atmosphere of his homeland less than congenial, he chose, like Musgrave, to live elsewhere.

So it was by a sublime irony that his latest work was commissioned by the Robert Burns Federation in conjunction with the Edinburgh Festival. What the Burns Federation, not famed for breadth of vision, expected of Hamilton is easy to imagine – a couthy sequence of familiar ditties, romantically orchestrated. But what Gibson conducted at the Usher Hall to celebrate the bicentenary of the poet's birth was not like that at all. Hamilton, in his programme-note, warned the audience that the music was 'a tribute to a great poet' but that there was 'no relationship between it and the poet's work'. Burns's supporters, feeling betrayed, spluttered with rage.

To be fair to them, they had been previously sheltered – as had Scotland in general – from the more uncompromising trends in modern music. The Edinburgh Festival was not famed for encouraging vanguard composers. The SNO had no experience of playing their works. And readers of *The Scotsman*, to judge by some of their letters to the editor, still thought even Bartók a fraud.

Against this background, then, Gibson's championing of Hamilton's Sinfonia was bound – as Peter Heyworth delicately put it in *The Observer* – to leave the audience 'slightly stunned'. It was, after all, the Usher Hall's first brush with anything even faintly avant-garde. And though Noël Goodwin in the *Daily Express* claimed it to be the most significant event in the entire Edinburgh Festival, the Burns Federation contemplated demanding its money back. In the words of its president: 'It is rotten and ghastly ... there were no tunes ... of Burns there was not a trace.' Hamilton's fee – 'a good one', the president added balefully – was likely to be reconsidered at the Federation's annual conference in Ayr.

But Gibson had begun his conductorship of the SNO the way he intended to continue. Though one listener complained that he had expected melodious music – 'Burns liked melodious music' – Iain Hamilton's Sinfonia was ruthlessly repeated during the winter season, and subsequently recorded. A shake-up was in progress which the critics did not fail to note.

In the *Daily Telegraph*, Martin Cooper admitted that he had always found the SNO's Edinburgh Festival appearances something of an embarrassment, the orchestra being 'a comparatively inexpert and inexperienced body inviting inevitably odious comparisons' with its European counterparts. But under Gibson, he declared, the orchestra had moved into a quite different class. His words may have seemed premature, yet by the spring of 1960 Gibson had conducted the British première of Schoenberg's Violin Concerto, with Wolfgang Marschner as soloist, in the first of several Musica Viva concerts. Hailing the programme as being 'singularly well devised', and paying tribute to the 'storms of applause', Peter Heyworth said he wished that some of the London concert organisers responsible for withholding the concerto for twenty-four years could have been in St Andrew's Hall that night. 'Hats off to Glasgow,' he added, for the first but by no means the last time in his career.

But Gibson had other Scottish ambitions, about which only a few people yet had any inkling, and he had been discussing them for years in secret nocturnal sessions with his London mafia. Midnight, as I have discovered, is one of Gibson's times for making plans. In this he is like many other musicians who unwind after performances by airing ideas, saying 'let's try it', talking not so much about performances past as about performances future.

There have been occasions when, as a critic, my own ideas have converged with his, and we have let it be known to each other that we were on the same wavelength about something or other – perhaps the music that a forthcoming programme should contain, or who might be the next director of the Edinburgh Festival. It is then that I can expect my phone to ring at one o'clock in the morning, and a voice, as fresh as a daisy, to say 'About this idea . . .' I will then draw up a chair, top up a glass, and talk into the night as if we are both in the same room.

But in 1960 I was working in Holland, and had only a faint glimmering (via *The Scotsman*, which in those days was a truly international paper, available abroad) of what was happening at home.

Gibson's appointment had seemed a step so logical that I thought the SNO – not famed for doing the right thing – would never decide upon it. The news of his appointment, and of what he was doing, made me begin to wish I was back in Scotland. The Sibelius theme looked inviting (Amsterdam, unless George Szell was around, shunned Sibelius in the same way as Rankl did). On the other hand, Gibson did not conduct Bruckner, a great Dutch speciality; the Holland Festival, directed by Peter Diamand, was more challenging than Edinburgh; and the Netherlands Opera, for all its shortcomings, gave me a staple diet of masterpieces I would not have had back home.

Gradually, however, I became aware that Gibson's aspirations extended beyond concerts with the SNO. His late-night talks with London singers had been about something else. Their dream was nothing less than the formation of a Scottish national opera company. John Donaldson, Sadler's Wells's Glasgow-born staff producer, had urged Gibson to go for this particular jackpot. Harold Blackburn, William McAlpine, Ian Wallace, and David Ward had all said they would sing. Norman Tucker, managing director of Sadler's Wells, had pledged his support. Richard Telfer, in conspiratorial mode, was filled with quiet enthusiasm.

Even after Gibson left London, the talks remained secret. The Scottish tendency to bicker and to pour scorn on grand ideas has destroyed many a valiant scheme, and Gibson did not want his brainchild to be stillborn. But once installed in Glasgow – where, to prove that he was not just another conductor in transit, he had moved immediately into a handsome flat in Westbourne Gardens – he confided in a few friends he knew he could trust.

One of these was Ainslie Millar, chartered surveyor and opera buff, who had recently become Scottish director of the Sadler's Wells Trust. Another was Ian Rodger, a Glasgow solicitor with a special interest in the arts, who drew up a provisional constitution for a non-profit-distributing company called the Scottish Opera Society Ltd. A midnight meeting at the home of Alastair Dunnett, editor of *The Scotsman*, resulted eventually in the promise of a subsidy of £1,000 from what was then that newspaper's sister organisation, Scottish Television. Stewart Cruickshank, director of Howard and Wyndham, offered the periodic use of the King's Theatre, Glasgow, on favourable terms. William Fell, administrator of the SNO, recognised that work in the pit would be a financially beneficial way of employing the orchestra during off-peak periods. After much debate, an initial repertoire of Donizetti's *Don Pasquale* and a double-bill of Bartók's *Bluebeard's Castle* and Stravinsky's *The Soldier's Tale* was chosen, an earlier scheme to do *Il trovatore* having been reckoned riskily expensive.

Since Gibson had already conducted the Bartók and Stravinsky works in London, all he would have to learn was the Donizetti. David Ward, by then principal bass at Covent Garden, agreed to sing Bluebeard. Ian Wallace, one of Glyndebourne's most experienced comic basses, offered his services for Don Pasquale, with Duncan Robertson, Gibson's old school chum and fellow-gondolier from Motherwell, in the romantic tenor role of Ernesto. Gordon Jackson, already established as one of Scotland's leading actors and film stars, would appear in Stravinsky's spoken anti-opera.

With so strong a Scottish bias, it was hoped that the plans for a total of six performances in Glasgow would qualify for a much-needed grant from the Scottish Committee of the Arts Council of Great Britain, precursor of what is now the Scottish Arts Council. The estimated deficit, after all, amounted to less than £2,000 – not a lot for such an event, even in 1961. But it was not to be. Employing a long familiar ruse, the Committee replied that the application had come too late to be included in the Council's annual budget. No doubt the Committee's director, Dr George Firth, lost no sleep over the fact that he had stymied the most important cultural development in Scotland since the foundation of the Edinburgh Festival. A dedicated bureaucrat, Firth was the man who liked to send part of his budget back to London at the end of the financial year.

But Gibson and his team were not disheartened for long. The conductor himself had the challenge, in February 1961, of his first North American guest conducting trip, from which he returned with an invitation for the SNO to perform there, if funds could be found for the flight. Alas, the orchestra's large and pusillanimous board of directors, accustomed to a life of inexertion with Rankl and Swarowsky, turned down the opportunity, even though STV offered to donate £1,000 towards the cost (William Fell, the orchestra's administrator, was 'not available to comment'). Gibson, with dates that year in Brno and Rotterdam, and an invitation to return to Sadler's Wells to conduct the première of a new opera by Richard Rodney Bennett, must have wondered if, after all, Scotland was going to be a lost cause. But it was at this demoralising moment that the nocturnal meeting in Alastair Dunnett's house finally paid off. The money that STV had agreed to give to the SNO went to Scottish Opera instead.

Scotland's entire musical future now rested, in one way or another, upon Gibson's brainchild. It was not simply that the foundation of Scottish Opera had been secured; it was that out of the new company a whole new musical network would soon develop. The creation of Scottish Opera created a climate which itself brought about the creation, in the years ahead, of three new orchestras and a variety of ancillary projects such as the transformation of a Victorian variety theatre into an opera house and the development of an opera school under the auspices of the Royal Scottish Academy of Music and Drama.

The orchestras, it's true, were not formed purely to satisfy the demands of an increasingly voracious opera company. The Scottish Baroque Ensemble, founded by Leonard Friedman in 1969, primarily played for John Calder's Kinross-shire festival, Ledlanet Nights. The Scottish Chamber Orchestra, founded five years later, had concert-giving ambitions. Both depended for their survival on regular dates with Scottish Opera, and it was only when the SCO ultimately withdrew from the pit, that the opera company was forced to recruit its own full-time orchestra.

In 1961, however, Scottish Opera's own future rested on the immediate availability of the SNO, and it was Gibson's conductorship of both organisations that made the project artistically possible. The last remaining stumbling block was the attitude of the Scottish Committee of the Arts Council. Would it be blinkered enough to refuse a second time to provide support? To prevent this happening, Gibson favoured the formation of a determined Advisory Council which, if the worst came to the worst, would shame the no-sayers into submission. Accordingly, Robin Orr, professor of music at Glasgow University, was invited to become the company's first (and, as things later turned out, unquestionably its best) chairman, and Lord Harewood its honorary president. In a letter to the new director of the Edinburgh Festival – as Harewood had now become – Gibson declared: 'From the moment I left Sadler's Wells I have felt that if I have a mission in life it should be to further the cause of opera in my present sphere of activities.' Words as potent as these ensured Harewood's instant acceptance.

With time to plan a 1962 season, the new company used it to advantage. The idea of a *Don Pasquale* combined with a twentieth-century double-bill, all based to some extent on Sadler's Wells resources, no longer seemed so attractive. Something more original was called for, and it was Richard Telfer who planted a time-bomb in Gibson's mind. Emerging from St Andrew's Hall after one of his Saturday night concerts with the SNO, the conductor found the soft-spoken, diminutive figure of 'Uncle Dick' waiting for him. 'I think,' he murmured from the shadows, 'I have an idea for you.'

Having been a tourist guide in Paris before the Second World War, Telfer had developed a taste for French opera. Aware that 1962 would be the centenary of Debussy's birth, he proposed that Gibson conduct *Pelléas et Mélisande*, a music drama which had not been seen in Scotland for almost half a century, and which was even absent at the time from Covent Garden's repertoire. The fact that Mary Garden, Debussy's mistress, and creator of the role of Mélisande, was by then living in retirement in her native Aberdeen added piquancy to the idea. When Mary Garden first sang Mélisande in 1904, she inspired the composer to say that here indeed 'was the gentle voice I heard in my innermost soul'.

Today, Debussy's masterpiece is no rarity in Britain. Covent Garden with Claudio Abbado as conductor, and Welsh National Opera with Pierre Boulez, have both staged notable performances of it in recent years. The Lyon Opera, with no more than black curtains and tall French windows as decor, brought it to the 1985 Edinburgh Festival, using Debussy's little-known first version of the score, conducted by John Eliot Gardiner. From Paris, Peter Brook took his controversial truncation of it to Glasgow's Tramway in 1993.

In the early 1960s, however, the work was seriously neglected. Would a production by a novice company with severe financial restrictions be a feasibility, or mere madness? The idea, in any event, caught everybody's fancy. Gibson, who had never conducted it before, got down to learning Debussy's delicate but steel-strong music. Yet there were worries that, in a country lacking in operatic experience, so oblique a masterpiece might prove caviar to the general. In case *Pelléas* proved too specialised, a crowd-puller, which could be performed on alternate evenings, seemed desirable. Gibson's thoughts returned to the first opera he had ever seen, the one that was already recurring at key points in his career. He chose *Madama Butterfly*.

But the blessing of Dr George Firth had still to be obtained. Costs were rising. Firth was discouraging. Fearing that *Pelléas* might have to be replaced by something less ambitious, Gibson and his directors – long before corporate funding had become a way of life for the arts in Britain – recruited a number of private individuals and organisations to make guarantees against loss. In the end, the figures added up and the plans for a 1962 season went ahead.

Amazingly, all this was done in the strictest secrecy. Nobody leaked the story to *The Herald* (which in 1961 did not possess a staff music critic). And though Alastair Dunnett of *The Scotsman* knew what was happening, he kept his own counsel in a way that an editor today might be less disposed to do. Meanwhile, Gibson's early seasons as conductor of the SNO had been so filled with new ideas that nobody could have imagined that he had even bigger plans.

The Musica Viva performance of Schoenberg's Violin Concerto – 'a landmark in Scottish musical history', proclaimed Christopher Grier – quickly led to other events of its kind. In October 1960 a heady mixture of Webern (Variations, Op 30), Schoenberg (Piano Concerto), and Stravinsky (*Jeu de Cartes*) prompted *The Times* to express the forlorn hope that London would shortly follow suit. But the biggest Musica Viva venture of all, and the one that really made history, took place the following spring when Gunther Schüller's *Spectra* and Thea Musgrave's *Obliques* served as the prelude at St Andrew's Hall to the British première of Stockhausen's *Gruppen*.

A total of 110 players and two extra conductors were required to produce the resounding, challenging new timbres of this twentieth-century masterpiece, which the German composer had completed four years earlier, and which London audiences would not hear for a further six years. It proved, if proof was still necessary, that Gibson's 1959 performance of Iain Hamilton's Sinfonia for Two Orchestras had been no mere flash in the pan but a clear statement of intent.

A return to London to conduct a revival of *Madama Butterfly* at Sadler's Wells, this time with Victoria Elliott in the title-role, would have seemed no more than a bagatelle if Puccini's opera were a work Gibson treated in that sort of way. In fact he treated it just as seriously as *Gruppen*, and had the good fortune to have Charles Craig as his Pinkerton. It was a role Craig would soon sing, to sterling effect, for the as yet unformed Scottish company, before unleashing his glowing voice upon Otello and Siegmund, in which his rapport with Gibson went from strength to strength.

During the early 1960s Gibson remained closely in touch with his old company, and hardly a season went past without his being invited back to make a guest appearance. He conducted performances of Rossini's ravishing last comedy, *Le Comte d'Ory*, that were highly prized. Of Richard Rodney Bennett's *The Ledge*, in which a would-be suicide struggles to fling himself from a high building, he was inevitably unable to make so much.

There must have been moments when the struggle to make Scottish Opera a reality seemed equally suicidal. But in the end, four months before the curtain was due to rise at the King's Theatre, Glasgow, the new company felt brave enough to disclose its plans. The Debussy and Puccini productions would be 'in the nature of a pilot scheme'. If Glasgow's response was encouraging, performances would spread to Edinburgh and other Scottish centres with short opera seasons to supplement the work of Sadler's Wells. Then, if all continued to go well, the scheme would 'become a significant feature of the musical and cultural life of Scotland in general and Glasgow in particular'. Gibson would be musical director, and the 'whole project would be built on the growing strength and reputation of the Scottish National Orchestra'.

Few of Scotland's subsequent musical schemes would be such well-kept secrets, or would be so grandly creative. In recent years, indeed, some have been quite negative. But the 1960s, for Scotland at least, were a time of glorious expansion. By 1964 the new Labour Government had given Britain, in the person of Jenny Lee, its first minister of the arts, and her policies and aspirations were as sensationally far from Thatcherism as it would be possible to imagine. Already, Scottish Opera had become an unstoppable force which would gather momentum from season to season until – as is the unfortunate nature of Britain's cultural life – it began to go into what, it was hoped, would be no more than temporary confusion and decline.

Its launch, however, was an event so sure-handed, and so conspicuously successful, that it could only be hailed a musical milestone more important than the much more uncertain launch in 1891 of the orchestra that would eventually become the SNO. As Magnus Magnusson, at that time a features writer on *The Scotsman*, exclaimed: 'This is Scotland's chance.' It was, he said, one of those immensely bold and imaginative breakthroughs that can revitalise an area of a nation's cultural life, 'the final act of faith that caps long months, even years, of dreaming and planning'.

Viewed from abroad, which was where I still was at the time, the scheme looked less than watertight. Magnusson's words had a romantic impulsiveness about them that suggested, to my cynical mind, the gush of an enthusiast rather than the rigour of a critic, though the journalistic support he provided in those early days was invaluable.

Much as I admired Alexander Gibson's achievements, I suspected that the new company might turn out to be no more than the Edinburgh Opera Company, or the Glasgow Grand, with knobs on. True, his conducting of *Nabucco* at the Usher Hall in 1957 had worked wonders with inexpert local resources, but Debussy's *Pelléas et Mélisande* was a work in a quite different league of difficulty and subtlety.

It was a doubt I evidently shared with at least one fellow critic, Edmund Tracey, who confessed in *The Observer* that when he first heard that a short experimental season of Scottish opera was to be given in Glasgow he grew faint with apprehension. Would Tovey's *The Bride of Dionysus* or MacCunn's *Jeanie Deans* be forced upon him? Fortunately, these phantoms were soon put to flight.

The crucial factor, clearly, was Gibson's drive, intelligence, and belief in what he was doing. Today it is hard to remember the state of music in Scotland before his time. The availability of a revitalised SNO was also important, and William Fell, prudent though he tended to be, had given the plans his full support. But what of the casting? Gibson had made plain that he wanted Scottish Opera to be the Covent Garden rather than the Sadler's Wells of Scotland. In other words, his aim was opera sung in the original language by a cast of international calibre. In 1962, however, good French singers were almost as hard to come by as they are today. Nevertheless, an almost entirely French, or French–Canadian, team was somehow recruited. Casting proved to be one of the company's great strengths in its early years and added to the air of excitement. 'International opera cast gather in Glasgow' stated one headline, bringing an air of excitement to the whole project.

But the first work Gibson conducted for Scottish Opera was not, as is nowadays assumed, *Pelléas et Mélisande*. It was with his old friend and faithful companion *Madama Butterfly* that he and his company made history on 5 June 1962. And in this production, too, the cast was international. Taking the advice of Lord Harewood, Gibson invited a New York soprano, Elaine Malbin, to sing the title-role. Charles Craig, as already stated, was Pinkerton, but an opportunity was given to a young singer from Wishaw to play the Bonze. His name was William McCue, and he went on to be one of the excellent resident Scottish singers the company would regularly employ.

Yet for all the pressure of rehearsals, Gibson still had space in the spring of 1962 for another meaty Musica Viva programme with the SNO. This time the concert opened with a new Scottish work, Thomas Wilson's Variations for Orchestra, followed by Bartók's First Piano Concerto (featuring the 25-year-old John Ogdon as soloist, fresh from winning the Tchaikovsky Prize in Moscow) and an austere early work by Peter Maxwell Davies, *St Michael* for seventeen wind instruments, written long before his much-publicised move to Orkney. Later, Gibson would conduct a large-scale survey of Bartók's music, with Vladimir Ashkenazy as soloist.

Gibson's tirelessness, and desire to put Scotland firmly on the musical map, was already a potent combination of qualities. Yet he never took himself too seriously, or boasted of his achievements. His matter-of-fact sense of humour, which has been described as a Scottish birthright, was seldom absent, even when he announced to an assembly of solemn London critics, 'From the moment I left Sadler's Wells I felt something should be done to decentralise professional music in this country.'

With the exception, all too briefly, of John Pritchard in Liverpool, no other musical director of a British orchestra was devising concerts of the sort Gibson was. No London orchestra, indeed, would have entertained the idea, and, when the London Symphony Orchestra was engaged to give the belated London première of Schoenberg's Violin Concerto with Wolfgang Marschner as soloist, it offered Gibson rehearsal facilities that were disgracefully inferior to those he was now accustomed to in Scotland. Not until the foundation of the London Sinfonietta in 1968 would the metropolis have an orchestra – admittedly of less than symphony orchestra proportions – with a flair for contemporary music. Not until Simon Rattle took command of the City of Birmingham Symphony Orchestra in 1980 would there be an English symphony orchestra with a sustained policy of adventurous programming.

But, inevitably, Gibson's operatic achievements won him greater public esteem than his belief that the orchestral repertoire required replenishing. No conductor in the 1960s would gain more than a handful of new friends for his championing of Schoenberg. Verdi's *Otello* was another matter altogether. This, along with Mozart's *Die Entführung aus dem Serail* and a pairing of Dallapiccola's *Volo di notte* with Ravel's *L'Heure Espagnole*, was to be the substance of Scottish Opera's second season, which this time would include Edinburgh as well as Glasgow.

'TONIGHT, OTELLO' proclaimed the poster in huge letters, dazing London visitors with the idea of a city like Glasgow creating its own production of late Verdi. When Gibson stepped into the orchestra pit, and the SNO unleashed the full fury of the opening storm music, it was plain that the success of the new company had been fully confirmed. But there was more to it than that. Gibson himself had shouldered most of the administration of Scottish Opera's first season as well as conducting all but one of the performances. He knew he could not continue to do this but he knew somebody who could. That somebody was Peter Hemmings, a Cambridge post-graduate who had been president of the University Opera Group and had recently been appointed repertory and planning manager at Sadler's Wells. Gibson persuaded the London company to release Hemmings on a temporary basis. The seasons grew year by year until Hemmings moved to Glasgow as Scottish Opera's full-time administrator in its first office in

Holland Street. Thus began a partnership that lasted fifteen years and built Scottish Opera into a permanent company with its own theatre in Glasgow.

CHAPTER SEVEN

The Great Days

What were the attributes that made Gibson, at the age of thirty-seven, the man Neville Garden called Scotland's Mr Music? To say simply that he was the right person in the right place at the right time might seem too much of a cliché, but it was certainly true. Had Willem van Otterloo become conductor of the SNO in 1959 there would have been no Scottish Opera and no Musica Viva. But apart from being inspirational in his ideas, and apart from the ability to attract people around him who could in turn inspire him, he was a visionary conductor, a likeable personality, and a true Scot in the best sense of the expression.

Attracting the right people was important to him. A conductor with ninety instrumentalists, a hundred or so choristers, and a variety of soloists in front of him can feel nerve-rackingly isolated. In Glasgow, in the foyer of the Theatre Royal, there is a lofty portrait of Gibson, one of two painted by David Donaldson, the Queen's Limner in Scotland, showing him in the orchestra pit, poised on a stool. The painting originally caused Gibson embarrassment, since such tributes tend to be posthumous. But before the move to the Theatre Royal had been thought about, Donaldson had asked him to sit for a portrait. When, as part of a fund-raising campaign for the theatre, a number of Scottish artists were invited to donate their commission for the sale of their work, Donaldson generously donated his as yet unpainted portrait of the conductor to the Theatre Royal. Later, when the manner of opening the theatre was discussed, the cutting of a ribbon across the orchestra pit was jettisoned in favour of the unveiling of the Donaldson portrait. Twelve years later, in the company's jubilee year, a bust of Gibson's head, shoulders, and arms was also unveiled. This was commissioned by Scottish Opera from Archie Forrest.

In Donaldson's portrait, no orchestral players are visible. Costumed figures in the background carry a whiff of what looks like *A Midsummer Night's Dream*. Gibson's face, with just the faintest trickle of a smile, is enigmatic.

I have seen him look like that before, usually when he has been unhappy with one of his own performances, or when he has been unable to draw from his performers the sounds he has desired. Occasionally, I have met him afterwards and he has asked me what I have thought of it. He does not ask this question lightly, and he knows that, as a critic, I could be embarrassed by it. Critics do not like giving opinions before committing them to print. But I am aware at such times that he does not expect me to say 'very good' or 'I enjoyed it'. To anything resembling a bromide, he will riposte: 'Come on, you know that's not what I'm asking.'

Once, in this respect, he took me by surprise. It was after Scottish Opera's first, much-loved, long-remembered performance of *Così fan tutte* at Perth in April 1967. Elizabeth Harwood and Janet Baker, Ryland Davies and Peter van der Bilt, Jenifer Eddy and Inia Te Wiata had formed the incredibly perfect cast, who were simultaneously serious and funny, romantic and poised, in the way that Mozart in this work intricately demands. In the intimacy of Perth's lovely little Victorian theatre the humour and sadness of the music had been eloquently conveyed. And the sparkling streets of the lovely town, that moonlit night, had seemed the best place in the world to walk along at the end of an entrancing performance of Mozart's most human opera.

Yet when I encountered Gibson afterwards in the lounge of the Royal George Hotel, where the whole company seemed to be staying, I found him downcast. Had I really enjoyed it? He seemed anxious to know. I extolled the singing. I praised the uncommon truthfulness of the performance, every aspect of which, I said, meshed with success. But surely he knew all that for himself.

What was bothering him, it turned out, was whether I thought he had been able to get what he wanted, and/or what I wanted, from the orchestra. I confirmed that he had, allowing for the fact that there was space in the auditorium for only a handful of players, and that the string tone, as a result, was somewhat thin. And that was the crux of the matter. He considered that he had failed to get exactly the instrumental sounds he desired. He was right, of course. When, later in the run, I heard it again, the playing was inarguably better.

With Peter Hemmings at Scottish Opera, and with Robert Ponsonby now at the SNO, Gibson had administrators who were friends as well as colleagues, and who encouraged his talents to blossom. Ponsonby, a former director of the Edinburgh Festival, had been earmarked by Gibson, with the full support of the orchestra's board of directors, as soon as William Fell (who by then was finding developments like Musica Viva more than a man his age could handle) decided it was time to retire. It was an astute appointment. He already knew a bit about the orchestra. And he loved opera. A man of impeccable breeding (Eton, Oxford, and The Guards) he had previously shown his mettle by endorsing the commissioning of Iain Hamilton's potentially outrageous Sinfonia for Two Orchestras in 1959. He had encouraged four unknown young men called Alan Bennett, Peter Cook, Jonathan Miller, and Dudley Moore to stage an irreverent revue called *Beyond the Fringe* at the last Edinburgh Festival over which he presided. And in appearance he was imposing enough (at a height of more than six and a half feet) to have been mistaken by Tertia Liebenthal for a policeman.

Gibson, with whom he already had some musical empathy, was entrusted with the task of approaching him on behalf of the board and succeeded in enticing him back to Scotland. For eight years their rapport yielded bold, fascinating, often risky programmes, in which Henze and Stravinsky were vigorously spotlit, and the orchestral works of Schumann, rather than of Beethoven or Brahms, were considered a suitable theme to run through one entire season of concerts.

As Ponsonby was to say later, Gibson at the time was in the prime of his abilities, with a distinctive style of his own, constantly eager to do new things and to develop Scotland's musical resources in fresh ways. When it became plain that the Edinburgh Festival had outgrown the increasingly geriatric vocal support of the Edinburgh Royal Choral Union, Gibson persuaded Lord Harewood – who had established himself as the most comprehensively ambitious of the Festival's chain of directors – to form a brilliant new Festival Chorus recruited from the whole of Scotland, with Arthur Oldham as director.

When Musica Viva seemed in need of revitalisation, Gibson transformed it into Musica Nova, which, with the support of Frederick Rimmer of Glasgow University's music department, became a triennial festival of modern music, presenting seminars, lectures, and public rehearsals, and commissioning major works from the cream of modern composers. When the need arose for the services of a chamber orchestra, for Lord Harewood among others, Gibson split the SNO in two. Sometimes, during the off-season, he would take one half of the orchestra on a tour of small halls in the Highlands while an associate conductor took the other half to the Borders.

The last of these ideas formed part of what was gradually emerging as one of Gibson's most ambitious plans: to turn the SNO into a vast musical pool out of which a symphony orchestra, opera orchestra, and chamber orchestra could be drawn according to demand. His model was the Vienna Philharmonic, which had the resources to serve the needs of concert hall and opera house simultaneously in Austria's cultural capital.

But though he managed gradually to increase the SNO's overall strength to ninety-six players, complete with ten double basses and extra woodwind, thus making it one of the biggest orchestras in Britain, he never got farther than that. The Scottish Arts Council, which had grown out of the old and less autonomous Scottish Committee, deemed the scheme dangerously monopolistic. A separate self-governing chamber orchestra was favoured, and subsequently emerged as the Scottish Chamber Orchestra in 1974. But the question of a separate opera orchestra – though this, too, was eventually formed – remains to this day a controversial issue, which the adoption of Gibson's plan might have averted.

Any success with a large pool would in any case have depended on the SNO's continuing willingness to accompany opera as well as give concerts, and this was something that remained uncertain. No matter how often Gibson cited the Vienna Philharmonic, the players remained unconvinced that their future should lie so substantially in opera. In this, as in other ways, Britain was different from the rest of Europe. Opera and concerts here were simply not, and still are not, integrated in the same way. There was no tradition of symphony orchestras spending half their life in the pit, and, as a result, players accustomed to performing Brahms looked down on practitioners of Verdi in much the same way as journalists on broadsheet newspapers are sometimes snooty about their tabloid colleagues.

Musically it was a silly schism, but nobody who sat regularly on the ample space of a large concert platform was prepared to see it as such. What was good enough for the Duisburg Symphony Orchestra (which performs for the Deutsche Oper am Rhein) or for the Munich Philharmonic (which has links with the Bavarian State Opera) was not acceptable to the SNO.

Even the limited amount of opera they were performing in the

1960s appears to have displeased many members of the orchestra – or so Gibson began to believe. And though the players today deny that they ever wanted to opt out of opera (they claim that they simply wanted to play less often for the opera company than was being forced upon them) it is evident that their relationship with their conductor became strained because of this. But in Ponsonby's time, at least, the rumbling volcano in the orchestra pit never actually erupted. Scottish Opera still seemed so new, so exciting, so worth while and so well run that even traditionally dissatisfied orchestral players were elated by it.

And despite the tendency of British orchestras in recent years to be disparaging about their conductors, there was little the players could find fault with in Gibson's handling of Gounod's *Faust*, Verdi's *Otello* and *Falstaff*, and Musorgsky's *Boris Godunov* (a work presented in the darker, sharper-edged, more pared-down original version which Gibson preferred to the glitzy Rimsky-Korsakov arrangement more usually employed). Returning to Scotland to become music critic of *The Scotsman* in time to review these events, I became an instant convert to the company's aims and ambitions.

Yet the choice of *Faust*, I confess, had continued to make me fear the worst right up to the rise of the curtain. How could a progressive company possibly contemplate performing Gounod's scented French distortion of Goethe, an opera that surely deserved to sink without trace? But the truth was that I had allowed my judgment to be coloured by old memories of how I had seen it treated by local amateurs, and how I had slumbered through interminable performances of the Garden Scene.

When I attended the first night of Anthony Besch's strong, stylish, and colourful production at the King's Theatre, Glasgow, I was bowled over by it. Gibson, in the pit, conducted it with fire, not the French romantic limpness I had prepared myself for. Robert Ponsonby, sitting across the aisle, made murmurs of approval. A dedicated opera buff, who had brought some excellent European companies to the Edinburgh Festival in the 1950s, he knew quality when he saw it.

Today, more than a quarter of a century later, he says he still remembers the pleasure of working with Gibson, and how much he admired him. 'I am so grateful he persuaded me to work in Glasgow. Those were great times. The themes we pursued! The way-out rarities we programmed! The modern music we performed! London should have been ashamed of itself. And when, in the end, I left, he made me play piano duets with him at my farewell party. By then he had completed his *Ring* cycle with Scottish Opera, and what did we play? We played *The Ring*, or at any rate Chabrier's *Souvenir de Bayreuth*, based on *Ring* themes. The first ten years of Scottish Opera, you know, were quite faultless. Peter Hemmings, Robin Orr, and Alex formed a masterly troika, but it was Alex who put it together.'

Working so closely with Gibson, however, also made Ponsonby aware of other, sometimes perplexing aspects of the man. For all the elegance of his conducting, for all his charm, for all his mastery in the boardroom – 'he had all the cleverness of an important diplomat, and indeed he *is* an important diplomat' – Ponsonby detected in him some unexpected uncertainties.

'He seemed to find it incredibly difficult to raise a controversial issue with colleagues. I remember once he rang me up. There was clearly something he wanted to say. He suggested we go for a walk. Now, you will know as well as I do that Alex never walks. But it was a nice day and we went to the Queen's View. We struggled up the hill. Pleasantries were exchanged, a bit of gossip. Then we walked down again. We drove back to Westbourne Gardens. Still nothing. We sat in the garden. Eventually, after three or four hours, he raised the issue, though I can't now recall what it was that was costing him so dear. A lot of things cost him dear. He suffers from nerves much more than people imagine, a reluctance to commit himself, and has all kinds of internal problems with which he somehow copes, though nobody knows at what cost.'

These, certainly, are among the areas of Gibson which, as a journalist, you probe at your peril, the ones that prompt him to ask you to switch off your tape recorder – a device I had abandoned using anyway, early on in our sessions, because it seemed to make him so uncomfortable. Once, coming unexpectedly into the room and finding us at work, his wife burst out laughing. 'Alex,' she exclaimed, seeing him sitting stiffly and earnestly on his chair while I fired questions at him, 'you look so *miserable.*'

Had Ponsonby not been tempted back to London by the opportunity to run classical music on Radio Three and, with it, the Albert Hall Proms, would he have continued to find life in Glasgow as congenial as Gibson did? Or would he, in the end, have sought some other outlet? The fact that the conductor belonged to Glasgow – or, at any rate, to one of its satellite towns – placed him in an altogether different position from the administrator.

For Gibson, Glasgow was home. Quite apart from having a job he enjoyed – two jobs to be exact – he felt securely in place in a way that none of his predecessors had done and none of his successors would do. Certainly, in SNO terms, he represented a break with tradition. Of his immediate predecessors, Swarowsky stayed two years and Rankl five (though both would have been prepared to stay longer). Walter Susskind, having won the old Scottish Orchestra its 'National' status, resigned after six years. Of the thirty-or-so previous resident or semi-resident conductors, none had stayed longer than that, and many had stayed for an appreciably shorter time.

Moreover, none had had Gibson's personal commitment to Scotland. When Ponsonby departed in 1972, Gibson had already been on the podium for thirteen years. When David Richardson, Ponsonby's Manchester-born successor, departed in 1980, Gibson was still there. His role model, as everyone by then knew, was Sir John Barbirolli who, though he had been in charge of the Scottish Orchestra for only a few (but crucial) seasons in the 1930s, had been conductor of the Hallé Orchestra from 1943 until his death in 1970. During his long reign he had shaped the Hallé in his own image, teaching it to play Elgar, Mahler, and Sibelius – curiously enough a repertoire similarly favoured by Gibson, albeit in a different way – with the big phrasing, the grand sweep, the measured tempi (which, even within a single performance, were capable of growing progressively slower) for which he became famed.

Though Barbirolli stayed even longer with the Hallé than Gibson stayed with the SNO, both of them were exceptions to the British rule of change. During Gibson's period with the SNO, the London Symphony Orchestra had six conductors, and the London Philharmonic the same number. Even the Hallé, since Barbirolli's death, has had three; so, too, has the SNO in the nine years since Gibson's resignation in 1984. There have always been two opinions about the value of long-term resident conductors. On the positive side, they are said to provide stability of style, aim, and programme planning, and to have time in which to work out their ideas and impose their distinctive sound upon an orchestra. Barbirolli did that in Manchester, as did Gibson in Scotland.

'Thinking back,' Ponsonby said to me recently, 'we had a very beautiful sounding orchestra at the end of my days in Scotland. Alex had a physical style one could recognise. Though there were players who complained that his left hand contradicted what his right hand was doing, he did have the ability to make his hands do different things, which not many other conductors possess. As he said himself, he was not a bandmaster. Andrew Porter, a music critic who has written about him on a number of occasions, has pointed out how physical style affects the sound an orchestra makes, and it's a principle which I myself certainly accept. Charles Münch's high-tension conducting of the Boston Symphony Orchestra brought great French brightness of tone.

Karajan, with his horizontal beat, obtained thick, plush playing from the Berlin Philharmonic. Alex's beat, and sound, have always been round, not edgy, very pleasant and warm.'

Viewed from different sides of the podium, any conductor's beat admittedly conveys different messages. What to a member of the audience may be meaningful may to an orchestral player be meaningless, and vice versa. Gibson's beat, which has been much discussed and much criticised, can look obscure. But it is certainly utterly individual. Hans Gal, an Austrian refugee and senior lecturer in music at Edinburgh University, was prone in his old age to sit immediately behind my critic's seat on Friday evenings at the Usher Hall. An old friend of George Szell, and a scathing critic of the Second Viennese School, he was a famously pernickety musician who scribbled fierce notes in the margin of his programme, perhaps for communication to abstruse and severely Teutonic quarterly music magazines. If the piece, or the performance, was not to his taste there would be dark but audible mutterings in German. Guest conductors, even those of the old school, did not invariably win his approval. Rudolf Serkin's Mozart playing, at one of Lord Harewood's Edinburgh Festivals, provoked quiet but prolonged rage. Yet on one occasion Gal went backstage to congratulate Gibson for being one of the few conductors he had ever encountered who got the accents in the opening bars of *The Marriage of Figaro* overture correct. But his admiration went further than that. 'That man,' he once leaned forward and remarked to me, 'has the most subtle beat I have ever seen.'

Not every orchestral player, waiting for a clear-cut cue for a vital entry, would have agreed about the value of subtlety. But the SNO, however grudgingly, got used to Gibson's beat, even if it sometimes infuriated them, and experienced players instinctively understood what it was saying. Other orchestras, with which Gibson has made guest appearances, have sometimes been less patient, although a second performance, or series of performances, with him has been known to do the trick. Players begin to perceive what he is trying to convey.

At different times in his career, Gibson has had productive relationships with orchestras other than the SNO. One of these, in recent years, has been the English Chamber Orchestra, with which he worked initially as a replacement for an ailing Benjamin Britten, but which later invited him to appear on his own terms, giving concerts, making recordings, and going on tour. One Stravinsky disc, a coupling of *Pulcinella* and the *Danses Concertantes*, won special praise, with Paul Griffiths of *The Times* hailing a subsequent live performance (at the

Barbican Hall in London) of *Pulcinella* as 'one of the finest I have ever heard, not only of this work but of anything by Stravinsky'.

Since Griffiths' review went on to say some acutely pertinent things, not only about Gibson but about Stravinsky in general, I shall quote it further. The performance, he wrote:

> had the beauty of all great art, in that it stated the obvious at the highest level of achievement, realising a truth about the performance of Stravinsky that has been staring us in the face. What the music needs is not briskness, even if the staccato style is sometimes supported by the composer's own recordings. What it needs is a just marriage, a balance not a blend, of twentieth-century precision with eighteenth-century qualities of sensibility, cultivation and flow. Alexander Gibson provided the framework of regularity that alone could support such a rich and diverse abundance of imaginings, and so aptly encouraged his players to let their solos and ensembles breathe free of the straitjacket normally imposed on this music, as to make the work a jostling marketplace of musical transactions.

It was, admittedly, a marketplace filled with the highest quality goods, both in terms of music and performers. The English Chamber Orchestra in 1982, when these recordings were made, contained peak players in peak form. But this does not lessen Gibson's achievement, which lay, as Griffiths pointed out, in his ability to encourage them and let them interact with each other. It is a quality he is not always sufficiently acknowledged as possessing, though those who are on his wavelength recognise it to the full.

John Currie, who has served as chorusmaster of the SNO Chorus, Scottish Opera Chorus, and Edinburgh Festival Chorus, as well as being director of his own John Currie Singers and Perth Festival Opera, has his own definition of the Gibson magic.

'A conductor,' he recently said to me, 'should be someone who knows how much to make things happen and how much to let things happen. Alex is singularly good at striking that particular balance. In the days when I trained the Edinburgh Festival Chorus, I could expect Giulini, for instance, to send me a score to work on, always carefully marked and amended. That was his way. But Alex had the talent to use a kind of perception. He would be extremely tolerant of my own sometimes daft suggestions. He was good at not being uppity, at sometimes taking advice, at not putting you down, the way Maestro A, B, or C might do.'

Gibson's beat, he agrees, is controversial, but he can almost always follow it. 'I'm not of the bandmaster school either. Yet I'll admit that there have been times when the shape Alex was looking for did not appear to be clearly conveyed, and he does like to shape things. I have been in awe of what players have been able to do for him when I myself couldn't have done it. Sometimes when working with amateur singers I've had to act as an interpreter between him and them. It's not a problem, and it's not a deficiency on his part; it's simply the man's style.

'As with Rozhdestvensky, Alex's centre of activity is the actual performance. He hates rehearsing with the piano, particularly opera. Yet when he tackled Schoenberg's *Gurrelieder*, which is a huge cliff-hanger of a piece, at the Edinburgh Festival, it was grammatically clear from beginning to end. Barenboim would not have been one bit clearer. Neither would Muti or Abbado. So obviously, in Alex's case, it is not a technical lack. One of the most intelligent members of the chorus said to me after the performance, "*There* was a conductor who had complete mastery of the score." And the Festival Chorus, bear in mind, sings with the very best people.'

John Robertson, who has sung principal roles and served as a chorister with Scottish Opera, says the same: 'Apart from being profoundly musical, Alex has a sense in the back of his neck what an audience is about. He is a very good singer's conductor. I sometimes think of him as the male ballet dancer in the *pas de deux* – he's there to show off whoever he is partnering. If a clarinettist has a solo, he lets the performer be. The complaints about his beat carry no weight with me. People say he never gives a downbeat. But he gives an upbeat, and that's what matters. It took me six months to work this out, but once I had done so I no longer found him hard to follow. Those who do find him difficult are those who expect all the time to be told what to do.

'There are times when Alex doesn't seem to want to beat at all. Sometimes he stops if things are going well. If the music seems to be making its own way, he doesn't want to interfere. Shaping and moulding are his main concern. In one of Scottish Opera's recent revivals of *La Bohème*, another conductor was in charge. I was talking later about it to Joseph Ward, the Manchester singing teacher who once played Loge in Alex's *Rheingold*, and I told him that this particular conductor beat the performance up and down. We both agreed that *Bohème* simply can't be done that way.

'Alex has never been an up-and-down conductor. What I'm really saying is that, for a singer, the building block is the phrase. Alex conducts all the time in phrases, and in Puccini the phrase is paramount. That's why he is so good at it. But the alchemy only works with those who are prepared to go along with him, and benefit from his beat. Yet you can tease him about it. When he received his knighthood, and was about to set off for Buckingham Palace, I asked him if he knew what happens at an investiture. I told him he would be shown into the Queen's presence, that he would kneel down, and that the Queen would raise her sword. At that point, I said, he should glance up, because what he would see would be a downbeat.

'It's easy to share jokes with him, even on potentially tense occasions, like the first night of *Così fan tutte* in Perth. I was one of six male choristers who in Act One had to march on as soldiers. The producer, Anthony Besch, had arranged us in order of size. The tallest of us being nearly seven feet, there was scope for humour. Alex looked up and saw us and *leaned sideways* as he was conducting.

'There were times, too, when we tried to make him laugh. In Peter Ebert's production of *The Trojans*, which was very famous, serious, and special, Norman White and John Lawson Graham played the roles of a pair of sentries who paced slowly and gloomily back and forward, from the left and right of the stage, while singing a duet about how hard their lives were. After many nights of doing this, they decided they would reverse sides and see if Alex noticed. He spotted it right away, of course, but remained totally unruffled. I really owe him a great debt of gratitude. But for him, I'd never have become a singer.'

Anecdotes like Robertson's and Currie's pay testimony to the pleasure of making music with Gibson. But though they were only two of the many people I spoke to while gathering material for this book, they were, I found, absolutely typical in their responses to him. John Lawson Graham, one of the sentries who reversed sides, subsequently in real life changed roles entirely and now plays an important administrative part in the company. But he shares with Robertson an almost total recall of what Scottish Opera was like in its first years under Gibson, of the idealism and sense of achievement created by these early productions that led, in the course of the 1960s and early '70s, to Britain's first modern *Ring* cycle outside London, to a Berlioz centenary production (complete on a single evening) of *The Trojans*, and to an Edinburgh Festival debut with *The Rake's Progress* by Stravinsky.

Today, with its new generation of singers, choristers, conductors, producers, orchestral players, and administrators, and with the latest in a long line of chairmen, the company has almost totally changed, and Graham fears that the original feeling of elation is in danger of being forgotten.

'It was such a special time, and it was good to be part of it. There was a great feeling of pioneering. It was never parochial. Suddenly we were confronted by Dutchmen, Germans, Danes, Australians, New Zealanders, French–Canadians, Americans, all singing for Gibson, perfectly naturally as part of the company. But we as Scots were part of it, too. Gibson, from a young singer's point of view, seemed a giant in the 1960s. He was still a young man, and you felt that in working with him you were in a very serious business which was also fun. You knew that at the helm there was someone who really knew what it was all about, and that's why the company was immediately so successful. And to have a symphony orchestra in the pit was priceless – you simply can't quantify that sort of advantage.'

Though Graham modestly says his own singing career was nothing special (I remember him, all the same, as a frightening Hobson in *Peter Grimes* and a sonorous, black-voiced Priam in *The Trojans*) he felt thrilled simply forming a part, however small, of such a team. 'In those days Gibson took great interest in young singers, as he still does.'

Like all the singers I have spoken to, Graham has one particular observation to make about Gibson: 'He has always been a singer's conductor.' But more than that: 'You could always rely on him to get you out of a mess. I've seen him conduct people who went completely awry, but he invariably has the ability to adjust and get them back on the rails. More important than that is his awareness of breathing. He always senses the breath in every phrase, and it's a great comfort to know that he's breathing with you and anticipating you all the time. Some conductors refuse to budge in this respect. Also he seems always to know how well or unwell you might be on a particular evening, and he adjusts to that, with a sympathetic understanding of whether you're in good form or otherwise.

'As for his beat, well, I had few problems with it. I always accepted that the way he shapes the music is more important than whether it is clear in absolute terms. If ever you look at him in consternation, if ever he feels you are in trouble, his beat instantly becomes very clear. If he knows you need extra clarity you will get it from him. But in general he isn't in the business of being a strict time-beater in that sense. Some singers, especially if they come from abroad and have their eyes on the pit more than is necessary, can't always handle that. Those who expect a constant beat from him simply aren't on the same wavelength. He's in the business of making music rather than of pedantry.'

In response to my question: 'Which of his performances have you admired most?' Graham replied: 'I would say *Otello*, *Fidelio*, and *The Ring*. I also liked his *Rosenkavalier*, *Peter Grimes*, and *Meistersinger* – the kind of pieces that have breadth to them are right up his street. He can see the music from beginning to end. But also *Così fan tutte*, in which the ensemble and blend were quite exceptional. Yet today, if you talk to people about Alex Gibson and Scottish Opera, they don't always seem to realise how much he has done. This never ceases to surprise and even annoy me, but perhaps he is to blame as much as anybody – if blame is the word – for being, as he has always been, so self-effacing. You would never guess, in speaking to him, that in Scotland there would be no opera-going habit without him, that he created whole generations of people who now go to the opera as a matter of course. It's quite remarkable when you think of it.'

Gibson's self-effacement, as I wrote earlier, can be one of his most attractive characteristics. But it can also be aggravating, in that he has allowed it to impede his progress. As a critic, accustomed to the hype that surrounds conductors who are far less talented than he is, I am aware of his failure to project himself and his achievements in a way which, had he done so, would have won him many more laurels. 'Alex, I wish you'd told me,' I have said to him more than once on hearing something about him that would have given me the substance of an article or a review. Perhaps he has simply grown to accept that he is the prisoner of his own reticence. Perhaps he genuinely believes that none of it really matters. As was said of T. E. Lawrence, he is someone who backs into the limelight. The difference is that, in Lawrence's case, it was a form of conceit, the equivalent perhaps of Carlo Maria Giulini – in Peter Heyworth's famous phrase — 'wearing his modesty with a capital M'. With Gibson, the modesty is real.

CHAPTER EIGHT

Was It Really Like That?

People who never experienced Scottish Opera's early years sometimes ask me, 'Was it really like that?' With the proviso that I missed
the first two years myself, I reply that yes it was. There were flaws.
Casts — even the remarkable *Così* on some of its revivals — contained
weak links. The visual aspect sometimes failed to rise to the standards
of the music-making: some of the most important productions,
including *The Ring* and *The Trojans*, are remembered, by me at any
rate, more for how they sounded than how they looked. Yet the
overall achievement was colossal, thanks to Gibson's deep personal
involvement with all the major events of the first two decades, not
only the works already mentioned but Henze's *Elegy for Young Lovers*,
Gluck's *Alceste*, Berg's *Wozzeck*, Puccini's *Manon Lescaut*. There was
even a second production of *Pelléas et Mélisande* which in terms of
beauty and radiance of tone was among the best things he ever did as
the company's artistic director, and there was the merriest of *Merry
Widows*, an operetta for which, at Sadler's Wells, he had already
shown a special flair.

In these and other productions, but especially in the Henze,
Scottish Opera's early virtues as an ensemble company could be
experienced at their best. The trouble was that, with one artistic success
after another providing an incentive, the company's expansionist
ambitions grew harder and harder to control. Seasons grew longer and
more numerous. There were more theatres, including new ones in
Stirling and Inverness, to perform in. No opera was deemed too

difficult to stage. Gibson talked of conducting Strauss's *Der Frau ohne Schatten* and Verdi's *Don Carlos*, two of the most notoriously exhausting, expensive and, in terms of casting and performing, treacherous works in the repertoire.

In fact, the great 1971 *Ring* cycle, the fruit of five years of labour, brought Scottish Opera's wave to its crest, with *Rosenkavalier* the following year providing a fine flurry of spray. The Scottish Arts Council's sermons about money, until that time audaciously ignored, now had to be heeded. The *Ring*, once assembled, was never repeated. And though, in later years, there would be other triumphs – not least the acquisition of the Theatre Royal as Glasgow's opera house – the early zeal, the ability to do (almost) no wrong, never quite returned. Though Gibson and Hemmings remained in charge, Scottish Opera had entered the second phase in its history. Things would never be quite the same again.

There were changes, too, at the SNO, whose brilliant and beneficial marriage to Scottish Opera was by now heading towards a ridiculous divorce. Though Ponsonby's successor, David Richardson, was at first happy to sustain the status quo, he felt increasingly threatened by Hemmings's requests for more and more of the orchestra's time, and increasingly irked by what he construed to be Gibson's divided loyalties. Yet, at least initially, he went along with the scheme to enlarge the orchestra to Vienna Philharmonic proportions, and he developed – to the point where it very nearly happened – the idea of forming, with Gibson, a chamber orchestra under the aegis of the SNO itself.

Had they succeeded, or had the Scottish Arts Council not preferred the idea of a wholly separate Scottish Chamber Orchestra, who knows in what direction music in Scotland would have gone? Since the SNO in recent years has suffered constant financial, managerial, and industrial problems, whereas the SCO has not, perhaps the Scottish Arts Council's veto was wise. On the other hand, had the decision gone the SNO's way, perhaps none of the problems would have arisen.

Richardson, however, was probably too ambivalent about the whole project to see it through to a productive outcome. He undoubtedly had successes whilst working with Gibson. The repertoire grew even bolder than it was in Ponsonby's time. Musica Nova flourished, with performances under Gibson of Peter Maxwell Davies's *Stone Litany*, Luciano Berio's *Still*, and György Ligeti's Double Concerto for Flute and Oboe. Even the SNO proms – those 'purveyors of mindless pap', as I had once insultingly described them – won new respect (mine at any rate) when Gibson conducted Mahler and Tippett symphonies, and Berlioz's Requiem, to a vast Glasgow audience. And, as the crowning event of the Richardson regime, there was the first American tour, which took Gibson and the orchestra from Toronto and Ottawa to New York and Washington, with a repertoire including, not just safe international favourites, but genuine Scottish music in the form of two fine works (one of them brand new) by Iain Hamilton, who, being resident in the United States at the time, went to hear them.

But between Richardson's arrival at the SNO and his departure eight years later, tensions developed in his working relationship with Gibson that had never occurred between Gibson and Ponsonby. 'It never became so difficult that it turned into a he-goes-or-I-go situation,' Richardson recently told me (though in fact Richardson went). 'But tactically I didn't handle it as well as I should have done.'

The problem, as Richardson saw it, lay largely in what he considered to be 'Alex's conflict of interests between the SNO and Scottish Opera. There were times when he was late for SNO rehearsals and was known to have been at Scottish Opera. Even if he was just late, for whatever reason, it began to be assumed he'd been giving Scottish Opera his time. I had the feeling that the orchestra was not being played fair.' Members and ex-members of the orchestra to whom I have spoken tend to support Richardson's judgment: 'He had a way of being invariably six minutes late for us – we could set our watches by him – but he was never late for an opera rehearsal.'

Gibson, for his part, insists that he was equally late for both! Indeed, he says, he has spent the greater part of his life in Scotland making sure that he was 'wearing the right hat at all times', though, as we shall see later, Richardson was not the only person to consider that the conductor had overstayed his welcome.

Gibson firmly believed that holding two major musical posts in a single city was a virtue and surely to everyone's benefit. It meant that he was on the spot, always ready to attend meetings, solve problems, give advice, exchange ideas, and dash from one rehearsal to another in a way he found exhilarating but which may have been more tiring than he thought.

To my eyes, he seldom looked tired. On Friday evenings, he strode on to the platform of the Usher Hall with all his familiar verve. His platform manner was true to both the man and his performances: always to the point, never ostentatious. He did not enter at a run, as does Rafael Frühbeck de Burgos. He did not leap on to the podium, as Karajan did. He did not hold a handkerchief limply to his mouth, as if, like Yuri Temirkanov, the act of conducting might place him in imminent danger of death. He simply got on with it.

Nevertheless, there have been times when Gibson has conducted a performance on what seemed like auto-pilot, then suddenly galvanised himself and the orchestra when he has realised that the plane was dangerously losing height. Resident conductors, especially those who are long-term residents, must have difficulty keeping their rapport with their orchestras alive and meaningful. And though their understanding of each other, and the recognisable house-style that derives from it, should count as a plus point, it easily degenerates into boredom when an orchestra decides a conductor has become too predictable.

But though he could not have been unaware that freelance conductors often get all the fun, Gibson preferred to persevere. If ever he felt he was doing too much, he would never have admitted it. John Currie can recall times in Glasgow when Gibson conducted an opera matinée in the afternoon and a concert in the evening, yet never seemed to be under strain: 'indeed, maybe that's been when he's at his best'.

Yet the result seldom seemed superficial. To quote Currie again: 'I've never known a conductor whose performances are more his own. In the prelude to *Tristan und Isolde* he chooses a speed where the push and pull of the music could not have been done by anyone else. His long-range shaping gives me the sort of shivers that are the token of all real performances, and he can do the same in the Verdi Requiem and the Rakhmaninov symphonies. And as a chorusmaster I wouldn't expect to prepare a better performance of *The Dream of Gerontius* than the one Alex conducted at the Royal Albert Hall in London during Ponsonby's period. It was the first time an Albert Hall prom had taken place on a Sunday, and the performance was characterised by that beautiful and utterly individual soft-grained sound that Alex can produce, which the orchestra lost after he left and Järvi and Thomson developed a much brighter tone quality.

'I trained the SNO Chorus to produce a crescendo of a sort which many choirs can't manage – and that was something which really suited Alex. A turning-point in the chorus's development was the Verdi Requiem they sang for him in memory of Barbirolli, with Luisa Bosabalian, Janet Baker, Ronald Dowd, and Marius Rintzler – most of them from Scottish Opera – as the soloists. At last, it seemed to me, the choir contained real male voices, not ragged ones. The sound was fully balanced, and that was because of their good relationship with Alex. I knew then that we could create a first-class symphony orchestra chorus in Glasgow. After this, Alex wrote me a letter saying, "Don't go and work in England", which I was planning to do at the time, but I'm afraid I did and was committed to that for five years.'

Like all conductors, but perhaps more than most, Gibson seems always to have enjoyed a nucleus of friends and fellow musicians whom he could trust, work with happily, and confide in. And when separations came, as they often did, he invariably seemed the loser. His biggest loss – and it did seem to be a sadly unnecessary one – was when Peter Hemmings, having organised the purchase of the Glasgow Theatre Royal from Scottish Television, and then settled Scottish Opera into its new home, decided it was time to quit.

It is a subject to which I shall return, because it marked a major change in both their careers, and each suffered as a result of it. Happily, it was not the end of their friendship, which has continued from different sides of the world. But each of them needed the other perhaps more than they knew at the time. Indeed, after two ill-starred appointments – the first with the Australian Opera in Sydney, the second with the London Symphony Orchestra – Hemmings seemed on the verge of sinking into obscurity when he moved to California to take command of the Los Angeles Opera.

Perhaps because it is a more many-sided organisation, Scottish Opera has provided Gibson with more friends than has the SNO. But many of them are now, like Hemmings, spread around the world. Peter Ebert, Hemmings's successor and director of many of the company's early successes, now lives in semi-retirement in Umbria. Thomson Smillie is in Kentucky, Robin Orr in Cambridge. Leonard Hancock and Catherine Wilson – a husband and wife team who contributed much to the success of the Gibson era, he as head of music staff, she as the company's most romantic soprano in roles ranging from the Countess in *Figaro* to Rosalinda in *Die Fledermaus* and Hanna Glawari in *The Merry Widow* – commute between England and Italy. Janet Baker, who rated Gibson as one of her favourite conductors, retired from opera in 1982 and from the concert platform seven years later. Catherine Gayer, the Berlin-based American exponent of tortuous modern roles, drifted into cabaret after a series of Scottish Opera successes.

Of the original London-based mafia, David Ward and Harold Blackburn are dead. So are Peter van der Bilt, Scottish Opera's first and best Don Giovanni, and Elizabeth Harwood, the golden young Fiordiligi of the first *Così fan tutte*. Others who have died include such devoted advisers and background influences as Ainslie Millar, Gavin Boyd, and John Boyle. There have been times in recent years when

Scottish Opera's early glories have seemed transformed into an endless funeral cortège.

Compared with Scottish Opera – on whose behalf Gibson once personally signed 20,000 letters, night after night, in order to raise funds for the Theatre Royal endowment, just as his wife, in earlier years, had taken part in sewing sessions to provide costumes for *Falstaff* – the relationship between the conductor and the SNO was cooler and more formal, or so it seemed to an outsider. Though Gibson has never shown himself to be status-conscious in the manner of other conductors (even the cheerful James Loughran, when he was in charge of the Hallé, had his own chauffeur-driven limousine as one of the perks of the job), he has nevertheless found himself victim of all the traditional British orchestral jealousies. Robert Ponsonby (who himself could hardly claim high popularity among the players) recalls the time he saw the postal code of Gibson's house listed on the staff noticeboard, its letters, OPU, amended to read OPUlent.

But as Ponsonby says: 'There is always resentment of a chief conductor who is well-to-do when you yourself are on a rank-and-file salary and regard yourself as near the breadline. This is unavoidably true of any conductor. However charming he may be, there is no way in which he can be loved by the whole orchestra. Even Barbirolli suffered in this way. It is simply not in the nature of orchestral musicians – who having perhaps started out with aspirations of their own – to accept without rancour the fact that they are not allowed to interpret the music in their own way, not allowed to use the bowings they want, not allowed to answer back, not allowed a voice of any kind. There were some pretty rough diamonds in the SNO in my day, and Alex was not invariably charming. Like any other conductor, he could be surly, bad-tempered, and unco-operative.'

Asking players their opinion of a conductor is to remove the bung from what is usually a capacious barrel of woes. Conductors whom one admires, for whatever reason, are promptly rubbished. The great are more despicable than the lowly, but the lowly are mostly pretty useless. Almost everybody has feet of clay. Life would be thoroughly disheartening if, as a critic, one did not turn deaf ears to the litany of complaint. But however much a conductor's wretched rehearsal methods, faulty ear for intonation, ignorance of instrumental technique, feeble sense of rhythm, tendency to talk, tendency to remain silent and general unpreparedness may be despised, it is the sound that reaches the audience that matters.

Gibson's rehearsal methods, being as individual as his beat, do not win universal acclaim. At worst, he can be abrupt. To launch a rehearsal of Brahms's Second Symphony, to stop it after a few bars, to turn to the cellos and to exclaim 'What's the matter with you?' – perhaps an isolated example of Gibson in curt mode but one I have personally witnessed – is not necessarily the best way to get the show on the road. Yet old hands see him as no worse than anyone else, and in some respects better. Two ex-SNO players, now in the world of academe, have this to say:

Player A: 'He could be naughty, saying things like "Let's learn this together", which we construed to mean that he didn't yet know the music and was treating us like guinea pigs. Yet what always amazed me, even if you couldn't see what he was getting at in rehearsals, was his ability to get a real performance out of us when the moment came. He proved again and again that he could do this. Whatever emotion there was in the music, Gibson got it. I don't know how he did it, but he did it. Pathos, anger, jubilation, or whatever, he got it out. Yet at rehearsal he often hardly talked, it was as if he felt embarrassed to talk. I remember George Hurst once conducting Britten's *Four Sea Interludes*, and saying "It's not just about seagulls, you know". Alex would never say something like that. He doesn't like to say what he feels about a piece of music, not the way that Tortelier, say, would talk romantically about Bach. Alex doesn't give a *picture* of what he wants. He prefers to play it through until it's right, and then, on the night, he rises to the big occasion.'

Player B: 'People used to say he left all the work to the orchestra. That's partly because he would tell us it wasn't his responsibility to get us together. He seldom fussed about rhythm.'

Player A: 'Jerzy Maksymiuk fusses about rhythm with the BBC SSO, to the detriment sometimes of whatever it is he's conducting. Alex always wants to put the music first, and he wants the players to supply the rhythm.'

Player B: 'As a result, if it's a very rhythmic work, the sound can sometimes be mushy, through lack of bite. It's *legato* that interests him.'

Player A: 'Yes, he'll say, "I'm conducting the *phrase*". Even with the National Youth Orchestra of Scotland, he won't give that vital first beat in Sibelius's Second Symphony.'

Player B: 'Rudolf Schwarz wouldn't have given it either.'

Player A: 'Yet amazingly, after a few concerts with NYOS, you'd have thought they'd been playing together for years.'

Player B: 'You could never accuse him of doing anything unmusical.'

Player A: 'Now I've grown older, and realise what a conductor's job can be like, I'm a lot more sympathetic.'

Player B: 'I've never seen him show nerves, though I do remember once when he was conducting Shostakovich's Tenth Symphony at the Edinburgh Festival his baton shook. But that was because Shostakovich had arrived with all his bodyguards and was sitting in the front row.'

Player A: 'He once had a contretemps with the tenor, Richard Lewis. There was an argument about the tempo of a Handel aria. Alex let Lewis have his way. He tries never to upset soloists, though during a rehearsal of *The Trojans* he told the Australian, Ronald Dowd, not to be obtuse, and Dowd replied: "Are you calling me fucking stupid?" He's had some pretty bad soloists in his time, but he steers them all through.' [Gibson today regrets that solitary incident with Lewis, a singer he admired greatly and enjoyed working with many times thereafter.]

Player B: 'He's a fine accompanist, and infallible when someone gets lost. He'll instantly find the right place, give a flick, and bring them back in.'

Player A: 'He never has problems handling singers. When Alberto Erede, who was enormously experienced, replaced him as conductor of *Otello*, he drew a wonderful sound from the strings. He knew the opera inside out, and he would lift his arm up whenever Kiri Te Kanawa, who was singing Desdemona, sang flat, and lower it whenever she sang sharp. She was still young and inexperienced, and she burst into tears. But for all Erede's expertise, his performance was finally not as exciting as Alex's. There wasn't so strong a feel for the theatre.'

Gibson's operatic verve, indeed, was greatly appreciated by some members of the SNO, especially when it enabled them to perform the great nineteenth-century and early twentieth-century masterpieces – Berlioz and Verdi, Wagner and Strauss – which contained glorious orchestral parts they would otherwise be deprived of. But as Scottish Opera became increasingly a travelling opera company, so the SNO became increasingly a travelling opera orchestra – touring with Scottish Opera but receiving (or so the players surmised) none of the kudos it deserved. Richard Chester, who was principal flute for a large part of Gibson's reign, says that one year the orchestra devoted 36 per cent of its work to Scottish Opera – 'and for a symphony orchestra that was a lot of work'.

More and more operatic forays were being made into England, including, while Britten was still alive, what appears to have been an exhausting visit to the Aldeburgh Festival. Later, the great American concert tour of 1975 did something to restore the balance. For the orchestra it was a triumph, but it was also, says Chester, 'a milestone in Alex's career, the major event to which he'd been building up for some time'. Nevertheless, the prevailing problem remained unsolved and Gibson seemed content to leave it that way.

But David Richardson was less content. Indeed, his unhappiness ultimately triggered a rift between the SNO and Scottish Opera. Hemmings was by now proposing more short seasons in an attempt to make Scottish Opera as permanent a presence as possible. Richardson objected, saying so many interruptions would damage the SNO's concert schedule. It was plain, he said, that the parting of the ways was nigh – and in due course the opera company's acquisition of the Theatre Royal brought this about.

Since Scottish Opera by now was using more than one orchestra – the BBC SSO, Scottish Chamber Orchestra, and Scottish Baroque Ensemble between them were helping to create the illusion of the Vienna Philharmonic-style operation Gibson had desired – the loss of the SNO was not the disaster it might have been for the company. But there was no doubt that both organisations suffered as a result: Scottish Opera because the SNO had been such a vital ingredient in its early success and the SNO because it actually needed the operatic work. In later years, when times were harder and out-of-season activities had conspicuously diminished, the orchestra came to regret that it had irretrievably severed its connection with the opera company.

By then, had he still been the orchestra's musical director, Gibson could have said 'I told you so'. But at the time he simply accepted the new situation, and got on, as best he could, with business as usual. There was no doubt, however, that the split between the orchestra and opera company would eventually lead to a split between Gibson and Richardson. Neither of them being acrimonious men, it did not lead to acrimonious scenes – at least none that either of them would admit.

As Richardson says of Gibson: 'I felt I knew him well. It was a friendly relationship. I could tease him, if he was in the right mood. I could even tell him off. He is an uncommonly warm and generous man, who doesn't think ill of anybody. I've been amazed so often by his little generosities, like the time he sold me his Bechstein piano at a ridiculously low price. Not that it was low in value to him – it was simply something to do for a friend. I have never heard him talk maliciously or disparagingly of someone else. He always has time for other people, and tolerates their weaknesses to a fault.

'But that, it seemed to me, wasn't always a good thing. There were times when I thought he was not intolerant enough, and times when he didn't sufficiently put his mind to things he should have done. He never sufficiently recognised the increasing divergence between Scottish Opera and the SNO. He should have been able to tell the SNO that they would do better to cut themselves off from Scottish Opera, but he never did that. And it was then that he himself should have left the SNO. I could not help feeling that he loved Scottish Opera more than the orchestra, that it was more in his soul. In comparison, the SNO sometimes got short-changed, even if he didn't see it that way.'

Gibson certainly did not see it that way. He was, he says, the first to recognise that full opera seasons which coincided with the orchestral winter season would mean dispensing with the SNO's services in the pit. Much as he regretted this, he felt that the SNO under his guidance had reached a point where it needed space to fit into its diary the kind of work he had been building up with it over the years in the spheres of international touring and recording.

However, the Richardson–Gibson years were so orchestrally productive that Gibson's ability to ride the operatic problems seemed, incredibly, to pay off. Anyone who conducted Tippett symphonies, Britten's touching valedictory cantata *Phaedra*, with Janet Baker as soloist, Iain Hamilton's *Circus* (a work, in spite of its name, that is as serious as the Robert Burns Sinfonia), Elgar's First Symphony in Brussels, Panufnik's *Sinfonia Sacra* in Warsaw (a supercharged emotional occasion), Thea Musgrave's Horn Concerto in Vienna, Monteverdi's *Ulysses* (its American premiere) in Washington, Walton's *Belshazzar's Feast* at Hollywood Bowl, Verdi's Requiem in St Louis, Harrison Birtwistle's *Melencolia I* at the London Proms, and Debussy's *Pelléas* and Janáček's *Glagolitic Mass* at the Edinburgh Festival, all to high acclaim, would be entitled to believe that all was for the best in the best of possible worlds.

Simply in terms of his appearances with Janet Baker, this period in Gibson's career must have given him immense satisfaction. Ever since her 1967 *Così fan tutte* in Perth, they had developed a musical partnership based on absolute trust, extending into the realms of Berlioz's Dido, Strauss's Octavian, and Gluck's Orpheus, portrayals as scrupulously prepared, vividly voiced, and sympathetically accompanied as one could possibly hope to encounter.

Some projects that were seriously discussed between them – for example Bizet's *Carmen*, Gluck's *Alceste*, Rosina in *The Barber of Seville* and the title-role in *Cenerentola* – remained tantalisingly unfulfilled, more because Baker was uncertain whether they would suit the tessitura or character of her voice than because she feared she would seem in some way dramatically miscast. Indeed, Baker as Carmen would surely have been fascinating. She was utterly at home in French music; she had the right timbre for the role; and she would have brought to it the passionate seriousness it deserves, yet which it receives from so few who do perform it.

107

But at least, on an SNO trip to London in 1972, she took part with Gibson in a choice performance of what is now a great rarity (much loved by Kathleen Ferrier), Chausson's *Poème de l'Amour et de la Mer*. Philip Hope-Wallace, a connoisseur of French music, said the beauty of the performance of this *fin-de-siècle* example of hothouse nostalgia made him think of a painting by Monet. 'As for showing the quality of the orchestra,' he reported in *The Guardian*, 'the occasion was most remarkable.'

Having been principally known as a concert singer before Gibson made her less opera-shy, Janet Baker does not conceal the gratitude she owed him at a crucial point in her career. 'When he asked me to sing Dorabella in *Così*,' she told me, 'it was something nobody else thought I could do. Before the season was over he went on to ask me to sing Dido in *The Trojans*, which was another act of faith.'

Had he done nothing more than act as operatic midwife to Janet Baker, Gibson would have earned his place in musical history. At this time she was singing operatic roles for him every second year – a typical conserving of her talents when other stars of the period were being recklessly prodigal. Saying that she found him marvellous to work with, she added that it was vital to have the right conductor, and Gibson possessed a complete understanding of the kind of voice she had.

'Singers,' she told me, 'are childish people. We need to feel liked, that we're welcome, that we get on well with that man who is wielding the stick. I can nowadays afford to go to places where I get that feeling, and Glasgow is one of these places. Alexander Gibson understands singers. He works against odds in a very remarkable way. At times when you are putting an opera together, calm deteriorates. The thing explodes. But Alexander Gibson keeps things together. If you have a disagreement with him, it's over in a moment. He realises that we're babies who need nursing. He's aware of what we're going through. I admire the feeling of building something new which he has been able to provide. That's something to be preciously guarded.'

For his part, when he was interviewed by Roy Plomley on *Desert Island Discs*, Gibson confessed to being Baker's greatest fan. But if Baker was Gibson's star, just as she had previously been Barbirolli's, there were many other singers with whom he had a special rapport. Jessye Norman, who performed Berlioz's *Summer Nights* and Tippett's *A Child of Our Time* with him at the Edinburgh Festival, once insisted that he, and only he, should be the conductor of a disc of sacred music she was contemplating. The songs, with a strong French bias, included an excerpt from Gounod's fragrant St Cecilia Mass, along with a cluster of spirituals. The performances avoided sentimentality and were highly praised for their restraint and sincerity. It was clear that Norman knew the sort of accompaniments she wanted, and knew that Gibson could give them to her.

Helga Dernesch, the German soprano, developed under Gibson into a Wagnerian of sterling presence and lustrous beauty of tone, first in the relatively minor role of Gutrune in *Götterdämmerung*, and later as Brünnhilde, Isolde, Fidelio, and the Feldmarschallin in *Der Rosenkavalier*, opposite Janet Baker's Octavian and Elizabeth Harwood's Sophie, before Herbert von Karajan grabbed her and overstrained her voice (he did the same to Harwood's, exquisitely though she recorded *The Merry Widow* for him).

Catherine Gayer and Jill Gomez, other members of the Gibson galaxy, contributed greatly moving Mozart portrayals, but did not shirk the modern repertoire. Both appeared to potent effect in Scottish Opera's Edinburgh Festival production of Hans Werner Henze's *Elegy for Young Lovers*, helping to champion a piece that had flopped at Glyndebourne a decade before and had thereafter been cold-shouldered by Covent Garden and Sadler's Wells.

Gibson, who had already established himself as Britain's leading conductor of Henze's orchestral music, having introduced the Fourth Symphony and the monolithic Second Piano Concerto to this country, could not wait to do one of the operas. Instinct led him to choose the German composer's waspish tragi-comedy, with its libretto by Auden and Kallman, in which an egocentric elderly poet draws inspiration from the people around him, to the extent that he jealously sends his young mistress to her death on a Swiss mountain because she has switched partners. The resultant 'Elegy for Young Lovers' is recited by the great man at the end of the opera.

Though Gomez and Gayer were just two of the moths that fluttered around the hypnotic head of John Shirley-Quirk in the central role, they contributed greatly to the allure of an evening as notable as any in Scottish Opera's early history. Henze, who came to Edinburgh to produce his own opera, later wrote to Gibson from Rome, saying:

'I really loved every minute of these times, and I think a great deal of the delight was due to your good humour. I'll never forget you even sat in at the tedious lighting rehearsals. Needless to say I'm proud the show came off so well. The first time in my life I sat through the whole thing three times! Just enjoying every bit, and how the sound of the orchestra matched with the goings-on on stage.'

Indeed, this was one of those special occasions when every aspect of the performance – cast and orchestra, conductor and producer, designs and lighting – worked to perfection and provided a justification of the whole complex and expensive art of opera. It was through a typically clever piece of casting, too, that Gomez as the doomed Elisabeth Zimmer was partnered by David Hillman as Toni, her equally doomed lover. Only a few months earlier, they had sung very different love music and, as Pamina and Tamino, played a very different pair of young lovers in Scottish Opera's first production of *The Magic Flute*, again with Gibson as conductor.

Of the other stars that blazed in Gibson's sky, David Ward was undoubtedly one of the most intense. Though born in Dumbarton, he had spent most of his operatic career in London, where he and the young conductor in the 1950s began to confide their Scottish ambitions to each other. Yet neither of them could have guessed that they would all be so grandly realised, first in *Boris Godunov*, then in *The Ring*, and finally in *Tristan* and *Die Meistersinger*.

Ward, a pupil of Hans Hotter, possessed a huge personality along with a voice like burnished gravel – smooth enough to bring a tragically sombre mellowness to his Wotan and Boris, yet with an edge of vulnerability that made each of those portrayals extraordinarily touching. Pogner the goldsmith, the first role he sang for Covent Garden, was also his last for Scottish Opera. But no matter whether he was singing Eva's father in *Die Meistersinger* or Brünnhilde's in *Die Walküre* (or, indeed, Feodor's in *Boris Godunov* or Donna Anna's in *Don Giovanni*), he invariably found his finest form. The role of a father, perhaps because he had no children of his own, brought out something profound in him, especially when Gibson – who seemed to have an instinctive ability to play on his most powerful feelings – was conducting. When, in his fifties, Ward ultimately forsook this gallery of rich operatic portraits to become a sheep farmer in New Zealand, he died before he had time to adjust to his new and very different role in life.

Even the bass Hans Hotter, though of an earlier generation, could sometimes be found in the Gibson firmament, most recently, at the age of seventy-four, as the speaker in the 1983 Edinburgh Festival performance of Schoenberg's *Gurrelieder*. But earlier, when he had sung 'Hotter's Farewell' at the Paris Opera, it was Gibson who conducted this performance of *Die Walküre*, in which a different bass had sung the long and exhausting second act while Hotter conserved his flagging energy for the finale.

For Gibson, it was his first, and last, experience of the faded luxury and complex musical politics of the Palais Garnier, where *Walküre* had had its first Paris performance in 1893, and where long-retired singers were still entitled to their own dressing-rooms. Gibson, who was accustomed to performing Wagner's operas uncut in Scotland, was dismayed to find that the French did not share his respect for the letter of the score.

'We follow the cuts observed by Maître Cluytens,' he was informed on arrival. (André Cluytens had been the first French conductor ever to appear at Bayreuth, and was the Paris Opera's Wagner specialist until his death in 1967.) Even more disconcerting, Gibson found, was the habit of French orchestral players to switch off the lights on their music stands when they were not playing. As a result there were occasions, in the course of a work he had been contracted to conduct nine times, when he was not quite sure whether they were there or not.

CHAPTER NINE

A Charismatic Conductor

Only once, when the SNO hired an American publicist called Danny Newman, was Gibson a victim of the sort of hype that many other conductors regard as nothing less than their due. But to be advertised as 'charismatic', as he was in the mid-seventies, was hardly the Gibson style. When this form of marketing was finally abandoned, and things returned to normal, he sighed with relief.

Yet in his ability to attract and hold an audience, charismatic is exactly what Gibson is. A journalist colleague of mine, not a music critic but a literary editor, once found himself in the front row of the stalls at the King's Theatre, Edinburgh, for a performance of Verdi's *Falstaff* which Gibson was conducting. Though his seat was far too near, he said he did not mind in the slightest, because watching Gibson enjoying himself gave him as much delight as anything that was happening on the stage. There have been times when I myself have welcomed the sight of him in the pit, finding it by far the most compelling aspect of, say, the umpteenth revival of some tired production that should have been shelved years ago.

And in the concert hall there is charisma, too. Though he never makes a drama out of his entrance, the audience's warmth of feeling for him is always perceptible. The SNO's subscription bookings and single-ticket sales were never higher than when he was fully established as musical director, making recordings, taking the orchestra on tour, but above all simply being there. By today's standards, he conducted more of the winter concert season than any of his successors, and infinitely more during the summer. He was convinced that a musical director, in order to justify his name, should be a visible presence, able to advise as well as conduct, to take part in local activities, to oversee programme policy as a whole. Gibson did this selflessly and to admiration.

Nobody, even now, can estimate how much he has done for music in Scotland, and how much he continues to do. The honorary appointments he holds — including, since 1963, the presidency of the Scottish Musicians' Benevolent Fund — are not, for him, mere titles. He lends his name to charities and other good causes. He does his bit for musical education. First as a governor of the Royal Scottish Academy of Music and Drama, and now as honorary president in succession to Ralph Vaughan Williams, Sir Adrian Boult, and Dame Janet Baker, he is said to take a keen interest in all its activities. In the words of one senior teacher: 'We're lucky to have him. He's terrific, for example, with the junior orchestra, and has far more patience than we might have expected. We can phone him and he'll come in and take the players through a Sibelius symphony. We thought that if we pestered him he would blow up, but not at all. Perhaps it's because, now that he's in his sixties, he doesn't need to prove anything any more. People say he's mellowed.'

But on his return to Glasgow in 1959, it was ever his aim, at whatever level, to serve Scotland to the best of his abilities. As a guest in his house while working on this book, I became increasingly aware of how many demands there are on his time and how willingly he deals with them. The planning of a Glasgow charity concert will receive as much of his attention as an invitation to tour France or to conduct an opera.

Not all conductors are so equable. I can think of one London-based British celebrity with whose secretary I was friendly. Having accepted an invitation to give an Albert Hall Prom with one of the top orchestras on a certain date, he subsequently received a more attractive offer from abroad. When he discovered that his secretary, acting in good faith, had said he was already booked that night, he promptly sacked her.

It would be hard to imagine Gibson doing something like that. Indeed, in order to attend a Glasgow press conference in 1993 for an event in which he was closely involved, he had turned down — as I discovered later — two performances of Beethoven's *Missa Solemnis* in Stockholm. The Glasgow engagement had come first and he was not prepared to cancel it. Few other conductors, one suspects, possess so honourable a sense of priority. Consult Norman Lebrecht's book, *The*

Maestro Myth, on the subject of the saintly Bruno Walter and you will wonder if conductors have any honour at all.

Not that Gibson could be called a soft option. Sharing the closing concert of the 1971 Edinburgh Festival with Luciano Berio, who had come to conduct his own *Sinfonia*, he found that the Italian composer wanted the place of honour at the end of the evening, with Gibson's performances of Stravinsky's *Ode* and Janáček's *Sinfonietta* relegated to the beginning. A battle of wills began which was still raging one day before the concert.

Gibson's argument was simple. Being a stickler for programme balance, he considered that, from the point of view of both the audience and the SNO, the Janáček would make the more celebratory ending to the splendid series of events Peter Diamand had compiled for the Festival's twenty-first birthday. Moreover, Gibson was the orchestra's musical director. But Berio (even though his *Sinfonia* is a work that rather fizzles out after its second movement) demanded his due as a distinguished guest of the Festival. Until they made up their minds, or Diamand intervened, the programme-notes for the concert could not be printed (I happen to know, because I was the Festival's programme editor and the printers, by then into double time, were waiting to go to press). It was Gibson who got his way.

Yet there have been occasions when his more characteristic willingness to please has seemed counter to his own interests. In the 1970s, when the SNO and Scottish Opera were vying more and more strenuously for his time, the fact that he was the only conductor in Britain to hold two jobs in the same city – which in the '60s had seemed such a boon – became increasingly a handicap. Conductors with separate appointments in the United States and Europe can easily isolate themselves from the one while attending to the other. For Gibson, there was no such respite. From opera rehearsal to concert rehearsal, from opera meeting to orchestral meeting, the Glasgow treadmill constantly turned.

Things he could have passed to others he did himself. Summer proms? He conducted them. Musica Nova? He learnt the new works. Performances in Edinburgh, Aberdeen, Dundee? All part of the job. An invitation to appear at an English festival? Yes, he would learn the new choral work by Richard Yardumian that was to form part of a concert with the Philharmonia Orchestra at the Sheldonian, Oxford.

Not everything worked to perfection. But when, week after week, audiences have a steady diet of a single musician, they must learn to take the rough with the smooth. No conductor is invariably in top form, or responds to all works with equal passion. Gibson, like Susskind before him, maintained a vast repertoire to which, especially in the 1970s, he was constantly adding. Other conductors swan around with a handful of works, of which they give practised performances. Walter Weller, the latest of Gibson's successors, makes do with a list of works that is quite astoundingly small. He shows little interest in modern music. His likes and dislikes are easy to detect. He conducts Bruckner with Viennese breadth; Mahler he shuns.

True, Karajan long scorned Mahler too; yet he was ultimately converted. But the groomed and brilliantined performances he obtained suggested that his heart wasn't in it. He did it because it seemed fashionable to do it. Gibson, even without the Berlin Philharmonic as the vehicle through which to express his ideas, built up a Mahler cycle infinitely more perceptive and poetic. He did it because he loved the music.

Yet all this was what one would, or should, expect of a busy conductor, working mostly in one place, with all his antennae out. To Sibelius's symphonies he added a growing enthusiasm for Nielsen's. To Mahler's symphonies he added some of Bruckner's. It was a gradual process, and Scottish audiences could follow him through it and benefit from it. Nevertheless, in retrospect, it does seem that he was doing too much, and the strain sometimes showed. From a new production of *Così fan tutte* at the Holland Festival, he joined the SNO at the Bergen Festival for a pair of concerts that found him below his best. But Elgar's First Symphony, on a subsequent trip to Brussels, was a triumph, and just the right work to perform in a bass-rich auditorium built in Elgar's lifetime. 'How odd,' a member of the audience said afterwards, 'that a country like Scotland should have a symphony orchestra.' Though one could have said the same about Belgium, Gibson's tours with the SNO in these years did nothing but good. Two of them in particular stood out: the first trans-European one, in Ponsonby's time, which began in Vienna's golden Musikverein; and the first American one, in Richardson's time, which climaxed at Carnegie Hall, New York. After conducting Elgar's *Enigma Variations* there, Gibson, visibly moved, told his orchestra: 'I want to thank you for last night. I may not have been listening carefully enough in the past, but I cannot recall you ever playing better.'

If, as time passed, there grew a more noticeable divergence between the decisive and indecisive sides of Gibson's personality, and between his public and private personas, then that is often the way with conductors' lives. 'Are you trying to destroy me?' is a question with which Sir Colin Davis once stunned a London press conference, at a time, you would have thought, when he had built up all the self-assurance he needed. André Previn, a conductor of conspicuous public popularity and charm, has suffered badly at the hands of orchestras and administrators with whom he has worked. Even the skilful Lorin Maazel, if he had had fewer irons in the fire, might have found his career seriously damaged when he was ousted from the Vienna State Opera in 1984.

Giuseppe Sinopoli has been mercilessly attacked by the London critics ever since becoming conductor of the Philharmonia Orchestra but, perhaps because he is a trained psychologist as well as a conductor, he has survived up to now. Karl Rankl, as we now know, was forced upon the SNO in 1952, though to his audiences he seemed a considerable catch. Rafael Kubelik's career was twice brought to a halt, first by Covent Garden and then by the Chicago Symphony Orchestra, before he won the respect he deserved as a freelance.

Sir Malcolm Sargent, though adored by the public, was despised by his players. In Manchester there was talk of getting Barbirolli 'out' – 'he's been here far too long' was a familiar litany – though he was the public jewel in the Hallé's crown. Even the inexorable Karajan might ultimately have found himself rejected by the Berlin Philharmonic, had not death intervened in the nick of time. In spite of the glamorous aspects, conductors' lives are no more secure than anyone else's, and conductors can be as paranoid about their misfortunes as the rest of us. Carlos Kleiber has found a simple solution to the problem by not conducting until, as he puts it, he needs the money, and by holding no official appointments. But then, by common consent, he is a perfectionist, in a class of his own.

Though Gibson would be the first to admit that he is not in Kleiber's league – who is? – his charisma is sufficient for him to retain a large, loyal following and to earn the resentment of unappreciative members of the SNO, who have a tendency to claim that his low-keyed (as they see it) rehearsal methods do not justify the success of his performances. Yet the players themselves are a natural part of that success. If Gibson's methods, however 'unorthodox' they may be, gain results, that is what matters. And quite often the results are gloriously right. His conducting of Sibelius's Second Symphony, a work he must have tackled hundreds of times, continues to evolve, along with the rest of his substantial Sibelius repertoire.

So, too, does his interpretation of Rakhmaninov's vast Second Symphony, in which – like everyone else at one time – he used to make the standard composer-approved cuts, until his musical sensibilities (pricked perhaps by a fierce rebuke from William Mann in *The Times*, employing words like 'monstrous' and 'amputated' after walking out halfway through the performance) prompted him to change his mind.

Like other conductors, he admits even now to an occasional desire to bring back the scissors, thanks to the memory of Temple Savage, the Covent Garden librarian, telling him about the final rehearsal for a complete performance of the symphony under Sir Henry Wood at the Leeds Festival in the composer's presence. 'Do you want me to have no success?' Rakhmaninov cried to the conductor. 'Please observe my cuts.' With this in mind, Gibson says that he, too, 'cheerfully observed the cuts, believing them to be Rakhmaninov's wishes'.

Paul Kletzki, who won the gratitude of all Rakhmaninov-lovers by making the first uncut recording of the work, once confessed to me that the idea was forced on him by his Decca producer, whom he regarded as completely mad. But Gibson, a more patient interpreter, now sees the point of letting Rakhmaninov's great melodic reservoir overflow its banks. For all its self-indulgence, the work's basic structure makes perfect sense. Tampering with it can only mutilate it. When, in 1991, he was invited to take his old orchestra to the London Proms, John Drummond specifically asked him to conduct Rakhmaninov's Second Symphony, because he remembered a fine performance of it Gibson had once given in Bournemouth. So Gibson agreed to do it, and Drummond has been quoted as saying that no other Prom performance that year surpassed it.

By then, of course, Gibson was a freelance, and the rivalries between the SNO and Scottish Opera had dwindled. For Richardson twenty years earlier, however, they had begun to dominate everything else, until in despair he moved as far away from them as possible, by taking charge of an orchestra in Minneapolis.

'There wasn't,' he now says of that tense period, 'any suggestion that I fall upon my sword. My first few years with the SNO were mostly trouble-free. There was no falling out between me and Alex, but there was ultimately an awkwardness. I'd put it to him at one point that he ought to think about relinquishing the SNO in favour of Scottish Opera, but tactically it was the wrong moment. He argued against the idea. The feeling came around that it wasn't the right thing, or the right time.

'I can see now that if I'd put it another way it might have changed the situation. Alex is very keen on numbers. The figure twenty-five is important to him. His twenty-fifth anniversary with the orchestra still lay several years ahead. If I'd simply said to him that it might be a good idea to consider standing down when that point was reached, he might have responded. But I do think in some way I may have planted the idea in his head, because it was after twenty-five years that he did leave.'

Gibson himself agrees that in a way he is quite keen on numbers – he once successfully programmed the fifth symphonies of Schubert, Sibelius, and Beethoven side by side in a single concert – but says that in this context he was more interested in the figure sixty, bearing in mind what had happened to Sir Adrian Boult at that age (the BBC insisted that he was no exception to its bureaucratic rule that that was when its staff members should retire).

Today he admits that he always had a feeling inside himself that he should not exceed twenty-five years with the SNO, whatever happened, even though that would bring him to the age of only fifty-eight. He is not, however, prepared to admit that he was at the same time convinced he should do the same three years later with regard to the opera company he had founded.

Richardson is keen to stress that he never turned against Gibson. It was just that, with the huge expansion of Scottish Opera, the balance of Scotland's musical life unexpectedly and drastically changed. But there was another, more universal, yet for Gibson acutely personal, change that Richardson does not mention. It was simply that, since the time of Barbirolli's death in 1970, long-term conductorships had become a thing of the past.

In America, the long stayers – people like Szell and Ormandy – were either dead, dying, or retired. London was merely a merry-go-round. Colin Davis, having held four major British appointments, was more often abroad than at home. Andrew Davis, after twelve years with the Toronto Symphony Orchestra, began to think that enough was enough at the very moment when Toronto appeared to be thinking the same about him. Daniel Barenboim's French period, which was expected to lead him from the conductorship of the Orchestre de Paris to the glory of the Opéra-Bastille, ended in sensational disarray after fifteen years. Only Simon Rattle in Birmingham looked like having staying power, but who knew how long that would last?

Richardson believed that if Gibson was going to cut the Gordian knot he should do it sooner rather than later. As a conductor he had devoted much of his energy to the SNO, but in Richardson's opinion both he and the orchestra needed the mutual benefit of a change. The parallel with Barbirolli was obvious. Barbirolli had become conductor of the Houston Symphony Orchestra in Texas during the 1960s without quitting his Hallé appointment, which he had held since 1943. Then, when his Houston contract ended, he was, to quote Richardson, 'immovably in Manchester, except on his own terms, even though he wasn't concentrating his whole effort on the job'.

To Richardson, himself a Mancunian, it seemed clear what Barbirolli should do. The trouble was that Barbirolli never did it. He died suddenly in 1970, admired more by the Berlin Philharmonic – with which he made more than seventy guest appearances in his old age and recorded Mahler's Ninth Symphony with such emotion that nobody involved ever forgot it – than by the British orchestra to which he had devoted the best years of his life.

If Richardson could forecast the same sort of thing happening to Gibson, he felt powerless to stop it. 'Alex, in his quiet way, is a manipulator. His way of manipulating is doing nothing and letting things fall into place. It is useless trying to push him into a decision before he is ready. When the orchestra split off from the opera, he sat on the fence. And later, when he should have been thinking of leaving Scottish Opera, he stayed on. As he saw it, he was always there, guiding. In fact, it became one of those situations when the founder, for his own good, should let go, but doesn't know when to do so. He needed to get away from the SNO, from Scottish Opera, from Scotland.'

Whether or not these were correct observations, they were at least partly in keeping with Gibson's response to a questionnaire in the Edinburgh *Evening News,* where he listed among his bad habits: 'Putting off difficult decisions in the hope that the problems will solve themselves, which they often do'.

But Richardson, as an Englishman, did not wholly understand the strength of Gibson's Scottishness. Scotland was his home and, for all its faults, he loved it. He had his opportunities to leave, but did not take them. A brief flirtation with the Detroit Symphony Orchestra – with which, in 1969, he made eight highly successful guest appearances – did not develop into a commitment.

Though the conductorship was on offer, though Gibson went so far as to reposition the players on the platform of the Ford Auditorium during his stay, and though Detroit's principal music critic praised his 'lean, handsome, urgent' performance of Rakhmaninov's Second Symphony and the 'drama, breadth, and conviction' of Mahler's Ninth, Gibson was not sufficiently attracted to the American orchestral scene, to pledge his troth. And who would blame him? Giulini, after all, had been unable to bear life in Chicago, a city with a great deal more to commend it. Only someone with ambitions more ruthless than Gibson's – or with real devotion to Detroit's soaring, monolithic architecture – would want to live in the heart of the American automobile industry, where Trollope, in 1862, had found conditions 'harsh, crude, unprepossessing' (it seems ironic that Neeme Järvi, Gibson's successor with the SNO, is Detroit's current conductor).

In 1969 Gibson had had ample reason to stick to Scotland. The SNO's first exhilarating European tour was only recently behind him, the *Ring* cycle was halfway to completion and he was about to conduct the first ever complete performance of *The Trojans* to celebrate the Berlioz Centenary. But there was one job which, had he been offered it, might just have lured him away from the SNO. That was the Hallé Orchestra, whose management, in a discreet way, was beginning to cast around for someone to succeed Barbirolli when the time came (and the time was to come sooner than was expected).

Sir John had been suffering from heart trouble, and, to reduce the strain, had celebrated his twenty-fifth season by becoming the orchestra's Conductor Laureate for Life – a title that implied lighter duties. 'Who will take up Barbirolli's baton?' asked the *Sunday Times*, somewhat insensitively, around this time, listing a handful of names, one of which was Gibson. In *The Guardian*, Gerald Larner more thoughtfully stated that 'the only man who could replace Barbirolli is another Barbirolli'.

Yet Gibson, who for years had maintained a warm professional relationship with Sir John, and who had been guest conductor with the Hallé many times, could conceivably have been that man. His tastes were similar. He had always had the well-loved senior conductor's personal blessing. Sir John knew and liked the way he conducted, referring to him, even at the age of forty, as 'a good boy'. (After conducting Brahms's Second Symphony with the Hallé, he was told later by the leader, Martin Milner, that 'the old man was very impressed with your Brahms, and had said "that boy is very musical".') The critics were not seriously opposed to him. 'No superlative gestures, astonishing in one so young,' Ernest Bradbury had observed in the *Yorkshire Post*. And in Bradford, where Gibson once deputised for an ailing Barbirolli, he was remembered as the conductor who had stopped the orchestra during the overture while late-comers shuffled in embarrassment to their seats. Moreover, Manchester was not so far from Glasgow that he would feel cut off from the city he loved best.

Because, in 1969, the north of England did not yet possess an opera company, there was speculation as to whether Gibson might want to launch one there. But the likelihood of his giving up Scottish Opera, even if he moved to Manchester, seemed slight. The *Daily Mail*, which favoured his appointment, feared that 'it is love of opera that may keep Alexander Gibson away'. Gerald Larner, in *The Guardian*, put it more positively. Pointing out that Gibson's heart was in the opera house and that he had a perfectly good orchestra in Scotland, he added: 'Anyone who leaves Scottish Opera for what Manchester might offer in that respect is either an innocent idealist or plain mad. Mr Gibson is neither.'

In the end, his loyalties were not put to the test. Though the *Daily Express* explained why Gibson was '6–4 favourite for the Hallé', and though *The Guardian* printed pictures of Gibson and Barenboim (the latter running at 100–1 in the *Express*'s estimation) facing each other, Gibson posing with his hand beneath his chin, the appointment went to neither of these possible contenders, nor to any of the others nominated by newspapers at the time. As is so often the way, an outsider came in. James Loughran, Gibson's fellow Scot, did not turn out to be 'another Barbirolli', but he was at least sufficiently similar in his enthusiasms to provide a sense of continuity until, in 1983, he decided he had had enough.

Today, Gibson is able to look back on what he calls the combined 'pressures' of Scottish Opera and the SNO and ask me: 'Could I ever have been considered absolutely even-handed about them, even if that was what I was? Inevitably, in any kind of disagreement about the relationship between the two, it was taken for granted that I would be favourably disposed to Scottish Opera, since after all I'd started the thing. But it wasn't true. Inevitably, if you're holding two positions in the same city, each organisation is going to feel it's being neglected.

'For example, I might have been conducting rehearsals for a symphony concert on the same day as an opera was at floor rehearsal stage. [Floor rehearsals are ones in which the conductor can be replaced by a *répétiteur* while the cast act their roles. At Covent Garden, Otto Klemperer, no matter what sort of rehearsal was in progress, used to say: "What is this acting? It gets in the way of the music."] But often, because they knew I was in town and even although I was doing something else, the opera cast would want me to be with them at floor rehearsals. I found myself doing more than many conductors would be prepared to do simply because I was around. It gives me the heebie-jeebies now when I look at my old diaries. How did I get through some of these weeks? And not only in Glasgow, but in Edinburgh, Aberdeen, Newcastle. When we were building up the *Ring* cycle, I did every performance myself, whereas elsewhere another conductor might also be involved.

'Yet at the time I didn't feel my diary was overfilled, otherwise I wouldn't have been able to do it. Nor did I get the impression that the people I was working with felt I was doing too much – except perhaps Robert Ponsonby, who was a very sensitive, understanding man, and who would wonder about the wisdom of my doing *Così fan tutte* in Holland and then conducting at the Bergen Festival immediately afterwards, or would point out to me that the beginning of the following season looked dangerously busy. [It was also Ponsonby who, fearing it might distract the conductor's attention from Mozart's *Haffner* symphony at the Usher Hall, refrained from informing him that President Kennedy had just been assassinated.]

'When there were conflicts of interest between Scottish Opera and the SNO, I not only had to handle the orchestral side with Ponsonby or Richardson, I also had to fight and deal with Peter Hemmings over what was right and not right – whether the SNO's winter concert schedule should be interrupted for opera performances, what was to be done about the *Ring* cycle, and the eternal question of orchestral overtime and how it was to be paid for.

'I tended to look on it all as something in the old German tradition whereby the conductor was responsible in the end. But when Scottish Opera began to expand, it was obvious that difficulties would arise and I tried to resolve them. I do remember that when we did *The Trojans* at the Edinburgh Festival, there were members of the SNO who said they were not prepared to work the overtime involved and withdrew their services from certain rehearsals accordingly. And that was something that grew steadily more difficult whenever a long opera was being staged.'

Whatever the players claim to the contrary, Gibson remains convinced that many of them considered opera to be an unnecessary chore. When one instrumentalist around the time of the historic *Ring* cycle went up to him and said, 'It must be nice for you, having a symphony orchestra in the pit,' he says he felt inclined to reply: 'Yes, but it's also nice for you. When I came here from London, I took over an orchestra that had been operating full time for only eight seasons. Its profile was low. It still had immense trouble getting dates at certain times of year. I got you those dates. And I managed to raise the orchestral strength from seventy-four to ninety-six players.'

Not every member of the orchestra objected to opera, but even those who enjoyed the *Ring* experience were aware of the growing tide of disapproval. Sam Bor, the SNO's leader, objected on simple ideological grounds: he regarded Wagner's tetralogy as a repellent Nazi tract, in which Alberich and Mime were Jews in disguise. Bor's was an influential voice, but other players also had their own objections. For most of them it was principally a matter of timing. *Götterdämmerung* lasted as long as three whole concerts, and was performed under seriously uncomfortable conditions in theatres not built for a Wagner-sized orchestra. It was not, they said, what they had joined the SNO to do, and their voices carried weight. The fact that the performances made history, and that praise was heaped on them by critics and public alike, cut little ice. Wagner was being imposed on them, and they wanted something done about it.

Today some of those who took part in the juggernaut performances of Wagner, Berlioz, and Strauss have modified their views. Partly perhaps because they were no longer members of the SNO, and had either retired or moved into other branches of music, they were able to look back upon Scottish Opera's triumphs more objectively. Gibson? Well, he wasn't so bad. He was quite good, really, in the right music, and those big works were certainly his scene. Pity the orchestra couldn't do that sort of thing now, during those periods when their chief executive seemed unable to find them decent dates. Maybe they'd been a bit too hasty, breaking with Scottish Opera entirely. Maybe they should have left at least one iron in that particular fire.

Richard Chester, a player who moved into orchestral administration and now runs the National Youth Orchestra of Scotland after many years with the SNO, is able from his present vantage point to see both sides of the picture. Taking part in Gibson's *Ring* cycle was a privilege, he says – and an unforgettable one. But some of the Mozart performances were almost as fine, 'because Alex was extremely good at working with a small Mozart orchestra'.

Yet Chester is one of those who believe that, when the SNO was in the process of withdrawing from Scottish Opera, Gibson took the wrong messages. 'He kept telling us that we didn't want to work for the opera company, when in fact we were quite unanimous that we did. We simply wanted to cut back on the vast amount we were doing, but he seemed miffed that we should want to question the matter at all. And now today it could be said that everyone, in a sense, has lost. Today the orchestra is a symphony orchestra, and no more than that. As a result, in a funny way, it has become less attractive to a musician. The fact is, looking back, Alex was the resident conductor of an extremely attractive package.'

CHAPTER TEN

Decision Times

Whatever the tensions inside the SNO office, Gibson still had Peter Hemmings as his friend, ally, and confidant at Scottish Opera. And between them, in 1975, they brought off the most spectacular of all their coups through the acquisition of the Glasgow Theatre Royal from STV.

Though the handsome Victorian theatre in Hope Street had been used for studio purposes, the ownership of it was no longer necessary to the television company. New studios had been built next door, and the theatre was being used largely for storage. So when STV agreed to sell the site at its commercial value of £300,000, the chance seemed too good to lose. With the enormous goodwill that the opera company continued to generate, and with Gibson's and Hemmings's sort of contacts, there would be no problem about raising the basic cash.

The conversion costs and running costs would be another matter, but Hemmings handled the transactions with the sangfroid for which he was famed. The auditorium, in what seemed like the twinkling of an eye, was brought back to all its Victorian splendour. A real orchestra pit was sunk. The stage was rebuilt. Not until later did some of the early decisions seem to have been too hastily made. By 1993 it was finally admitted that the chasm-like pit, much of it beneath the lip of the stage, was unacceptably submerged, acoustically harsh, and physically cramped. The original plan, to narrow the gulf between stage and audience, may have been clever, but the wind players found their narrow slot ear-splitting to perform in, and the audience grew increasingly aware that what actually emerged lacked richness. But in 1975, at least, sheer euphoria prevented anyone – other than the players – from grumbling.

Happily for the SNO, other players by then provided most of the accompaniments. It was the recently-formed Scottish Chamber Orchestra and the larger Scottish Philharmonia (essentially the same team plus extras) that now took over Scottish Opera's pit work in Glasgow and elsewhere. They, too, would eventually opt out of it, but for the moment, at any rate, the problem seemed solved.

The theatre itself was a gem, and it provided the company with the chance to sustain a full-length and uninterrupted Glasgow season from the autumn until the spring. 'We want to get away from semi-festival opera,' declared Peter Hemmings, when the plans were finally made public. 'We were unable to find enough rehearsal time, far less extend our annual number of performances, at the King's Theatre, our original home, because it could not always be made available when we needed it, especially during the long-established pantomime season.' For anyone to have suggested that he might be mistaken in his objectives would have caused incredulity. Yet semi-festival opera – as I myself would be prepared to proclaim in 1993 after eighteen years of the other sort – was what Scottish Opera was best at.

In 1975, however, the transformation of the Theatre Royal into Scotland's first opera house seemed the realisation of all Gibson's and Hemmings's dreams. That the achievement of their long-sought desire would bring enormous new problems, both artistic and financial, was as yet neither known nor guessed at. When, in the gleamingly renovated theatre, the curtain went up on *Die Fledermaus* and *Otello*, both of them conducted by Gibson with all the panache at his command, it seemed as if the wonders of 1962 were happening all over again.

There was rejoicing in the foyers and there was rejoicing on the stage, where the party scene in *Fledermaus* was used as an opportunity for some of the company's founder members to pay tribute to its achievement with special solos (Charles Craig's 'Nessun dorma' was specially prized) and for Peter Ebert to step forward and say – to show-stopping applause – 'Well, we've done it'. Little did he know, as he uttered those proud words, that perhaps nothing would ever be quite so good again for Scottish Opera, and that quite a lot was going to be quite decidedly not so good – for himself, for Gibson, and quite often also for the audience.

But not yet. Though some would have preferred the opening night to consist of something more thrilling than a revival of *Fledermaus*,

Gibson and Hemmings knew exactly what they were doing in choosing it. On such occasions, the glare of publicity can make whatever is performed seem embarrassingly wrong. In America, Samuel Barber's *Antony and Cleopatra* had been a notorious disaster at the opening of the New Met. An established company success, with some bright new trimmings and a few little surprises, proved exactly the right answer.

One source of surprise was Bill McCue, one of a number of local talents who had soared to operatic fame on the wings of Scottish Opera, who sang 'Bonnie Strathyre'. Another was John Lawson Graham's translation of the jailer, Frosch, into an archetypal Glasgow drunk (a portrayal infinitely funnier and better timed than Billy Connolly's some years later). 'Viennese this production is not,' said *The Times*, 'except in the pit, where Alexander Gibson conducts a deliciously lilting, affectionately Straussian reading.'

Scottish Television's live relay enabled country cousins, and those who had failed to get tickets, to see the whole performance. Gibson and the Theatre Royal were together judged to be the stars of 'the biggest thing to hit Glasgow since St Mungo'. David Donaldson's revealing life-size portrait of the conductor was unveiled on the scrubbed stone staircase between the stalls and circle. The theatre's plaster mouldings, restored to their original elegance, were admired. Harold Rosenthal of *Opera* magazine, not pitching enthusiasm too high but catching the flavour precisely, said it felt just like being in Brescia or Reggio Emilia. The only thing missing, as Desmond Shawe-Taylor sharply remarked in a *Sunday Times* review headed 'Glasgow Glory', was the SNO.

Did members of the absent orchestra note this patrician critic's gentle rebuke, and did they grasp its implications? Certainly, the sound of the Scottish Philharmonia in *Otello* could only remind opera-goers of happier days, when the national orchestra was in the pit and, in a new production of *Pelléas et Méslisande*, had been playing for Gibson with fresh finesse, enabling him to capitalise on his 1962 performances, adding new depths of darkness, new intensities of light, new tang to the sea textures, new shades to the forest music, and a fateful new sense of suffocation to the work as a whole.

It was this production that Scottish Opera took on its first, greatly (but quite sensibly) delayed excursion to London, coupling it with Wagner's *Tristan und Isolde*, and revealing, as never before, the one to be the psychological obverse of the other. And it was again this *Pelléas* which Peter Diamand, a great Scottish Opera supporter, invited the company to revive when, in 1978, he bade farewell to the Edinburgh Festival.

After the last of the three performances at the King's Theatre, Gibson, though pale with fatigue (the subdued Act Five of *Pelléas* being one of the hardest of all stretches of operatic music to sustain successfully), had to sprint to the Usher Hall to take part in 'A Garland for Peter Diamand', a concert party featuring Fischer-Dieskau, Teresa Berganza, and others who had glittered for the Festival director during the preceding thirteen years. Gibson's contribution, with the London Philharmonic Orchestra, was the 'Sentimental Sarabande' from Britten's *Simple Symphony* – just the sort of piece, and just the sort of occasion, to which as a conductor he invariably rises.

Had Scottish Opera not acquired the Theatre Royal in 1975, would things have gone very differently for him? That is one of the four big questions – the others concern his move from London in 1959, his failure to transform the SNO into a multiple orchestra in the 1970s and the wisdom of his staying in charge of it for twenty-five years – that still hang over his career, and to which the only answer is that he did what he did because he believed that what he was doing was right. He certainly felt he had to stand by Scottish Opera in its new premises. Without the Theatre Royal he thinks the company might not have survived and would certainly have been more vulnerable to takeover bids from across the border.

Yet Scottish Opera now found itself travelling along a quite different path from the one it had trod until 1975. Gary Bertini, the SNO's Israeli-born principal guest conductor who had performed various Mozart works with Scottish Opera, once stated his belief that all the company's troubles (and in recent years there have been many) began at that point. Speaking with an outsider's objectivity, he thought it a dangerous decision.

Though it grieves me to say I agree – and though I do so without the sanction of the subject of this book, who is appalled at my suggesting such a thing – it is a belief I have gradually come to share. Time, it's true, will move on and, via the succession of musical directors and administrators who now pass steadily through the company, Scottish Opera and the Theatre Royal may come to seem the mature integer that Gibson and Hemmings originally wanted them to be. Meanwhile, in spite of recent improvements, the acrid air of wrong decisions has not yet been swept away.

Having established the company in its new home, Hemmings left. Perhaps, as he said at the time, it was the right moment. He had helped to bring Scottish Opera to its moment of triumph. But if he was to build up his career as an international administrator, he needed a change. Cynical people might say that he simply saw trouble ahead, and that he deemed it prudent to get out before the euphoria wore off. If that is so, he made it in the nick of time.

Once he announced he was leaving, a successor had to be found fast. Thomson Smillie – a Glaswegian who, on the evidence of his recent American career, would have been an excellent choice – applied but failed. In the end the job went to Peter Ebert, an old friend of the company and formerly its director of productions, who in due course arrived from Germany with German expectations as to how things should be run. What he expected was a staff who would look after much of the administrative work while he himself devoted his attention to opera production.

Ebert's was the classic German conception of an *Intendant* who would not only choose the repertoire but grab the best bits of it for himself. In Britain it was not only unprecedented but, for financial reasons, it could not work. Nor, unfortunately, did it always work artistically. Though he had been responsible for several of Scottish Opera's greatest early successes, his production of Gluck's *Orfeo* – even with Gibson as conductor and Janet Baker, Margaret Marshall, and Marie McLaughlin as its sterling cast – failed to suggest that he had had time to exploit his creative talents to advantage in the midst of his administrative duties.

Even if there were no votes of no confidence in him, confidence, nevertheless, was gradually lost. Nobody seemed to be in charge of the shop. The Scottish Chamber Orchestra withdrew its services with the blessing of the Scottish Arts Council. A new full-time nucleus of an opera orchestra had to be recruited in haste (ironically, at the very moment when the BBC was trying, as it periodically did and still does, to get rid of the BBC Scottish Symphony Orchestra). But within a season or two the new opera orchestra was threatening strike action in mid-season because, among other things, it thought it deserved more pay for its performances of lengthy operas.

On one occasion an Edinburgh audience was left sitting in the auditorium while the orchestra meditated on its options. When it eventually became clear that some members of the orchestra were not going to return, the audience was sent home. Gibson, at the start of the evening, had not been fully informed that the performance might be in jeopardy. Morale steadily sank. Soon Ebert resigned, leaving behind him financial chaos and some tantalisingly unfulfilled plans to follow his Berlioz centenary production of *The Trojans* with a new *Benvenuto Cellini* and *Damnation of Faust* with Gibson as conductor.

When Hemmings left Scottish Opera, his job was greatly coveted. When Ebert left, nobody of international consequence

With the concert pianist Clifford Curzon (1970s)

Gibson gives a downbeat to the SNO at rehearsal in the Usher Hall (1970s)

Gibson with Scottish baritone William McCue (1976)

Off duty at Scottish Opera with John Lawson Graham and Patricia Hay (1976)

Gibson after receiving the Sibelius Medal from the distinguished present-day Finnish composer Joonas Kokkonen (1978)

Gibson with Arthur Rubinstein (1970s)

Gibson with Shura Cherkassky

Gibson with chorusmaster Arthur Oldham

Gibson with the young John Ogdon

David Donaldson, the Queen's Limner in Scotland, painting Gibson's portrait

Gibson with Peter Hemmings (Photograph by Eric Thorburn)

Gibson (right) welcomes Robert Ponsonby (left) as the SNO's administrator. Between them are Sam Bor (standing), the orchestra's leader, and William Fell, the retiring administrator

The Gibsons relaxing during a rehearsal break in New York

Gibson with Jessye Norman after a concert performance of the closing scene from Strauss's Salomé *at Glasgow Royal Concert Hall after its opening in 1990*

seemed interested. For a while, members of Ebert's staff attempted to keep things going, but before long the company that had started so gloriously seemed to be on the brink of collapse. In partnership with Ian Rodger, who by then was acting chairman, Gibson knew that an operatic *deus ex machina* needed to be found. Various names were put forward, but one in particular began to recur. John Cox, director of productions at Glyndebourne, had let it be known that he might be interested in a change of scene.

Cox's lack of administrative experience was not necessarily thought to be a deterrent factor – though it ought to have been, considering the administrative mess the company was now in. Nor did anybody seem seriously to consider that, after Ebert, another producer-administrator was the last thing that Scottish Opera needed. Cox's Glyndebourne associations, and the fact that he actually appeared interested in the job, appeared to do the trick.

By chance I was in Ian Rodger's Glasgow office the afternoon Cox's appointment was confirmed. Rodger phoned Gibson to give him the good news, and added that Cox was so eager to get started that he was prepared to journey to Belfast – which, though dangerous, was a popular and enjoyable touring date for the company – to watch it at work and meet the performers.

'Isn't that just like the man?' said Gibson enthusiastically down the phone. They were words he would later eat. For within a couple of years, Cox and Gibson were on less amicable terms.

What triggered this is difficult to say. The gangling Bristol-born administrator, with his mild manner and designer hairstyle, was certainly no Hemmings, and perhaps that was part of the problem. But for a time, in his capacity as producer, he worked well with Gibson, and between them they presented a goodish *Manon Lescaut* at the Edinburgh Festival, even if it proved less durable than the company's other Puccini productions.

But the more one saw of Cox's own productions, the more they came to seem like boxes of soft-centred chocolates – nice to taste, easy to swallow, prettily decorated, but soon forgotten. Cavalli's *Egisto* was a case in point. It looked attractive, in a tinselly sort of way, but when it was toured to Venice an Italian voice from the stalls of the Fenice Theatre cried 'Merry Christmas'. What was worse about the company's new administrator, however, was his apparent lack of quality control. While he himself was a conservative producer, he left it to others to run riot and he gave them his blessing. This was the era of the auto-biographical Torre Del Lago *Turandot* (Tony Palmer), the lavatorial *Don Giovanni* (Graham Vick), and the Hollywood *Oberon* (Vick again).

Since Gibson conducted all three of these productions, he himself was hardly blameless. He could have declared them unacceptable, as Riccardo Muti was to do of a Mozart production at the 1992 Salzburg Festival. But that would not have been Gibson's style. A stoical Scot, he was prone to take whatever punishment a producer gave him, even if it meant providing *Turandot* with two separate endings and accepting that it was the story of Puccini, his wife, and the housemaid. Such an approach to the piece might have formed the substance of a speculative television programme or university paper entitled *The Truth about Turandot*, but as Scottish Opera's first shot at Puccini's last opera, it was a non-starter. Those who knew the work were outraged. Those who didn't were baffled. The pain for Gibson must have been severe, but he coped with it and earned his sliver of praise for a performance well conducted.

But what did he really think? There are times, he says, when outlandish productions have crept up on him unawares. By the time he has fully realised what is happening, they have become a *fait accompli*. Charles Mackerras is known to have loathed the Ruth Berghaus production of *Don Giovanni* which he conducted for Welsh National Opera, yet he did nothing to intervene with her conception of it. Carlo Maria Giulini did object, publicly, to Luciano Damiani's Holland Festival production of the same work. Yet he conducted the first few performances of it and his objections finally made things worse. By the time it reached the Edinburgh Festival two months later, Damiani had disowned it and, presented without its original scenery, it was no longer a production at all.

To suggest that a certain kind of producer deliberately keeps a conductor in the dark about his intentions would be to imply that there are in the world a good many blind conductors — which Gibson certainly is not. But, as he admits, it is possible to be deluded. In the case of Palmer's *Turandot*, the extent to which Puccini's opera would be distorted was not, he says, noticeable during the early rehearsals. At that time it appeared to be a *Turandot* like any other. Besides, there were unexpected musical problems to contend with, principally involving the work's ending.

As Puccini left the work unfinished (though not before he had written 'Nessun dorma') the traditional solution has always been to employ Franco Alfano's completion of Act Three, made after the composer's death. But Palmer had a more radical solution. He proposed that the Alfano ending be discarded and replaced by the unrolling a second time of Puccini's own grandly sonorous music from the end of Act One. In theory it was an interesting idea, and Gibson gamely went along with it, typically justifying his acquiescence by securing the approval of a member of the board – the well-known musicologist, Hugh Macdonald, at that time professor of music at Glasgow University – as well as that of Scottish Opera's own head of music, the highly experienced and respected Leonard Hancock.

Another conductor might merely have told Palmer to go to blazes. In fact, that was just what Gibson should have done, for suddenly there arose a problem which, amazingly, nobody had anticipated. Ricordi, the Italian publishing house, insisted on behalf of the Puccini – or was it the Alfano? – estate that a new ending would be illegal unless the Alfano one was performed as well. From this point on, it was obvious (or should have been) that the event was doomed. Gibson found himself in a position whereby he had to conduct the 'Palmer ending', which was by now considered vital to the producer's conception of the piece, and then, after a pause, conduct a concert performance of the Alfano ending, sung by two different singers in evening dress.

With all this on his hands, he could perhaps be forgiven for not realising until it was too late that the Palmer *Turandot* would be a write-off from page one. 'But when we were working on the floor,' he says, 'it simply wasn't obvious what he was going to do. And though it is always possible for a conductor to have access to drawings and so forth, precise recognition of what is actually happening, or going to happen, does not necessarily dawn at that point.'

As a thoroughly professional, rather than a temperamentally prickly, conductor, Gibson has never walked out on a production. Nor is he the sort of person who makes a fuss, except over small details on behalf of singers or the orchestra, and producers may trade on this. Moreover, many of the sessions a conductor attends are purely musical ones. When Gibson, after the *Turandot* débâcle, prudently asked Graham Vick when he was actually going to *see* something of Vick's forthcoming *Don Giovanni*, Vick nonchalantly replied: 'Oh you will, you will.'

Sometimes, too, there can be changes of tack. During preliminary meetings about a production of *The Magic Flute* which Jonathan Miller had been invited to do for Scottish Opera, Gibson learnt that Miller was planning to employ lots of little clocks and chronometers, all twirling away. Happily, as things turned out, the cost of these proved prohibitively expensive. Books were considered a cheaper alternative, and the action of Mozart's Viennese masonic opera was shifted to what looked like the Bibliothèque Nationale in Paris.

Miller's concept, whether or not one liked it, was at least something that worked. But there were times, considers Gibson, when John Cox – 'who after all was the company's administrator' – should have acted as a safety valve and didn't. The graffiti in Graham Vick's

Don Giovanni were a case in point. These, relentlessly daubed by stage-hands in the course of the performance, formed an intrinsic part of Vick's deconstructive approach to Mozart's opera.

'But in the course of rehearsals,' says Gibson, 'Cox decided that they were distracting. He came to me and asked if I found them distracting too. He proposed that we talk to Graham about them. By that time, as you can imagine, everyone was getting at Graham about all sorts of things. Since Cox had appointed Vick, I felt he was in a better position to deal with what was happening to the production than the conductor who was concentrating on the musical ensemble. So I told him to tell him himself.'

Cox, though he had arrived in Scotland in the role of the company's saviour, was someone I personally found hard to fathom. After the regimes of Hemmings and Ebert (with both of whom, as a critic, I got on well) I detected in my encounters with him a tendency to conceal himself behind a veneer of seemingly amiable soulfulness. He was the man who had rescued Scottish Opera from oblivion. Yet he accepted that it could be guilty of sin. Whenever I attacked the work of one of his guest producers – the Peter Wood production of Cavalli's *Orion* at the Edinburgh Festival comes specially to mind, since I disliked both the piece and the way it was staged – he was apt to come up to me and, instead of acting as counsel for the defence, say 'I so agree with what you wrote'. As a critic accustomed to abuse, I found it extremely disconcerting.

But if that was how he felt about it, why did he ever let it happen? More seriously, the old camaraderie that had existed in Scottish Opera between musical director and administrator was by now conspicuously dwindling. The big press conferences at which the following season's repertoire would be disclosed amid much jolly repartee, and in the presence of the chairman and key members of staff, were a thing of the past.

On one occasion the press brigade was kept waiting in the outer hall of the Scottish Opera Centre in Elmbank Crescent until well past the official starting time. Everyone shuffled around and looked at one another. What was the matter? We were then summoned into a room in which Cox, standing frigidly alone, delivered the information in a clipped voice. Question time was kept brief. Asked why he had chosen a tenor rather than a mezzo-soprano – musically the more appropriate choice – for the role of Idamante in his own production of *Idomeneo* (acquired second-hand from Glyndebourne) he replied crisply: 'Because I prefer a tenor.' Then off he went. Neville Garden, behind me, said 'Does this mean we're to go?' I replied that I guessed it did.

These were uneasy times, very different from the self-confident, affirmative Hemmings period. Even if, as some people thought, Gibson for some time had been too torn between Scottish Opera and the SNO to concentrate properly on either, he had continued to do a phenomenal amount of work. Some of his major achievements I have already mentioned, but there were many others over the years, not perhaps quite so memorable, yet evidence of what a Scottish conductor who cared about his homeland should have been doing. Then as now, he nurtured the work of his fellow Scots. The 1970s, which had begun with a number of notable orchestral premières, among them Martin Dalby's Symphony and Iain Hamilton's elegiac Shelley-inspired *Alastor*, subsequently generated an operatic project of even higher ambition.

Having already staged a number of Scottish one-act operas (the best of them being Robin Orr's *Full Circle*, a tense little Glasgow drama based on a radio play by Sydney Goodsir Smith), Scottish Opera, at the height of the Hemmings-Gibson period, had decided it was time to go a step further. Accordingly, it commissioned four full-length operas from four Scottish composers, each with a libretto by a Scottish writer. Gibson treated the project seriously. The composers would be the cream of the talent then available. The performances would be cast at strength. The company would show that its international credibility did not exclude a desire to cultivate its own garden. The varied choice of subjects – political, psychological, historical, and literary – looked promising.

In today's financial climate, so cornucopian – or, as some might say, reckless – a scheme would be stillborn. Yet in the 1970s, Scottish Opera was able not only to see it through to the end but to get two of the productions into the Edinburgh Festival. Gibson conducted two of the works himself. That the first of them, Iain Hamilton's *The Catiline Conspiracy*, turned out to be both the best and by far the most difficult looked like a mixture of good luck and bad luck for the large cast and orchestra involved alongside Gibson in its performance.

Bowled over not only by Hamilton's powerful, uncompromising music but also by his ability to draw political parallels between ancient Rome and modern Britain – the Heath government was in its death throes when the work was first performed – I threw moderation to the winds and proclaimed *The Catiline Conspiracy* a masterpiece when it was premièred at the recently-opened MacRobert Centre, Stirling University, in 1974.

A little moderation, it's true, might have been advisable. Scotland's first political opera proved musically too rigorous for its audience, who longed for identifiable arias, or at least the occasional recurring theme. Yet the main characters – who, besides the rebellious Catiline, included Caesar, Cato, Crassus, and Cicero – had strong music to sing. The plotting and counter-plotting, the changing loyalties, the treachery and rumour, erupting from time to time into fierce senatorial clashes, made for an enthralling music drama. In the *Financial Times*, Ronald Crichton considered it worth one-and-a-half columns of space. In *The Times*, William Mann compared it, a shade optimistically, with Verdi and Puccini. Yet the point was that he considered such comparisons valid.

For Gibson, the work's critical success convinced him that the company was on the right track. And if Thomas Wilson's *Confessions of a Justified Sinner* suffered from structural problems, at least Thea Musgrave's *Mary Queen of Scots* (with Catherine Wilson cast to perfection in the title-role) gave the audience the traditional opera, complete with tunes, that it was longing for. Neither of these was conducted by Gibson, who instead had the delicate task, at the 1975 Edinburgh Festival, of dealing with Robin Orr's *Hermiston*, the first full-length opera by his own chairman.

To say that Orr on this occasion had bitten off more than he could chew would be harsh but sadly true. The talent that had made *Full Circle* seem so taut was here seriously overstretched. The piece, based on Robert Louis Stevenson's unfinished novel, began with a *coup de théâtre* – a public hanging in Edinburgh's Old Town (a small mechanical mishap on the opening night nearly resulted in the demise of the ballet dancer who played the doomed man).

But the music failed to live up to its arresting opening. Even with a traditional operatic mad scene – a small treat for the beautiful Catherine Gayer – the work never became more than what Joseph Kerman, the American musicologist, has termed 'opera as a sung play'. It was a disappointing end to Orr's reign as Scottish Opera's first and most enlightened chairman, but the moral, one feared, was obvious. Composers and librettists (Bill Bryden in this case), but particularly company chairmen. tamper with great novels at their peril.

Yet the four-part exercise had been well worth doing, prompting *The Guardian* to state that 'Alexander Gibson is one of the contemporary opera composer's truest friends'. He gave *Hermiston*, like *The Catiline Conspiracy*, a fine send-off, and he did so at a time when he was devoting unstinted energy not only to his opera company but to his orchestra. He had included, in the Edinburgh Festival's opening concert that year, a work new to the SNO's repertoire. For the same programme he had devised his own extensive and exceptionally successful sequence of movements from Prokofiev's ballet, *Romeo and Juliet*. And, with his usual aplomb, he had also dealt with a double crisis, first when Claudio Arrau, who was to have been soloist in Beethoven's *Emperor* concerto, hurt his shoulder and cancelled his appearance, and then when Daniel Barenboim, Arrau's replacement, cut his finger just before the concert. The pianist was rushed to the doctor, the concerto was switched to the end of the programme, and Barenboim arrived in time to perform, complete with bandaged finger and with Gibson's watchful support, a truly imperial *Emperor*.

A week later, with two performances of *Hermiston* in between, Gibson was back at the Usher Hall to accompany Teresa Berganza in a variety of classical and pre-classical rarities, interwoven with symphonies by Haydn and C. P. E. Bach that lay outside the SNO's normal range. Nor could his Viennese night at the end of the Festival be called a doddle. With Gundula Janowitz singing Mozart concert arias, and with Johann Strauss's *Covent Garden* waltz and *Sängerslust* polka as proof that the programme had really been thought about, here was the sort of event that might have seemed more trouble than it was worth. But it was also the sort to which Gibson has always brought real finesse.

'I specialise in not being a specialist.' George Szell's dictum is one that Gibson has quoted more than once, applying it to himself and demonstrating its truth with the extraordinary variety of music he is willing and able to conduct. In Washington in 1974 he had conducted the belated American première of Monteverdi's *Ulysses* in the Raymond Leppard edition with sufficient intensity to suggest that baroque opera formed a regular part of his life. In fact it did nothing of the kind, and it still doesn't. *Ulysses* was simply something which, as a wide-ranging opera conductor, he was happy to undertake. (His association with the Washington Opera had started the year before with Stravinsky's *Rake's Progress*, in which the young baritone making his debut as Trulove was Willard White.)

In 1976 he celebrated his fiftieth birthday by conducting Berlioz's *Damnation of Faust* in Madrid, Stravinsky's *Persephone* (with Genevieve Page as speaker) at the Venice Bienniale, and Schubert's Great C major Symphony at the Caramoor Festival in New York State, interwoven with Verdi's *Falstaff* in Scotland, performances of Iain Hamilton's *Aurora*, Balakirev's First Symphony, and Vaughan Williams's Ninth Symphony in Manchester, as well as other events already mentioned. His efforts were rewarded by the Incorporated Society of Musicians, who named him Musician of the Year, and the medal was presented to him by the society's president at the time, Richard Lewis.

Yet Gibson's belief that he is not a specialist is characteristic of his modesty. If he is not a specialist in Sibelius, why was he awarded the Sibelius Medal? Why do Scandinavian orchestras invite him to appear with them? If he is not a Berlioz specialist, why was he at such pains to conduct every note of *The Trojans*, a Berlioz masterpiece that had previously suffered death by a thousand cuts? Why, even in his youth, did he conduct Elgar's *Enigma Variations* to such perfection that he received a letter signed 'Dorabella' (the composer's friend Dora Powell, immortalised in the most fastidiously written variation of the set) telling him that his was the best performance she had ever heard? It has been Gibson's way of demeaning his own achievements, by the simple method of never proclaiming them to the world at large, that has made people sometimes fail to appreciate how remarkable a musician he is. And in the 1980s alas, this was to tell against him.

CHAPTER ELEVEN

Sir Alex

For a conductor, it is said, life begins at fifty – or is it sixty, seventy, or eighty? For every Mark Wigglesworth or Franz Welser-Möst who emerges in his twenties as the latest wunderkind, there is a Gunter Wand (now in his nineties) who will gain a kind of conductorial patina in his old age, perhaps after a long period when he won no great recognition at all. Klemperer (in spite of his early achievements at the Kroll Opera) was a bit like that. So was Jascha Horenstein.

Would Gibson in his fifties enter a new phase in his career? Not, some people felt, if he continued to devote the bulk of energies to his two Scottish organisations. As musical director of each, he took his duties seriously. He involved himself in the working and the politics of each company. He attended meetings and auditions. He listened to other conductors' performances. He gave advice when it was sought from him. He believed in Scotland as a musical entity. He turned down operatic opportunities elsewhere, either because they clashed with his duties at home or would have meant his being away for weeks at a time from what he considered to be higher Scottish priorities.

These things he did ungrudgingly. He loved his job, but, as we shall see, he failed to watch his back. The awards he received in the 1960s and '70s for his services to Scotland made it seem by the 1980s that he had reached, perhaps even passed, the peak of his achievement. His CBE in 1967 had been an early token of official recognition, though the Freedom of Motherwell and Wishaw had come to him even earlier. Aberdeen University in 1968 made him – along with Joan Sutherland

and June Gordon, Marchioness of Aberdeen – an honorary Doctor of Laws, revealing in the ceremonial process the curiously prophetic contents of a boyhood article he had once written in his school magazine. Master Gibson, it emerged, had 'deplored the fact that nearly all eminent modern musicians bore foreign names and looked forward to the day when Scotland would have great performers and a distinct musical life of her own'. If that was a personal aspiration, he certainly lived up to it.

His awards from Glasgow University and the Royal Scottish Academy have already been mentioned. When Janet Baker became Chancellor of York University, she was allowed to nominate three people for doctorates. Gibson was one of them. In 1970 he received the St Mungo Prize – a gold medal and £1,000 – for the 'person considered to have done the most for Glasgow or to have enhanced its reputation in the preceding three years'. Doctorates continued to flow in, from Stirling (where he was honoured alongside the French anthropologist Claude Lévi-Strauss, the documentary film-maker John Grierson, and the Pitlochry Festival Theatre's founder, Kenneth Ireland), from Newcastle (where this time he found himself beside Lord Mackay of Clashfern, Lord Justice Taylor, Sir Leon Brittan, and Kate Adie), and from the Open University. In 1977, at the age of fifty-one, he was knighted.

With him, to Buckingham Palace, went his wife and mother, though the financial aspects of his journey from Glasgow were bureaucratically intricate. 'You may, if you wish to do so, claim towards certain expenses incurred in attending an investiture,' Gibson was informed by the Prime Minister's principal private secretary. A contribution 'not exceeding second-class rail fare' would be available to him. There was even the possibility of subsistence 'where absence from home is five hours and not more than ten hours'. If an overnight stay was unavoidable, the sum of £9.95 would be paid towards its cost. The figures seemed curiously reminiscent of the expenses paid by *The Scotsman* to its journalists at the time. Rather than indent for them, the newly-knighted conductor preferred to paste the application form into one of his albums of souvenirs.

Back home after the ceremony, he had an immediate date with the SNO Chorus's Gilbert and Sullivan splinter group. Chorusmaster Currie, reckoning that the knighting of a Scottish conductor was something rare enough to require acknowledgment, told his singers that 'it would be nice to greet him this evening with some applause', because, though his honour was personal, it 'reflects on the whole of Scotland'. No doubt the choristers, an enthusiastic lot, would have greeted him anyway, but Currie had more detailed plans. 'Because he sometimes sneaks in rather quietly,' the singers were reminded, 'I suggest that you applaud only as he goes on the rostrum. Also, as a joke, when the women come to sing "Over the bright blue sea/Comes Sir Joseph Porter KCB", please substitute (but at the rehearsal only) "Comes Sir Alex Gibson CBE".'

There were, during this period, rewards of other kinds, chief of which was the increasing recognition he was receiving in the United States. Both before and after the SNO's tour in 1975, he was in considerable demand. His Detroit concert series led to a St Louis series, and the St Louis series to the principal guest conductorship of Barbirolli's old orchestra, the Houston Symphony. Nor were these all. The Freeman of Motherwell and Wishaw also appeared with the Philadelphia Orchestra, the Caramoor Festival Orchestra and Opera, the Pittsburgh Symphony Orchestra, the Indianapolis Symphony Orchestra, the New Orleans Symphony Orchestra, and the Cleveland Orchestra at Carnegie Hall, New York.

Where another conductor, thinking of his international image, might have arrived in each of these places with a handful of glittering party-pieces, Gibson, characteristically, did no such thing. For his debut appearance in St Louis (where one of his SNO predecessors, Walter Susskind, was by then the musical director) he chose Stravinsky's Symphony in C, Sibelius's Fifth Symphony, and Mahler's vast and structurally complex Sixth Symphony – arguably the greatest of all his works, but by no means a popular favourite.

For his daring, as well as for his conducting, he won high praise in St Louis. Then, having shown his audience what to expect from him, he went next time with Sibelius's oblique Sixth Symphony, Hindemith's Viola Concerto, Haydn's little-known 61st Symphony, Holst's *Perfect Fool*, MacCunn's *Land of the Mountain and Flood*, and Elgar's First Symphony (its St Louis première, conducted with such breadth that Elgar was hailed as 'a sort of English Bruckner'). To the Caramoor Festival he took British music: Walton's *Improvisations on a Theme of Benjamin Britten*, Vaughan Williams's *London Symphony* (a work which means much to him, and for which he reserves some of his most poetic conducting), Britten's Piano Concerto and *The Rape of Lucretia*.

But if any of these dates could be called a triumph, it was evidently the one with the Cleveland Orchestra in Carnegie Hall. Sibelius's Fifth Symphony, one of his unfailingly fine interpretations, was the main work. Berlioz's *King Lear* opened the programme. And the concerto, by Paganini, reunited him with his old friend, Henryk Szeryng, with whom he had appeared at the Edinburgh Festival and had recorded all Mozart's violin concertos with the Philharmonia Orchestra for Philips.

Paganini's Third Violin Concerto, though no more than a showpiece, was a work with which Szeryng and Gibson were already associated; together they had recorded it for Philips and given its 'posthumous première' in London, after it had at last escaped the clutches of the Paganini family, who had jealously guarded it from the time of the composer's death in 1840. Whether its copious range of scales, arpeggios, pizzicati, and harmonics was worth guarding was another matter, but Szeryng and Gibson gave it a grand modern send-off that was televised across Europe. As *The Times* wittily remarked, the 'very scale of its release would surely have flabbergasted even the demon fiddler himself'.

But in New York, the critics gave more space to Gibson's Sibelius and Berlioz than to his Paganini, praising the way he controlled the symphony's long, graded *crescendi*, along with his ability, vital in a Sibelius conductor, to 'hold back, unleash, and scale back down again'. That was the voice of *Musical America*, but Winthrop Sergeant in the *New Yorker* magazine went further. 'I put it mildly,' he said, 'when I say that Alexander Gibson took the audience by storm. His absolute mastery over everything orchestral was manifest from the start.' Of the Berlioz he reported that he had never heard the work performed with comparable clarity and sensitivity of tone. For Gibson, whose 'batonry had hair-trigger alertness', the Clevelanders played, claimed Sergeant, with a more sensuous tone than they had ever produced for George Szell. Coming from an ex-orchestral player, a former member of the New York Philharmonic, this was praise of the choicest kind.

But at home there were good things too. An all-Berlioz programme, with Jessye Norman as soloist in an eloquent rarity, *The Death of Cleopatra*, was an event to equal anything Gibson did in America. The large Gibson repertoire grew larger. The Gibson knighthood was celebrated with a chain of premières – at the Cheltenham Festival Wilma Paterson's *Et in Arcadia Ego* and Alun Hoddinott's *Passaggio*, and in Scotland Zimmermann's Violin Concerto and Arthur Oldham's *Psalms in Time of War*.

The first public performance by a British orchestra of Tippett's Fourth Symphony (composed for Solti and the Chicago Symphony) took place not in London, Edinburgh, or Glasgow, but in Inverness. Later, Gibson and his players showed their mastery of this strong, sinewy music when they took it on tour to London, Lausanne, and Warsaw – where the Poles enjoyed the performance but thought the music old hat. A Nielsen cycle, including all the symphonies and concertos, was launched. Edward Harper's First Symphony, dedicated to Gibson and inspired, said the composer, by his performances of Elgar's First Symphony, had its first performance. The British première of Penderecki's neo-romantic Violin Concerto, with György Pauk as soloist, attracted *The Times* to Glasgow, and prompted its critic, William Mann, to declare that the SNO had pipped London's orchestras to the post yet again.

As Gibson himself was prone to say, there was always something new to do, and he was always happy to do it. Everything in Scotland's musical life now seemed to revolve round him. Yet around him, too, as became increasingly evident, there was also change. In the course of his long reign over the SNO, he worked with four different administrators. During the same period, the Edinburgh Festival went through four directors. When David Richardson left the SNO in 1980, and was succeeded by Fiona Grant, Gibson knew that he, too, would soon have to decide whether he would stay or go. The orchestra was restless. Their conductor's rehearsal methods, though accepted by older players, made newcomers impatient. So did their new administrator's managerial manner, though her credentials (the Edinburgh Festival and Philharmonia Orchestra) were excellent. Richardson's parting advice to Gibson – that he should get away from Scotland – quietly simmered. Gibson did not get away from Scotland. Nor, with his first *Wozzeck* on the stocks, did he – not yet anyway – get away from Scottish Opera. But on 18 December 1981 he announced that he would resign from the SNO.

He says his decision finally crystallised during a programme planning session with Fiona Grant. He enjoyed such sessions and always took them seriously. Jean Mearns, who had been a member of the SNO's office staff since Susskind's time, has told me that nobody planned the way Gibson planned. 'He was very articulate and amusing – which made office meetings a pleasure – but a discussion of programmes could take hours. It could go round and round and sometimes even end up where it started, yet usually it had a purpose behind it. Alex has always loved to talk about programmes.'

Recognising, not for the first time, that his twenty-fifth season was approaching, he steered the discussion on this occasion in a different direction. Elgar, his favourite British composer, was to be the theme of his jubilee season, and a complete recording of Sibelius's symphonies was scheduled by Chandos. What better way to sign off? Fiona Grant agreed that it ought to be then or never. But it was a decision which, to use Robert Ponsonby's expression, must have cost him dear.

Orchestras, famously, are hotbeds of rumours, and Gibson wanted to tell the players personally of his decision before news of it leaked to the press. His announcement, when it came, took them by surprise. He journeyed from his home to the SNO Centre – the orchestra's headquarters and rehearsal hall whose acquisition he had personally supervised in 1979 – to tell them while they were rehearsing with the sombre Kurt Sanderling, who was making one of his periodic guest appearances in Scotland. 'It was,' says Richard Chester, 'an incredibly emotional moment, especially for him. I shall never forget it. Veronica was by his side, and the fact that she was there with him seemed to highlight the finality all the more. Yet he is still here, still conducting in Scotland, and he now seems much calmer, more settled in himself.'

In a public announcement, Gibson said that though he held the British record for longevity with an orchestra, 'there comes a time when the infusion of new blood is needed'. In giving two and a half years' notice, he was providing time for the right successor to be found. 'If one doesn't stop at twenty-five years,' he added, 'one feels one should see it through to thirty, and so on.'

He still had two major tours with the orchestra, both sponsored by General Accident. The first, a British one, went well and included what Malcolm Rayment hailed in *The Herald* as the best performance of Mahler's Fourth Symphony, in terms of insight and magic, since the time of Bruno Walter. Twenty concerts were given throughout England to great acclaim. The subsequent American tour, containing the same symphony along with works by Gibson's beloved Sibelius, proved more uneven.

Whether he was wise to remain with the orchestra another two and a half years was a moot point. On the one hand, it gave Fiona Grant time to find a successor, an appointment which, after much speculation, eventually went to a very different sort of conductor, the Estonian Neeme Järvi. On the other hand, it meant prolonging an uneasy relationship when a quick severence might have been better for all concerned.

The SNO was still playing for Scottish Opera, however, and the Edinburgh Festival *Wozzeck* gave the 1980s a searing send-off. Gibson was praised for his vehement and uninhibited conducting, which released all the 'whips and scorpions' of the score. Astonishingly, Berg's masterpiece, one of the milestones of twentieth-century opera, had been staged only once before by a British company, and that was nearly thirty years previously, at Covent Garden, with Erich Kleiber as conductor. Now, thanks to John Drummond's acumen as Festival

director, that production had a worthy successor. Though there were
initial problems over who should produce it (Peter Ebert, who had
allotted it to himself, had just resigned), the opportunity went in the
end to the American *enfant terrible* David Alden. Happily, he contented
himself with a starkly Brechtian treatment of the work's fifteen short
scenes, staging them without an interval ('regretfully', said a notice in
the foyer of the King's Theatre, whose management was more
concerned about the loss of bar revenue than about dramatic tension)
and permitting the music, for the most part, to make its proper point.
True, there was no window for Marie to slam, which meant that one of
Berg's instrumental masterstrokes – the sudden cut-off of the sound of
the street band – failed to register. Even worse, on the opening night, a
technical delay just before the two overwhelming orchestral *crescendi*
on the note B natural (which link Marie's murder with the succeeding
tavern scene) led to some audibly impatient cursing from Gibson in the
pit.

When Alden's production, now with some vulgar accretions, was
revived a year or so later, Gibson passed it on to Simon Rattle, who
brought his own flair and integrity to the music in sometimes difficult
circumstances. Yet Gibson's *Wozzeck* was the one that stuck in the
mind. He had wanted to conduct it ever since, as a student in Salzburg,
he had felt totally overwhelmed by Karl Böhm's conducting of it, and
had groped his way into the daylight afterwards, completely shattered.
His own performance combined the heat of Böhm with the iciness of
Boulez, and possessed a frightening force and pungency. It unleashed
the expressionistic fury of the music in a way that Simon Rattle, at that
stage in his career, could not match.

With the company's second *Madama Butterfly* and first *Tosca*,
Gibson had been continuing to champion Puccini. Inspired by notably
perceptive productions – the first set in a Gorbals-like tenement that
stripped it of Japanese prettiness, the second modishly but effectively
updated to the Mussolini period – he showed his ability to bring fresh
insights to music he loved. But other updates, such as the crass film
studio version of Weber's *Oberon*, inspired him less. This was the sort
of pre-Wagnerian score to which, in other circumstances, he might
have brought the right sense of romance, but the music was hamstrung
by a production that set out to unearth qualities the opera did not
contain.

Whatever state of backstage unease was by then building
up between Gibson and John Cox, it did not seriously affect the quality
of *The Flying Dutchman*, which showed that Wagner was still one
of Gibson's fortes, as did a series of grandly spacious concert

143

performances of Act One of *Die Walküre* with Jessye Norman. With the double basses facing straight out into the audience, and with Wagner's chords planted like huge trees in the earth, the sound of the SNO in Glasgow City Hall was rich and majestic, with Norman's great soprano voice magnificently burnished.

Sadly, Gibson's promised *Parsifal* was postponed for financial reasons (it never took place in the end). After his *Ring, Tristan* and *Die Meistersinger*, this was to have formed the climax of his Wagner cycle for Scottish Opera. An inspiring cast, with Norman Bailey and Pauline Tinsley in major roles, and Elijah Moshinsky as producer, had been assembled. A new *Ring*, again with Gibson as conductor, had also been planned, but big-scale opera was for the moment beyond the company's reach, and some years would pass before, under another conductor, Wagner was performed again.

Happily, Gibson's period as the Houston Symphony Orchestra's principal guest conductor had served to remind him that there was life beyond Glasgow. Having conducted Janáček's *Jenufa* and Verdi's *Falstaff* for Houston Grand Opera in 1978, and a variety of concerts (including a Wagner night) during the same period, he had been invited in the early 1980s to establish a closer association with the Texan orchestra. It was just the sort of challenge he needed. The programmes were intended to explore specific areas of music – the Sibelius symphonies backed up with established British masterpieces – in which he specialised. The planning of them would divert his attention from troubles in Scotland, but the opportunity to become the orchestra's resident conductor was not taken up.

An intricate non-chronological running order for the seven symphonies was devised, one programme beginning daringly with the terse and little-known Symphony No 3. Shorter Sibelius works, such as *The Swan of Tuonela*, were added. Holst's *Planets* and a liberal splash of Walton represented Britain, and space was found for uncommon odds and ends – Haydn's 84th Symphony, Beethoven's *Choral Fantasia*, and Szymanowski's Second Violin Concerto – that lay outside the proposed categories. These were truly integrated concerts, not just ordinary guest conductor fare, with the Sibelius performances capturing, it was said, the 'total mood' of the music even if its edges were sometimes rough. As one critic mused: 'Gibson seems to conduct notes not beats, but if his beat is vague his body language is eloquent.' This was well put, and akin to what Mary Miller, my successor as music critic of *The Scotsman*, would say about him in the 1990s.

Increasingly today, biographers like to demonstrate that poets are like their poems, and that composers are like their music. But can it be said that conductors are like the way they conduct? Boulez's geometric hand signals, Toscanini's rigidity, Furtwängler's quiver, Bernstein's leaps, Boult's long and waggling fishing rod, Beecham's cut and thrust, Szell's aquiline hover, Barbirolli's sweep, and Berglund's left-handed awkwardness all suggest that there is some truth in the theory, in spite of obvious exceptions such as an almost immobile Richard Strauss unleashing torrents of sound. Gibson, in earlier days, was often described as elegant. Later, by fellow Scots, he would be accused of 'porridge stirring'.

But not by me. Once, waiting backstage at the King's Theatre, Edinburgh, to interview a singer for an article I was writing, I found my attention attracted by the sight of a conductor on the TV monitor. I could not remember who was on the podium that night, and his face was in shadow. Seldom, as a critic, do I have a chance to view a conductor from the front. This one's beat looked wholly original, idiosyncratic, expressive, indeed mesmerising. I had never, I thought, seen it before, yet there was something curiously familiar about it. Could it possibly be? Surely it wasn't! But yes: it turned out to belong to Alexander Gibson.

CHAPTER TWELVE

Moments of Truth

Music being a profession as treacherous as any other, Gibson has been an unusually forgiving member of it. He rarely speaks ill of his enemies. He bears no obvious grudges. He defends what he perceives to be musical justice. When Neeme Järvi, after only four years, resigned from the SNO before his contract had expired, Gibson felt angry. Though he admired his successor's achievements, he considered the players had been let down. His old orchestra, upon which Järvi had imposed a brand-new sound and style, did not deserve to be thus abandoned, and to award Järvi the Laureate Conductorship struck him in the circumstances as 'a kind of reward for desertion'.

Yet there was no personal animosity between Gibson – who was by then the orchestra's president – and Järvi. Musically they respected each other. They got on. If, finally, Järvi did what he did, then that was what ambitious conductors often do. The trouble was simply that he did it to what until recently had been Gibson's orchestra. Nevertheless, after Järvi's resignation and Bryden Thomson's appointment as his successor, some jolly photographs were taken of all three of them wagging their batons at each other outside the SNO Centre. As a study in conductorial style, it was amusing but also revealing. Järvi, in terms of weight and swagger, looked the dominant figure. Yet he had ruthlessly pursued his own interests, and had done less than either of the others for Scottish music.

Between Gibson and John Cox, on the other hand, antipathy increased. And though the conductor characteristically prefers not to talk about what went on, it is easy to deduce – because the abruptness with which Gibson refers to him implies it – that Cox has yet to win forgiveness for the role he played in the affairs of Scottish Opera and in Gibson's fortunes, or misfortunes, as musical director.

If Gibson remains tactful about Cox, Cox before he left Scotland proved increasingly tactless about Gibson. To describe the company's founder, in an interview, as a 'sacred cow' was hardly the best way to sustain their already cooling operatic partnership; nor was his criticism, at the time of the lavatorial *Don Giovanni*, of what he described as the 'old guard' in the company's board of directors, who desired a return to the early days and the values they represented. 'They don't want the company to grow up,' he was quoted as saying. But whether the above-mentioned production, in which Giovanni sang the Champagne Aria in the loo and pulled the plug at the end of it, could be considered as evidence of Scottish Opera's adulthood, Cox forebore to mention. Indeed, the urinary *Barber of Seville* of the same period implied that the company had gained a seriously retrogressive lavatorial fixation.

With his twenty-fifth opera season now approaching, Gibson's love of numbers must again have been telling him it was time to go. But with Scottish Opera, even more than with the SNO, he still believed in what he was doing. Admittedly, his faith was being put to the test. Quite apart from its new desire to be merely trendy, Scottish Opera was no longer the company it had once been. It was faction-ridden. It was in financial disarray. Its artistic policy was a shambles. Good productions, far from being taken for granted, had become more a matter of luck than of judgment. The only stability lay in the music, and that was what some people apparently wanted to destroy.

The problem was an international one, and not confined to Scotland, but it was a pity that a company once famed for its good judgment had become infected with what seemed a particularly virulent form of the disease. Increasingly, during this period, Gibson welcomed his opportunities to escape to the United States, to Spain, to Israel, in all of which he had important dates as guest conductor. But his absences left his position weaker, and the knowledge that the knives were out for him when he was not there did not help. A rearguard attempt to bring back Peter Hemmings sounded like a panic measure. It did not succeed. But the appointment of a new managing director in the person of Richard Mantle seemed to do little more than create a top-heavy and potentially explosive division of power. In the reshuffle, Cox took over Gibson's somewhat nebulous title of 'artistic director' (which the conductor had never really liked), and Gibson himself became musical director – a more explicit title to describe his contribution to the company, though not one that suggested an increase in his influence.

While Cox spoke of a need for new perspectives and redefinition, the newly-appointed Mantle, whose previous operatic experience was scanty, more ominously told *The Scotsman* that a time might come when Gibson would 'want to stand aside'. Why the company's founder should want to do so, except through sheer frustration over what was happening to all his ideals, was never explained. Meanwhile, a tip-off I received at *The Scotsman*, saying that Gibson's successor had already been chosen, and identifying him as John Mauceri, gave substance to Mantle's remark. After comments from Cox about the company's need for 'new blood', I promptly wrote a speculative piece, which *The Scotsman* front-paged, alerting readers to the danger. It drew an outraged mailbag but, as is often the way, otherwise achieved nothing.

Why did Gibson not defend himself, the way a Lorin Maazel would have done in newspaper and television interviews if his position were threatened? All that can be said is that he is not that sort of person. He would rather resign than retaliate. Public brawls have never been his *métier*, any more than they have been that of Claudio Abbado, a conductor whom, in some ways, he resembles. Both are quiet men of music. Both detest displays of authority. Both are deeply reticent about the art they practise. Both are simply more interested in conducting than in playing the power game. Both, when faced with base and vulgar attempts to oust them from their posts, withdraw with dignity. Abbado, when he was plotted against by deceitful Viennese factions, bade a gentle farewell to the Vienna State Opera in 1991.

In the words of John Lawson Graham: 'Whether Alex was right to stand down from Scottish Opera will always remain the big unanswered question. It was, of course, typical of the man to do so. If he had been a different character and had resisted other people's ambitions, who knows what other achievements he himself could have brought to Scottish Opera? For twenty-five years he had completely dominated the musical life of Scotland, but that doesn't account for the fact that he had unselfishly brought so many other people into the picture. He seemed quite content to see other people's careers promoted, sometimes at the expense of his own, and he was always faithful to those he worked with. He trusted Peter Hemmings implicitly, and the trust was returned. But his position when Peter left was less strong.'

Hemmings himself, having failed to make headway in Australia and soon equally uneasily in charge of the London Symphony

Orchestra, now had so many problems of his own that he had little time to spare for those of his old friend and colleague in Glasgow. But John Duffus, Hemmings's former personal assistant at Scottish Opera and subsequently administrator of the Hong Kong Philharmonic, seemed to have plenty of time and an indignation so strong that it blazed its way from one side of the world to the other.

Born and brought up in Aberdeen, Duffus was someone whose career had benefited from his period with Scottish Opera, and in letters to the editor of *The Scotsman*, to me and to others, he made his feelings unmistakably clear. It was not merely that he thought Gibson was being shabbily treated. He was convinced the company was going collectively crazy (if he had seen the production of Handel's *Orlando* around that time, much of it set in an asylum, he would have felt even more certain).

Since then, we have kept in touch by letter and telephone. And since his letters are so revealing, both about Gibson and about Scottish Opera, I have received his permission to quote them.

Though he now deals in celebrity tours of Asia, with Pavarotti, Carreras, and Kiri Te Kanawa among his star singers, Duffus was no more than a novice when he joined Scottish Opera in 1971. He was initially in some awe of Gibson, yet his first impressions were of 'a man who had immense charm, was forceful in meetings when it came to matters of standards, yet who seemed outwardly shy'. His respect increased a few weeks later when he was asked if he could deliver a score of *Der Rosenkavalier* to Gibson's home that evening after work. As it happened, Duffus got caught up in other duties and it was nine o'clock before he reached Cleveden Gardens.

'V [Veronica] opened the door, asked me where I'd been, and said "Thank goodness you are safe". I did not quite understand what she meant until Alex himself came to the door. He had expected the score three hours earlier and had planned to spend that evening, his only free one prior to the start of *Rosenkavalier* rehearsals, working on the cuts. They had thought I might have been in some accident, as there was no answer from either the office phone or my apartment.'

Being a newcomer to the company, Duffus was terrified that he had not only ruined the conductor's evening but had given him the problem of having to find time to work on the cuts in this encyclopedic opera some other day. A George Szell, or even a Karl Rankl, would have torn him apart. But instead of being shown the door by a furious maestro, Duffus was invited in, offered a drink, put at his ease, and spent the next three hours talking about Scottish Opera. 'That entire evening was devoted to making me feel a part of the company, and an important part at that. Not surprisingly, it was at this time that I developed an intense loyalty to Alex as well as a strong bond of affection.'

They were both, they realised, Aquarians – Gibson was born on 11 February, Duffus the following day – and they recognised that they possessed similarities of temperament. Both could be stubborn, and both had their private sides. One day they talked about Duffus's early experiences as a studio manager with the BBC in London. 'What can I do with these tapes?' Gibson suddenly asked him, drawing his attention to the multiple rows of audio tapes of Gibson performances on the shelves of his study. 'They are in no order and I never know what is on each of them. Would you like to catalogue them for me?'

Thereafter, for many months, Duffus went to Clevedon Gardens after work, and listened to each tape, trying to determine not only what music was being performed, but when it was made and with what orchestra. 'I learnt a great deal about Alex's career, but I was never quite sure if he really wanted the tapes catalogued or whether it might just have been one of his ways of getting me a little more income.'

Their working relationship survived inevitable moments of tension. By 1978, Duffus had become the company's technical controller, and on one occasion a visit to Her Majesty's Theatre, Aberdeen, was being disrupted by industrial action. During a performance of Janáček's *Jenufa*, the local stage crew had walked out. Wagner's *Die Meistersinger*, due to start (because of its immense length) at 4.30 p.m. the following day, was seriously under threat.

'As things turned out,' Duffus told me, 'we could not get the show started on time, and we were about fifteen minutes late in going up. We also had a slight additional delay at the first interval, when I began to get extremely worried. The orchestra – and I think also the chorus – were on maximum six-hour calls. In other words, if the performance went over six hours, we had no provision in the contract for determining payment, nor in fact any agreement that the players would stay in their seats.

'By the time we were halfway through the second interval, it was obvious that we were in danger of exceeding the six-hour limit. Alex, as the conductor, had to be made aware of this, and so I went to his dressing-room and quietly explained the situation. I then quite seriously suggested that, whilst I had no right to interfere in artistic matters, he literally had it in his command to solve the problem if only he could take the very long last act of the opera at a slightly faster average tempo.

'Understandably he became angry, and gave me hell for

suggesting that he might compromise his performance because of blunders in the technical department. Yet, when he conducted it, the performance of Act Three turned out to be several minutes shorter than in previous performances and we evaded the six-hour limit by five clear minutes. Later, Alex came to me and apologised for being angry. He said I'd had a nerve to suggest such a thing to him but commended me for ensuring he knew about what could have been a major problem. He then insisted I go back to the hotel, where we had an excellent meal.'

As an example of operatic professionalism, as well as of Gibson's affection for his colleagues, the outcome of the Aberdeen *Meistersinger* would be hard to surpass. How, then, did the crisis of the 1980s ever occur? Duffus still believes that its root cause lay in what he calls the financial 'black hole' that resulted from the purchase of the Theatre Royal. Then, in the crisis of confidence that gradually followed, first after Hemmings's departure and then after Ebert's, Gibson inevitably became the key figure around whom the company had to unite.

'But Alex has never been that kind of figure. A figurehead, yes, but he is too shy to feel comfortable in such a role. I feel that the extra burden of just keeping the company going had a very big effect on him. Scottish Opera desperately needed a strong decision-maker, a leader who could rally the staff and the board of directors and influence public opinion. I know that the problems and responsibilities weighed extraordinarily heavily on him at this time.

'I know he felt that it was a good time to go. As a loyal company servant, he would never wish to outstay his welcome. But equally, I do not think some of his own supporters really knew what they were doing, simply because there was nobody there to point it out to them.'

Like almost everyone else to whom I have spoken, Duffus was acutely aware of Gibson's indecisiveness, a trait which – because in one sense it can seem like a brick wall – some people like to term 'passive aggression'. 'His staying on with the Scottish National Orchestra when everyone was urging him to resign was the most obvious case of this. He and I spoke at length about it on many evenings over several years. Most people were aware that as Scottish Opera established itself, especially in the 1970s, Alex's devotion to both his domains could engender conflicts of interest. Given that he had founded Scottish Opera, the feeling was – and I think it was true – that in any conflict, the SNO's interests would have to take second place.

'Alex worked hard to see this did not happen, but it was inevitable that it occasionally did. Many people suggested that he should consider giving up one or other organisation, and deep down I am sure he was often tempted to agree. I tried many times to make him see the sense of leaving the SNO, but he would always bring up arguments as to why he should continue.'

When, on behalf of *The Scotsman*, I asked Gibson about his future in Scotland at the time it was under threat, he predictably declined to comment. Later, he said that he would always do what was best for the company. In any event John Mauceri, a Bernstein protégé from New York, was duly appointed. Whether he was better for the company, or represented just one more wrong decision, was a moot point. Cox, before long, drifted away. Mantle's exit, a few years later, proved sensationally abrupt (he now runs a company in Edmonton, a city once described by Alistair Horne in *The Spectator* as the Siberia of Canada). Mauceri, too, has gone, leaving the way clear for a further redefinition of Scottish Opera, this time by a team consisting of Richard Armstrong and Richard Jarman, recently nicknamed the 'two Richards' (though which of them is the Lion-Heart remains to be seen). If they succeed – as their Welsh National Opera and Edinburgh Festival backgrounds suggest they might – Gibson will be the first to congratulate them.

Back in 1985, however, things looked bleak. A company statement, though reassuringly headed 'Sir Alexander Gibson to Remain with Scottish Opera', simply confirmed that he was leaving. Since he was out of the country at the time, nobody could ask what he himself thought about it. The terms in which it was couched were, in any case, masterly in their use of double-speak. With massive generosity, the company announced that their founder's contract would be extended by one year, after which he would continue to work closely with the company as principal guest conductor. His decision to do so, said the latest chairman, Raymond Johnstone, boded well for the future of Scottish Opera. The reality behind the message, however, was that he would hardly be appearing at all, that he would not be given one single new production to conduct, and that there would be seasons in which he did not appear even once with the company he had formed and nurtured.

Plainly, the conductor's supporters on the board had been duped into believing that he would benefit from the new arrangements. At least one of them, indeed, was naive enough to believe Gibson would continue to be given the pick of the new productions. But though, in the years immediately after his resignation, the repertoire included several works, including *Das Rheingold* and *Die Walküre*, in which he had previously specialised, it was his successor who usually conducted them. Since Mauceri was the new musical director, this was of course his right and he would have been curiously altruistic if he had not exercised it. Nevertheless, Gibson was invited to conduct the new staging of *The Trojans* (this time seriously weakened by being spread over two evenings) that Scottish Opera was to share with Opera North and Welsh National Opera, but a long-standing prior engagement to spend three weeks in Japan with the NHK Orchestra in Tokyo could not be adjusted to make this feasible.

What Mauceri seemed best at, ironically, was music not strictly relevant to a company whose repertoire at the time contained some conspicuously gaping holes. The fripperies of Bernstein's *Candide*, the stylistic conflicts of Weill's *Street Scene*, and the clumsy amateurism of Blitzstein's *Regina* might have been all very well in the United States, but they hardly made up for the absence of the *Parsifal*, *Don Carlos*, and *Die Frau ohne Schatten* that Gibson had promised but was no longer in a position to give. Blitzstein's attempt to make an opera out of *The Little Foxes*, Lilian Hellman's rip-roaring vehicle for Tallulah Bankhead, proved a major disaster, and only a company with an artistically floundering management would have permitted its performance (it was, in fact, withdrawn before it reached Edinburgh).

If these words sound harsh, it is to emphasise that Scottish Opera was then in no position, either financially or artistically, to make boobs of the above sort. But, happily, there were good things too, including an occasional appearance by Gibson to remind audiences what opera — especially Puccini — was all about. In 1987, the year of his resignation, it was apt and touching that his last performance as musical director was of Nuria Espert's keenly characterised and radical production of *Madama Butterfly*, the work that keeps turning up at key moments in his career. The decor may have been a shock to old *Butterfly* hands, but it undoubtedly teemed with life; and Gibson's conducting, as shimmering and truthful as ever, confirmed where operatic priorities should lie. The subsequent revival of *Tosca*, too, had its priorities right, and wholly justified the vast number of performances Gibson was invited to give. These, moreover, eloquently demonstrated that in music he loved, and with a production that inspired him, his prowess as an opera conductor was as strong as ever.

Yet he was only scratching the surface of his operatic abilities, even though he fully demonstrated that Puccini, when performed well, is an experience not to be demeaned. What he needed, as a demonstration of the company's faith in him, was an invitation to do all three parts of *Trittico* or *The Girl of the Golden West* — major absentees from the Scottish Opera repertoire — of which he would have been the perfect exponent. As John Lawson Graham has pointed out: 'It would be true to say that there is a large part of his reservoir that remains untapped, just as there could yet be a wider dimension to his place in musical history.'

But how is that dimension to be exploited when Gibson remains so diffident? It is not that his confidence has been seriously damaged, though there have been moments when it might have appeared so, and when his beat has looked not so much vague as uncertain. But to hear him unleash the black violence of Act Two of *Tosca* provides the proof, if proof is needed, that he is still a conductor to reckon with, a man in complete control of the dramatic situation and of the fiery interplay of good and evil in Puccini's music.

And the Scottish Opera Orchestra senses this, to the extent that it has asked to work with Gibson more often. 'The man seeps with musicianship, really,' says the leader, John Doig. 'As a member of the audience, the only time I've been on the edge of my seat at a Scottish Opera performance was when Gibson was conducting. And now, in the pit, it's the same. Things work, in spite of the wavery beat. The secret of his success is that you never know exactly how or why it happens. It's a strange alchemy. There's so much about his music-making which I can't explain, though I rack my brains. You know that every performance is going to be different, some, indeed, very different from others. The players have a high regard for him. He represents stability. In Puccini's operas, they've worked with many conductors. But when Alex comes in, right from day one, he shows his love for the music. He knows it backwards, and you know that it's going to be something special.

'When he conducts opera, you have to breathe with him. The most impressive thing is his control of the spacing of the music. Yet at the same time he allows you to express yourself musically the way you've always wanted to. And though I can get annoyed by some of the things he says or does, the end product is what counts. He is certainly in command of the situation. In the two years I've been leader, there have been no great problems. There is simply respect. Things have grown.

'Yet you must watch out for the things that annoy him at rehearsal, like newspaper reading, or in performances, like audience noise. I remember him stopping the orchestra when he spotted a player reading a paper. "How many years do I have to work here for you to know that I hate that?" he exclaimed. "You must stop doing it." There was a terrible silence. Yet later, during the break, I saw him chatting cheerfully to that very same person. He's not a conductor who says things just to keep an ego trip going.'

As for the audience, Doig says Gibson can be very funny, even in anger. 'Above all he hates coughers. On one occasion, during a slow aria, there was a lot of coughing right behind him. You could see him seething. Suddenly he said "Oh for God's sake," took out some of the blackcurrant pastilles he likes to suck, and passed them over his shoulder.'

For Doig, playing for Gibson has become the natural extension of listening to him conduct. 'He is his own worst critic, which is what any great conductor ought to be, and I would call him great without any hesitation, even if he has along with it a degree of insecurity. But he produces the goods. His *Butterfly* has never been better. He's stress-free these days, at home with the operas he conducts, and he can't fail to be successful under these circumstances.'

CHAPTER THIRTEEN

Quiet Man of Music

Gibson, in one of his dialogues with me, defined guest conducting as 'power without responsibility', which suggests that some small part of him is still undecided about whether being a guest conductor is what he really wants. Having held staff appointments for more than forty years, and having been on his own for only six, he has found it hard to get used to a life of freedom. But there is no doubt that his career is the better for it.

He has more time to read, to study, to listen to music, to see his family, to play the piano – a noticeably growing interest again, to judge by the ever-changing albums of solos and duets that lie on its lid ('I do it as therapy,' he says). He can decide which concert and opera invitations attract him. When he conducts abroad he knows that he no longer has to slot it into an overwhelming schedule of day-to-day events in Scotland. Yet he still has a hankering for his past life. On one of my visits to his home in 1992 I found him divided as ever between a series of concerts with the Royal SNO and performances of *Tosca* with Scottish Opera. He seemed extremely busy, and he seemed content. 'It's just like old times,' he said. For Gibson, old habits clearly die hard.

Yet at the age of sixty-seven he is not as brisk as he was. His progress on to the platform has become rather stately. Americans refer to him, without difficulty, as 'Sir Alexander', and some would probably think it rather rude to call him Alex. Recurrent back trouble – the fate of many conductors – has noticeably stiffened him. Guest conducting, once he is fully used to it, will surely suit him very well. True, he misses

156

the opportunity to do, say, Verdi's Requiem whenever he wants to, which was one of the primary assets of full-time employment as a musical director, but there are constant surprises and pleasant treats.

From France in 1992 came an invitation to conduct a series of performances of *Don Giovanni* in the handsome Bordeaux Opera. To conduct 'Finch'han dal vino' in claret country must have been inspiring, even if North Italian Marzemino, a brackish wine, was Giovanni's tipple. From Scandinavia in 1993 came an invitation to conduct *Peter Grimes* in nautical Copenhagen at the Royal Danish Opera – the first foreign company to stage Britten's masterpiece, two years after its première. Without a company or orchestra of his own, he can now more easily accept time-consuming trips, which may take him away for a month at a time. And because the children are grown up – though there are now two grandchildren – his wife can go with him.

Everyone says he is more relaxed, and his performances more positive. A profile of him in the fortnightly magazine *Classical Music* describes him as busier, fitter, more abstemious. He has gained a new lease of life, it says, and is getting out of Scotland more often. On each of my visits while writing this book some new invitation has arrived, and he warns me that he will be away in Metz, in Geneva, or on some tour with the London Philharmonic.

The English Sinfonia, a chamber orchestra with which he has struck up an association, has asked for a more permanent relationship with him. The players, a self-governing group, have voted unanimously in his favour, and he has agreed to succeed Sir Charles Groves as their principal conductor.

Kentucky Opera phones, proposing a choice of operas for his next visit. The Philharmonia Orchestra wants him to record Beethoven rarities. A conference of virologists – or could it be marine engineers? – make a date with him for a private concert to include Britten's *Four Sea Interludes* and Handel's *Water Music*. The Royal Scottish National Orchestra and Chorus book him to do Berlioz's Te Deum. Scottish Opera asks for another series of performances of *Madama Butterfly*, and offers a new production of *Hansel and Gretel*. English National Opera is in touch about its new production of *Tosca*, with Rosalind Plowright in the title-role.

Oh, and will he, with three associates, be prepared to play eight-handed piano music in aid of the Sir Malcolm Sargent Cancer Fund at Scone Palace? Two of the other pianists, he learns, are old friends: John Birch, who succeeded George Thalben-Ball as organist of the Temple Church in London, had been at college with him and played for his wedding at Old Chelsea Church; Roderick Brydon is a colleague from early Scottish Opera days; the third, Peter Evans, is the only 'real' pianist among them. Gibson accepts.

A logistically complex scheme to merge, though only for one night, Scotland's four main orchestras to celebrate the seventy-fifth anniversary of the Scottish Musicians' Benevolent Fund seems right up his street. With two hundred players involved, and Glasgow's new concert hall at his disposal, he can devote hours, probably days, to programme planning. Barber's *Adagio*, played by a hundred strings, seems irresistible. Judith Weir's *Music Untangled* looks like a suitable, relatively new, Scottish piece. Tchaikovsky's *1812* must be the finale, but, with John Lill, an old friend, as soloist, some late-night conferring is needed to choose a concerto.

Gibson's full-time secretary, the meticulous Helen Brebner, types and photocopies all his schedules on inverted foolscap pages, giving dates, names, places, and programmes. Even concerts of operatic excerpts are precisely annotated, with titles of arias and instrumental interludes. The BBC Scottish Symphony Orchestra is a name that has been occurring more often. Now that he is no longer exclusively committed to the Royal SNO, he has been able to strike up a fresh relationship with the rival band which, forty years ago, set him on the road to concert conducting. Its adventurous programme policy attracts him, and has enabled him to feature Scottish music the way he did in Ian Whyte's day. But even a Beethoven symphony, he says, becomes a fresh experience when you have been away from it for a few years and suddenly find yourself doing it with a different orchestra. 'For once you have time to reflect on it, and take pleasure in it in a way you may not have done for some time.'

The BBC players, for their part, are said to like him and — I quote a member of staff — to have gained 'unbounded respect' for him. If, as seems increasingly likely, the BBC and the Scottish Opera orchestras are forced to merge, and to share operatic and concert work, Gibson may find himself appearing with an orchestra of the sort he visualised, but failed to bring about, in his earlier days with the SNO. Though both orchestras deeply disapprove of such a merger, Gibson is one of those who might help it to work if in the end it takes place.

But discussions of the 'what if' variety have always stimulated him. It was thus, after all, that Scottish Opera was born, thus that Musica Nova was created, thus that the Edinburgh Festival Chorus was recruited, thus that the SNO made its first major foreign tours, and thus, on the long defunct Waverley label, that it made its first recordings, performing Prokofiev's Fifth Symphony rather than sticking to the commercial security of Beethoven's Fifth.

To people of my generation, Gibson's achievement speaks for itself — which does not make it any the less worth celebrating. But younger people have grown up unaware that it is to him that they owe gratitude for the existence of everything listed above. He himself will never tell them, though he will chat to them about other things on the last night of the Royal SNO proms. Were I to be asked whether, after all our conversations, I have got to know him any better, I would have to answer no. Perhaps I knew him well enough already — as well, at any rate, as a critic can ever know a distinguished performer — and I certainly now know more about the multiplicity of things he does but does not usually talk about.

But there is and there always will be a reserve about him, and an area that is probably unreachable. It does, however, expose itself in the best of his performances, in his *Falstaff*, his *Meistersinger*, his *Trojans*, his Elgar and Sibelius. And that, surely, is how it should be. It does not tell us everything about Alexander Gibson, but it will do.

World Premières and British Premières of Concert Works Conducted by Sir Alexander Gibson

Abbreviations

World premières **, first British performances*

BBC Scot	BBC Scottish Orchestra (before present BBC Scottish Symphony Orchestra)
CH	City Hall, Glasgow
ECO	English Chamber Orchestra
EFC	Edinburgh Festival Chorus
GCH	Glasgow Concert Hall (1963–8)
HWH	Henry Wood Hall, Glasgow
KH	Kelvin Hall, Glasgow
LFO	London Festival Orchestra
RAH	Royal Albert Hall, London
RSAMD	Royal Scottish Academy of Music and Drama
SAH	St Andrew's Hall, Glasgow
SCO	Scottish Chamber Orchestra
SNCO	Scottish National Chamber Orchestra
S Op	Scottish Opera
SPO	Scottish Philharmonia Orchestra
SWO	Sadler's Wells Opera – at Sadler's Wells Theatre unless otherwise indicated
UH	Usher Hall, Edinburgh

Berio, Luciano. ***Still. SNO/CH 1973

Birtwistle, Harrison. **Melencolia I for clarinet and strings*. Alan Hacker, SNO/ University of Glasgow 1976

Bourgeois, Derek. ***Organ Concerto. ECO/Oundle 1987

Brindle, Reginald Smith. **Cosmos*. BBC SO/Cheltenham Festival 1960

Butterworth, Arthur. **Overture: Solent Forts*. Wren Orchestra/Kenwood Bowl, London 1991

Dalby, Martin. **Symphony No 1*. SNO/UH 1970

—— **Tower of Victory*. SNO/CH 1973

—— **The Mary Bean*, SNO/RAH 1991

Dallapiccola, Luigi. **Sex Carmina Alcaei*. April Cantelo/SNCO/Leith Town Hall 1969

Davey, Shaun. **The Brendan Voyage*. ECO/Royal Festival Hall 1985

Davies, Peter Maxwell. **Stone Litany – Runes from a House of the Dead*. SNO/CH 1973

Forbes, Sebastian. **Symphony in Two Movements*. SNO/UH 1972

Gwilt, David. **Athletics*. BBC SSO/CH 1973

Hamilton, Iain. **Sinfonia for Two Orchestras*. SNO/UH 1959

—— **Écossaise for Orchestra*. SNO/UH 1959

—— **Piano Concerto*. Margaret Kitchin/SNO/SAH 1961

—— **Aurora*. SNO/Carnegie Hall, New York 1975

—— **Alastor*. SNO/UH 1974

Harper, Edward. **Symphony* SNO/UH 1979

Henze, Hans Werner. **Symphony No 4*. SNO/UH 1966

—— **Symphony No 3*. SNO/UH 1967

—— **Piano Concerto No 2*. SNO/UH 1968

—— **Cinque Piccoli Concerti*. ECO/RAH 1984

Hoddinott, Alun. **Passaggio*. SNO/Cheltenham Festival 1977

Holloway, Robin. **Concerto for Orchestra No 2*. SNO/HWH 1979

Ligeti, György. **Concerto for Flute and Oboe*. SNO/CH 1973

Lutoslawski, Witold. **Poèmes d'Henri Michaux*. SNO and SNO Chorus/UH 1972

McGuire, Edward. **Scottish Dances*. RSAMD Orchestra and Chorus 1990

Matthews, Colin. **Fourth Sonata*. SNO/UH 1976

Mellers, Wilfrid. **Yeibichai. SNO/RAH/1969

Musgrave, Thea. **Obliques*. SNO/SAH 1961

—— **A Festival Overture*. SNO/GCH 1965

Newson, George. **To the Edge of Doom*. SNO/CH 1975

Nono, Luigi. **Due Espressioni*. SNO/SAH 1961

O'Brien, Garrett. **A Lowland Rhapsody*. SNO/KH 1985

Oldham, Arthur. **Psalms in Time of War*. Thomas Allen/EFC/SNO/UH 1977

Orr, Robin. **The Book of Philip Sparrow*. Janet Baker/SNO/CH 1969

Paterson, Wilma. **Et in Arcadia ego*. SNO/Cheltenham Festival 1977

Penderecki, Krzysztof. **Cello Concerto*. Palm/SNO/UH 1972

—— **Violin Concerto*. Pauk/SNO/UH 1979

Petrassi, Goffredo. **Estri – for 15 instruments*. SNCO/Leith Town Hall 1969

Purser, John. **Opus 7 for Orchestra*. SNO/UH 1965

—— **A Comedy Overture*. SNO/UH 1972

Schoenberg, Arnold. *Violin Concerto.* Wolfgang Marschner/SNO/SAH 1960

Schuller, Gunther. *Spectra.* SNO/SAH 1961

Stevenson, Ronald. **Piano Concerto No 1.* Stevenson/SNO/Music Hall, Edinburgh 1967

Stockhausen, Karlheinz. *Gruppen for Three Orchestras.* Gibson/Del Mar/ Carewe SNO/SAH 1961

Sweeney, William. **Sunset Song.* SNO/CH 1986

—— **Air, Strathspey and Reel.* SNO/KH 1990

Wilson, Thomas. **Te Deum.* EFC/SNO/UH 1971

—— **Symphony No 3.* SNO/HWH 1979

Williams, Graham. **Symphony.* SNO/UH 1972

Wordsworth, William. **Confluence Variations for Full Orchestra.* SNO/Eden Court Theatre, Inverness 1976

Zimmermann, Bernd Alois. *Violin Concerto.* Gawriloff/SNO/UH 1978

Scottish Works Conducted by Sir Alexander Gibson

(The year of his first performance of each work is given)

Abbreviations as in Appendix 1
Dalby, Martin. *Conflict – Three Episodes for Orchestra.* SNO/UH 1965
—— ***Symphony No 1.* SNO/UH 1970
—— ***Tower of Victory.* SNO/CH 1973
Dare, Marie. *Highland Sketch No 1.* BBC Scot/Glasgow 1953
Davie, Cedric Thorpe. *Variations on a Theme of A. C. Mackenzie.* BBC Scot/ Glasgow 1953
—— *The Forrigan Suite.* BBC Scot/Glasgow 1953
—— *Variations on a Theme of Dr Arne.* SNO/UH 1968
—— *Fantasia on Four Scottish Tunes.* SNO/Kelvin Hall, Glasgow 1968
—— *Royal Mile – March.* SNO/RFH 1969
Dorward, David. *Concerto for Wind and Percussion.* SNO/UH 1968
—— *Ode.* SNO/UH 1971
Finlay, Kenneth G. *Prelude for String Orchestra.* BBC Scot/Glasgow 1953
Gwilt, David. ***Athletics.* BBC SSO/CH 1973
Hamilton, Iain. ***Sinfonia for Two Orchestras.* SNO/UH 1959
—— ***Écossaise for Orchestra.* SNO/UH 1959
—— *Violin Concerto.* Manoug Parikian/SNO/UH 1961
—— ***Piano Concerto.* Margaret Kitchin/SNO/SAH 1961
—— *The Bermudas.* SNO/UH 1971
—— ***Alastor.* SNO/UH 1974
—— ***Aurora.* SNO/Carnegie Hall, New York 1975
—— *Circus for Two Trumpets and Orchestra.* Philip Jones/Elgar Howarth/ SNO/UH 1973

—— **The Catiline Conspiracy.* S Op/McRobert Centre, Stirling 1974

Lawson, Gordon. *Divertimento for Strings.* SNO/GCH 1963

McCunn, Hamish. *Land of the Mountain and Flood Overture.* BBC Scot/ Glasgow 1952

—— *The Ship o' The Fiend.* BBC Scot/Glasgow 1952

—— *The Dowie Dens of Yarrow.* BBC Scot 1953

McEwen, J. B. *Solway Symphony.* BBC Scot 1952

McGuire, Edward. ***Scottish Dances.* RSAMD Orchestra and Chorus 1990

Musgrave, Thea. **Obliques.* SNO/SAH May 1961

—— ***Festival Overture.* SNO/GCH 1965

—— *Four Scottish Dances.* SNO/GCH 1963

—— *Sinfonia.* SNO/RFH 1963

—— *Concerto for Orchestra.* SNO/UH 1967

—— *Horn Concerto.* Barry Tuckwell/SNO/Musikverein, Vienna 1968

Orr, Robin. *Rhapsody for Strings.* SNO/UH 1963

—— *Symphony in One Movement.* SNO/UH 1964

—— *Prospect of Whitby.* SNO/UH 1969

—— ***The Book of Philip Sparrow.* Janet Baker/SNO/CH 1971

—— *Symphony No 2.* SNO/UH 1974

—— ***Full Circle.* S Op/Perth Theatre 1968

—— ***Hermiston.* S Op/King's, Edinburgh 1975

Purser, John. ***Opus 7 for Orchestra.* SNO/UH 1965

—— ***A Comedy Overture.* SNO/UH 1972

—— ***The Undertaker.* S Op/Gateway, Edinburgh 1973

Stephen, David. *Coronach.* BBC Scot/Glasgow 1953

Scott, Francis George. *The Seven Deidly Synnes.* BBC Scot/Glasgow 1954

Stevenson, Ronald. ***Piano Concerto No 1.* SNO/Music Hall, Edinburgh 1967

Sweeney, William. ***Sunset Song.* SNO/CH 1986

—— ***Air, Strathspey and Reel.* SNO/KH 1990

Weir, Judith. *Music Untangled.* BBC SSO/GCH 1993

Whyte, Ian. *A Scots Suite.* SNO/UH 1960

—— *Donald of the Burthens,* finale. SCO/UH 1991

Wilson, Thomas. *Carmina Sacra.* Chamber Choir/SNO/Music Hall, Edinburgh 1967

—— *Toccata for Orchestra.* SNO/GCH 1963

—— *Concerto for Orchestra.* SNO/UH 1969

—— *Touchstone – Portrait for Orchestra.* SNO/UH 1969

—— *Missa Pro Mundo Conturbato.* SNO/UH 1971

—— ***Te Deum.* EFC/SNO/UH 1971

—— ***Symphony No 3.* SNO/HWH 1979

Wordsworth, William. *Theme and Variations for Small Orchestra.* SNO/GCH 1963

—— ***Confluence Variations for Full Orchestra.* SNO/Eden Court Theatre, Inverness 1976

Operas Conducted by Sir Alexander Gibson

(The year of his first performance of each work is given)

Abbreviations
S Op   Scottish Opera
SWO   Sadler's Wells Opera

Bartók. *Bluebeard's Castle.* SWO 1957
Beethoven. *Fidelio.* S Op/Kings, Glasgow 1970
Bennett, Richard Rodney. ***The Ledge.* SWO 1961
Berg. *Wozzeck.* S Op/Kings, Edinburgh (Festival) 1980
Berlioz. *The Trojans.* S Op/Kings, Glasgow 1969
Bizet. *Carmen.* SWO/Coliseum 1974
—— *The Pearl Fishers.* SWO 1956
Britten. *Peter Grimes.* S Op/Kings, Edinburgh (Festival) 1968
—— *The Rape of Lucretia.* Caramoor Festival New York 1977
Dallapiccola. **Volo di notte.* S Op/Kings, Glasgow 1963
Debussy. *Pelléas et Mélisande.* S Op/Kings, Glasgow 1962
Donizetti. *Don Pasquale.* S Op/Kings, Glasgow 1972
Gardner, John. ***The Moon and Sixpence.* SWO 1957
Gluck. *Alceste.* S Op/Kings, Edinburgh (Festival) 1974
—— *Orfeo.* S Op/Theatre Royal, Glasgow 1978
Gounod. *Faust.* Glasgow Grand Opera/Kings, Glasgow 1954
Hamilton. ***The Catiline Conspiracy.* S Op/McRobert Centre, Stirling 1974
Henze. *Elegy for Young Lovers.* S Op/Kings, Edinburgh (Festival) 1970
Humperdinck. *Hansel and Gretel.* SWO 1956
Janáček. *Jenufa.* S Op/Theatre Royal, Glasgow 1978

Lehár. *The Merry Widow.* SWO 1958
Leoncavallo. *Pagliacci.* SWO 1955
Menotti. *The Consul.* SWO 1954
—— *The Telephone.* SWO 1957
Milhaud. *Salade.* Western Theatre Ballet and Rostrum/Empire, Edinburgh (Festival) 1961
Monteverdi. *Il ritorno d'Ulisse in patria.* Kennedy Centre, Washington, USA 1974
Mozart. *Così fan tutte.* S Op/Theatre, Perth 1967
—— *Don Giovanni.* S Op/Kings, Glasgow 1965
—— *The Magic Flute.* SWO 1955
—— *The Marriage of Figaro.* SWO 1956
—— *Die Entführung aus dem Serail.* SWO 1956
Musorgsky. *Boris Godunov.* S. Op/Kings, Glasgow 1965
Orr, Robin. ***Full Circle.* S. Op/Theatre, Perth 1968
—— ***Hermiston.* S Op/Kings, Edinburgh (Festival) 1975
Puccini. *La Bohème.* SWO 1954
—— *Gianni Schicchi.* SWO 1957
—— *Madama Butterfly.* SWO 1954
—— *Manon Lescaut.* S Op/Kings, Edinburgh (Festival) 1979
—— *Tosca.* SWO 1954
—— *Turandot.* S Op/Theatre Royal, Glasgow 1983
Purser, John. ***The Undertaker.* S Op/Gateway, Edinburgh (Festival) 1973
Rimsky-Korsakov. *The Golden Cockerel.* S Op/Theatre Royal, Glasgow 1975
Rossini. *Count Ory.* SWO 1965
Saint-Saëns. *Samson and Delilah.* SWO 1958
Schubert. **Alfonso und Estrella.* Usher Hall, Edinburgh (Festival concert performance) 1968
Smetana. *The Bartered Bride.* SWO 1952
Strauss, J. *Die Fledermaus.* SWO 1954
Strauss, R. *Der Rosenkavalier.* S. Op/Kings, Glasgow 1971
Stravinsky. *The Rake's Progress.* S Op/Kings, Edinburgh (Festival) 1967
—— *The Soldier's Tale.* S Op/Assembly Hall, Edinburgh (Festival) 1967
Tchaikovsky. *Eugene Onegin.* SWO 1955
—— *The Queen of Spades.* SWO 1966
Vaughan Williams. *Riders to the Sea.* SWO 1959
Verdi. *Aida.* SNO/Usher Hall, Edinburgh (concert performance) 1962
—— *Ballo in maschera.* S Op/Netherlands Op, Amsterdam 1974
—— *Falstaff.* SWO 1958
—— *Macbeth.* S Op/Kings, Edinburgh (Festival) 1976
—— *Nabucco.* Usher Hall, Edinburgh Opera 1957
—— *Otello.* S Op/Kings, Glasgow 1963
—— *Rigoletto.* SWO 1955
—— *La traviata.* SWO 1955
—— *Il trovatore.* SWO 1957

Wagner. *The Flying Dutchman.* SWO 1958
—— *Die Meistersinger.* S Op/Theatre Royal, Glasgow 1976
—— *Tristan und Isolde.* S Op/Kings, Glasgow 1973
—— *Das Rheingold.* S Op/Kings, Glasgow 1967
—— *Die Walküre.* S Op/Kings, Glasgow 1966
—— *Siegfried.* S Op/Kings, Glasgow 1971
—— *Götterdämmerung.* S Op/Kings, Glasgow 1968
—— *Der Ring des Nibelungen.* S Op/Kings, Glasgow 1971
Weber. *Oberon.* S Op/Theatre Royal, Glasgow 1983
Weill, Kurt. *The Seven Deadly Sins.* Western Theatre Ballet and
Rostrum/Empire, Edinburgh (Festival) 1961
Wolf-Ferrari. *The Jewels of the Madonna.* Glasgow Grand Opera/Theatre
Royal 1954
—— *School for Fathers.* SWO 1956
—— *Susanna's Secret.* LPO/Pavilion, Hastings (concert performance) 1957

APPENDIX 4

Discography

Abbreviations

CGO	Covent Garden Orchestra
ECO	English Chamber Orchestra
LFO	London Festival Orchestra
LPO	London Philharmonic Orchestra
LSO	London Symphony Orchestra
NPO	New Philharmonia Orchestra
New SO	New Symphony Orchestra
RPO	Royal Philharmonic Orchestra
SCO	Scottish Chamber Orchestra
SNO	Scottish National Orchestra
SPO	Scottish Philharmonia Orchestra

(Dates listed are those of the first issue of a recording)

Arnold, Malcolm. *Four Scottish Dances.* SNO 1962/Wav
—— *Tam o' Shanter.* New SO 1958/RCA/Decca
—— *Tam o' Shanter.* SNO 1981/Chandos
Beethoven. *Piano Concerto No 1.* Lill/SNO 1975/CFP
—— *Piano Concerto No 2.* Lill/SNO 1977/CFP
—— *Piano Concerto No 3.* Lill/SNO 1977/CFP
—— *Piano Concerto No 4.* Lill/SNO 1977/CFP
—— *Piano Concerto No 5.* Lill/SNO 1974/CFP
—— *Concerto in C for Piano, Violin and Cello.* Kalichstein/Laredo/Robinson
Trio/ECO 1986/Chandos
—— *Choral Fantasia.* Lill/SNO and Chorus 1976/CFP

Bennett, Richard Rodney. *Piano Concerto No 1.* Bishop/LSO 1972/Philips

Berlioz. *Overtures: King Lear, Carnaval Romain, Le Corsair, Béatrice et Bénédict, Benvenuto Cellini.* LSO 1970/EMI

—— *Overtures: Rob Roy, King Lear, Carnaval Romain, Béatrice et Bénédict, Le Corsair.* SNO 1982/Chandos

—— *Overture: Waverley.* SNO 1981/Chandos

—— *Damnation of Faust: Excerpts.* New SO 1958/Reader's Digest

—— *Les Troyens: Closing Scenes.* Baker/Greevy/Erwen/Howell/Ambrosian Singers/LSO 1969/EMI

—— *La Mort de Cleopâtre.* Baker/LSO 1969/EMI

Bizet. *Symphony in C, Suite 'L'Arlésienne'.* Suisse Romande Orchestra 1968/Decca

—— *Carmen: Suite.* CGO 1966/RCA/Decca

—— *Jeux d'Enfants: Suite.* SNO 1975/CFP

Britten. *Variations on a Theme of Frank Bridge, Matinées Musicales, Soirées Musicales.* ECO 1983/HMV

Bruch. *Violin Concerto No 1, Scottish Fantasia.* Hasson/SNO 1976/CFP

Chopin. *Les Sylphides.* LPO 1958/Reader's Digest

Debussy. *Fantaisie for Piano and Orchestra.* Kars/LSO 1970/Decca

Delius. *Piano Concerto.* Kars/LSO 1970/Decca

Dukas. *L'Apprenti Sorcier.* SNO 1973/MFP

Dvořák. *Carnival: Overture.* LFO 1958/Reader's Digest

—— *Carnival: Overture.* LPO 1968/WRC/MFP

—— *Symphony No 9.* LPO 1968/WRC/MFP

—— *Cello Concerto.* Walevska/LPO 1973/Philips

Elgar. *Symphony No 1.* SNO 1976/RCA

—— *Symphony No 2.* SNO 1977/RCA

—— *Coronation Ode.* Cahill/Collins/Rolfe-Johnson/Howell/SNO and SNO Chorus 1977/RCA

—— *The Spirit of England.* Cahill/SNO and SNO Chorus 1977/RCA

—— *The Dream of Gerontius.* Hodgson/Tear/Luxon/SNO and SNO Chorus 1977/CRD

—— *Overtures: In the South, Froissart, Cockaigne Overture, Handel in D minor,* SNO 1983/Chandos

—— *Pomp and Circumstance: Marches 1–5, Cockaigne Overture, Crown of India Suite.* SNO 1978/RCA

—— *Falstaff, Enigma Variations.* SNO 1979/RCA

—— *Cello Concerto.* SNO/Kirshbaum 1979/Chandos

German. *Welsh Rhapsody.* SNO 1969/EMI

Gounod. *Faust: Ballet Music.* CGO 1966/RCA/DECCA SPA 220

—— *Funeral March of a Marionette.* CGO 1966/Decca

Grieg. *Peer Gynt: Complete incidental music.* Cantelo/RPO 1963/WRC/MFP

—— *Peer Gynt: Suite No 1.* LFO 1958/Reader's Digest

—— *Norwegian Dance No 2.* New SO 1958/Reader's Digest

Hamilton. *Sinfonia for Two Orchestras.* SNO 1966/EMI

—— *Violin Concerto.* Parikian/SNO 1973/EMI

—— *Five Scottish Dances Op 39.* SNO 1961/Wav

Handel. *Entry of the Queen of Sheba.* SNO 1961/Wav

—— *Messiah: 'Thus Saith the Lord' and 'But Who May Abide'.* McCue/SNO 1961/Wav

—— *Ptolemy: Silent Worship.* McCue/SNO 1961/Wav

—— *Music for the Royal Fireworks, Oboe Concerto, Sinfonia – Acis and Galatea, Alexander's Feast: Overture.* SCO 1983/ASV

—— *Water Music* (complete). SCO 1985/Chandos

Harty. *With the Wild Geese.* SNO 1961/EMI

Holst. *The Planets.* SNO 1980/Chandos

Humperdinck. *Hansel and Gretel: Witches' Ride.* New SO 1958/RCA

Kabalevsky. *Colas Breugnon: Overture.* SNO 1962/Wav

Leclair. *Sonata No 3 for Violin and Piano.* Bress/Gibson 1961/WRC

Lehár. *Gold and Silver: Waltz.* SNO 1961/Wav

—— *Merry Widow: Highlights.* Wilson/Hay/Blanc/Hillman/McCue/S Op Chorus/SPO 1977/CFP

Liszt. *Mephisto Waltz.* New SO 1958/RCA/Decca

McCunn. *Land of the Mountain and the Flood.* SNO 1969/EMI

—— *Land of the Mountain and the Flood.* SNO 1981/Chandos

Mahler. *Das Lied von der Erde.* Hodgson/Mitchinson/SNO 1976/CFP

Mahler. *Symphony No 4.* SNO 1981/Chandos

Mendelssohn. *Symphony No 3* and *The Hebrides.* SNO 1977/CFP

—— *The Hebrides Overture.* SNO 1981/Chandos

Mozart. *Piano Concerto in A major, K 488; Piano Concerto in C minor, K491.* Hobson/ECO 1983 EMI/CFP

—— *Violin Concerto Nos 1 and 2, Rondo for Violin in B flat, Rondo for Violin in C major.* Szeryng/NPO 1970/Philips

—— *Violin Concerto Nos 3 and 4.* Szeryng/NPO 1970/Philips

—— *Adagio in E for Violin, Violin Concerto No 4.* Bress/ECO 1961/WRC

—— *Adagio in E for Violin.* Szeryng/NPO 1966/Philips

—— *Violin Concerto No 5.* Szeryng/NPO 1966/Philips

—— *Violin Concerto 271a.* Szeryng/NPO 1966/Philips

—— *Sinfonia Concertante for Violin and Viola.* Szeryng/Giuranna/NPO 1970/Philips

—— *Sinfonia Concertante for Violin and Viola; Concertone for Two Violins.* Brainin/Schidlof/ECO 1984/Chandos

—— *Concertone for Two Violins in C.* Szeryng/Poulet/NPO 1970/Philips

—— *Rondo from Haffner Serenade.* Bress/ECO 1961/WRC

—— *Don Giovanni: Highlights.* Armstrong/Mathes/Murray/Tear/Shirley-Quirk/Dean /SCO 1976/CFP

—— *The Marriage of Figaro: 'So, Sir Page'.* McCue/SNO 1961/Wav

—— *The Marriage of Figaro: 'Vengeance Aria'.* McCue/SNO 1961/Wav

—— *The Magic Flute: 'Isis and Osiris'.* McCue/SNO 1961/Wav

—— *Die Entführung aus dem Serail. 'When a Maiden Takes Your Fancy'.* McCue/SNO 1961/Wav

—— *Four German Dances.* SNO 1961/Wav

Musgrave. *Triptych for Tenor and Orchestra.* Robertson/SNO 1965/EMI
—— *Concerto for Orchestra.* SNO 1975/Decca
Musorgsky. *Gopak, Sorotchinsy Fair.* SNO 1960/Wav
—— *Night on the Bare Mountain.* New SO 1958/RCA/Decca
—— *Gnomus (Pictures at an Exhibition).* New SO 1958/RCA/Decca
Nielsen. *Symphony No 5, Helios Overture.* SNO 1978/RCA
—— *Symphony No 4, Pan and Syrinx, Rhapsodic Overture: A Journey to the Faroes.* SNO 1979/RCA
Orr. *Symphony No 1.* SNO 1965/HMV
Paganini. *Violin Concerto No 1.* Szeryng/LSO 1976/Philips
—— *Violin Concerto No 3.* Szeryng/LSO 1970/Philips
—— *Violin Concerto No 4.* Szeryng/LSO 1976/Philips
—— *Moto Perpetuo Op 11.* New SO 1958/Reader's Digest
Prokofiev. *Symphony No 5.* SNO 1963/Wav/HMV
—— *March and Scherzo ('The Love of Three Oranges').* SNO 1962/Wav
Puccini. *Tosca.* Milanov, Corelli, Guelfi. Royal Opera House/CGO 1957/ Standing Room Only
Rakhmaninov. *Piano Concerto No 1.* Binns/LPO 1968/WRC
—— *Symphony No 2.* SNO 1981/Chandos
Ravel. *Ma Mère l'Oye: Suite.* SNO 1975/CFP
Rossini. *Overtures: Barber of Seville, Thieving Magpie, William Tell.* LFO 1963/WRC
—— *Overture: Il Signor Bruschino.* SNO 1960/Wav
—— *La Boutique Fantasque* (arr. Respighi): *Excerpts.* SNO 1973/MFP
—— *Arias from: Barber of Seville, Italiana in Algeri, Semiramide, La Cenerentola, Stabat Mater.* Berganza/LSO 1959/Decca
Saint-Saëns. *Danse Macabre.* New SO 1958/RCA/Decca
—— *Danse Macabre.* SNO 1973/MFP
—— *Carnaval des Animaux.* Katin/Fowkes/SNO 1975/CFP
—— *Piano Concerto No 2.* Binns/LPO 1968/WRC
Shostakovich. *Festival Overture.* SNO 1962/Wav/EMI
Sibelius. *Symphony No 1.* SNO 1974/CFP
—— *Symphony No 1.* RPO 1990/Collins
—— *Symphonies Nos 1 and 7.* SNO 1983/Chandos
—— *Symphony No 2.* SNO 1973/CFP
—— *Symphony No 2.* SNO 1982/Chandos
—— *Symphony No 2.* RPO 1990/Collins
—— *Symphony No 3.* SNO 1966/Saga
—— *Symphonies Nos 3 and 6.* SNO 1984/Chandos
—— *Symphonies Nos 4 and 5.* SNO 1983/Chandos
—— *Symphony No 5.* LSO 1960/RCA/Decca
—— *Symphony No 5.* SNO 1975/CFP
—— *Symphony No 7.* SNO 1976/Saga
—— *Karelia: Overture.* SNO 1967/EMI/CFP
—— *Karelia: Suite.* LSO 1960/RCA/Decca
—— *Karelia: Suite.* RPO 1990/Collins

—— *Scènes Historiques: Sets 1 and 2.* SNO 1977/RCA
—— *King Christian II: Suite.* SNO 1967/EMI/CFP
—— *Valse Lyrique No 1 op 96.* SNO 1977/RCA
—— *Festivo.* SNO 1967/EMI/CFP
—— *Festivo.* SNO 1977/RCA
—— *Rakastava: Suite.* SNO 1977/RCA
—— *The Bard.* SNO 1967/EMI/CFP
—— *The Bard, The Dryad, En Saga.* SNO 1978/RCA
—— *En Saga.* SNO 1975/EMI CFP
—— *En Saga.* RPO 1990/Collins
—— *Finlandia.* LFO 1958/Reader's Digest
—— *Finlandia.* SNO 1978/RCA
—— *Finlandia.* RPO 1992/Collins
—— *Luonnotar, Night Ride and Sunrise, The Oceanides, Pohjola's Daughter, Tapiola, Varsäng (Spring Song).* SNO 1978/RCA
—— *Swan of Tuonela.* LFO 1958/Reader's Digest
—— *Four Legends.* SNO 1979/RCA
—— *Four Legends.* RPO 1992/Collins
Smetana. *The Moldau (Vltava).* New SO 1958/Reader's Digest
Smyth. *The Wreckers: Overture.* SNO 1969/EMI
Suppé. *Poet and Peasant: Overture.* New SO 1958/Reader's Digest
Strauss, J. *Waltzes: Emperor, Vienna Blood, Roses from the South, Wine, Women and Song, Annen Polka, Tritsch-Tratsch Polka.* SNO 1970/EMI/MFP
—— *Tritsch-Tratsch Polka.* NSO 1958/Reader's Digest
—— *Thunder and Lightning Polka.* New SO 1958/Reader's Digest
Strauss, R. *Der Rosenkavalier: Highlights.* Dernesch/Howells/Cahill/Langdon/Blackwell/Scottish Opera Chorus/SNO 1975/CFP
Stravinsky. *Symphony in E flat, Symphony in C, Symphony in Three Movements, Ode.* SNO 1981/Chandos
—— *Pulcinella Suite, Danses Concertantes.* ECO 1982/Chandos
Tchaikovsky. *Symphony No 4.* SNO 1976/CFP
—— *Symphony No 5.* SNO 1973/CFP
—— *Symphony No 6.* LFO 1958/Reader's Digest
—— *Capriccio Italien.* New SO 1958/Reader's Digest
—— *Andante Cantabile from String Quartet in D.* New SO 1958/Reader's Digest
—— *Overture Hamlet.* RPO 1989/Collins
—— *Overture Romeo and Juliet.* RPO 1989/Collins
—— *1812 Overture.* New SO 1958/Reader's Digest
—— *1812 Overture.* RPO 1989/Collins
—— *Rococo Variations for Cello and Orchestra.* Walevska/LPO 1975/Philips
Vaughan Williams. *Symphony No 5, The Wasps' Overture.* RPO 1983/EMI
Verdi. *La Forza del Destino: Overture, La Traviata: Preludes to Acts 1 and 3.* LFO 1963/WRC
—— *Macbeth Act III Ballet Music.* SNO 1981/Chandos

—— *Un Ballo in Maschera: Highlights.* Deutekom/Craig/Hay/McCue/SNO 1977/CFP

Wagner. *Lohengrin Act 3: Prelude.* New SO 1958/Reader's Digest

—— *Ride of the Valkyries.* New SO 1958/Reader's Digest

Walton. *Belshazzar's Feast.* Milnes/SNO Chorus/SNO 1978/RCA

—— *Coronation Te Deum.* SNO Chorus/SNO 1978/RCA

—— *Symphony No 1.* SNO 1984/Chandos

—— *Cello Concerto.* SNO/Kirshbaum 1979/Chandos

Weber/Berlioz. *Invitation to the Waltz.* New SO 1958/Reader's Digest

Miscellaneous Collections

18th century operatic arias: Gluck, Cherubini, Pergolesi, Handel, Paisiello. Berganza/COG 1961/Decca

Golden Treasury of Christmas Music. Cathedral Singers/Sinfonia of London 1967/WRC

Christmas Carols. SNO and SNO Chorus 1973/CFP

Great Scottish Songs. Morrison/SNO and SNO Chorus 1976/Polydor

Music for Royal Occasions: Matthias, Walton, Handel, Elgar, Davis. LSO 1981/ Pickwick International.

Jessye Norman, Sacred Songs. RPO/Ambrosian Singers 1981/Philips

†*Alexander Gibson: A Concert Tour.* Chesky

Coronation Celebration, 1953–1993 (including Elgar, Handel and Holst). Radio Times/Chandos

††**Berlioz.** *Five Overtures.* SNO 1982/Chandos

††**Sibelius.** *The Complete Tone Poems.* SNO 1977/1985/Chandos

† This collection includes items issued by Reader's Digest in 1958.
†† Listed separately in Discography.

APPENDIX 5

Sir Alexander Gibson at the Edinburgh Festival

1959

28 August
Berlioz. *Le Corsair Overture*
Beethoven. *Piano Concerto No 5* (soloist Wilhelm Kempff)
Iain Hamilton. *Sinfonia for Two Orchestras* (commissioned jointly by the
    Edinburgh Festival Society and the Robert Burns Federation)
Elgar. *Enigma Variations*

30 August, Usher Hall
Beethoven. *Egmont Overture*
Dvořák. *Cello Concerto* (soloist Pierre Fournier)
Sibelius. *Symphony No 2*

1960

28 August, Usher Hall
Schumann. *Manfred Overture*
Chopin. *Piano Concerto No 1* (soloist Claudio Arrau)
Mahler. *Symphony No 1*

31 August, Usher Hall
Mozart. *Symphony No 34*
Beethoven. *Piano Concerto No 2* (soloist Myra Hess)
Bartók. *Concerto for Orchestra*

174

10 September, Usher Hall
A Scottish serenade, with works by Iain Hamilton, Cedric Thorpe Davie, and
Ian Whyte (soloist Ian Wallace)

1961

24 August, Usher Hall
Britten. *Four Sea Interludes*
Mozart. *Piano Concerto in D minor, K466* (soloist Paul Badura Skoda)
Schoenberg. *Variations for Orchestra*
Liszt. *Totentanz*

2 September, Usher Hall
Berlioz. *Benvenuto Cellini Overture*
Schoenberg. *Violin Concerto* (soloist Wolfgang Marschner)
Liszt. *A Faust Symphony* (with Murray Dickie and Edinburgh Royal Choral
Union)

Week beginning 4 September, Empire Theatre
Milhaud. *Salade*
Stravinsky. *Renard*
Weill. *The Seven Deadly Sins*
(soloists Dorothy Dorow, Murray Dickie, Raymond Nilsson, John Lawren-
son, Trevor Anthony, Cleo Lane)

1962

2 September, Usher Hall
Delius. *Nocturne, Paris*
Mozart. *Concert Aria, Bella mia fiamma, K528*
Walton. *Cello Concerto* (soloist Joan Dickson)
Mozart. *Coronation Mass, K317* (soloists Stefania Woytowicz, Janet Baker,
Alexander Young, Thomas Hemsley, Edinburgh Royal Choral Union)

3 September, Usher Hall
Shostakovich. *Festival Overture* (British première)
Shostakovich. *Symphony No 10*
(Both in the composer's presence)
Brahms. *Violin Concerto* (soloist David Oistrakh)

1963

30 August, Usher Hall
Berlioz. *Roman Carnival Overture*
Bloch. *Schelomo, Hebrew Rhapsody* (soloist Leonard Rose)

Beethoven. *Triple Concerto* (soloists Isaac Stern, Leonard Rose, Eugene Istomin)
Prokofiev. *Symphony No 5*

1964

17 August, Leith Town Hall
Scottish National Chamber Orchestra
Mozart. *Symphony No 34*
Beethoven. *Ah perfido* (soloist Marilyn Horne)
Lampugnani. *Superbo di mi stesso* (soloist Marilyn Horne)
Haydn. *Symphony No 98*

27 August, Usher Hall
Berlioz. *Les Francs Juges Overture*
Webern. *Six Pieces, Op 6*
Schumann. *Cello Concerto* (Scottish première of Shostakovich arr.; soloist Rostropovich)
Berlioz. *Te Deum* (with Charles Craig and Scottish Opera Chorus)

29 August, Leith Town Hall
Scottish National Chamber Orchestra
Mozart. *Symphony No 32*
Britten. *Sinfonietta*
Rodrigo. *Concierto de Aranjuez* (soloist Julian Bream)
Haydn. *Symphony No 84*

1 September, Usher Hall
Berlioz. *Waverley Overture*
Janáček. *Cunning Little Vixen Suite*
Elgar. *Falstaff*
Beethoven. *Piano Concerto No 5* (soloist Rudolf Serkin)

1965

22 August, Usher Hall (Opening Concert)
Mahler. *Symphony No 8* (debut of newly formed Festival Chorus) (with Heather Harper, Gwyneth Jones, Gwenyth Annear, Janet Baker, Norma Procter, Vilem Přibyl, Vladimir Ruzdjak and Donald McIntyre)

24 August, Usher Hall (Sibelius Centenary Concert)
Sibelius. *Symphony No 4*
Sibelius. *Violin Concerto* (soloist Henryk Szeryng)
Sibelius. *Symphony No 5*

3 September, Usher Hall
Haydn. *Symphony No 61*
Tippett. *Piano Concerto* (soloist John Ogdon)
Robin Orr. *Symphony in One Movement*
Dvořák. *Symphonic Variations*

1966

21 August, Usher Hall (Opening Concert)
Britten. *Cantata Accademica*
Tippett. *A Child of Our Time* (with Elizabeth Vaughan, Janet Baker, Richard Lewis, Forbes Robinson, and Edinburgh Festival Chorus)

28 August, Usher Hall
Mahler. *Symphony No 8* (with Heather Harper, Gwyneth Jones, Gwenyth Annear, Yvonne Minton, Norma Procter, Vilem Přibyl, Vladimir Ruzdjak, Donald McIntyre and Edinburgh Festival Chorus)

3 September, Leith Town Hall
Scottish National Chamber Orchestra
Berg. *Chamber Concerto* (soloists Maureen Jones and Brenton Langbein)
Schubert. *Symphony No 5*

1967 – Stravinsky Year

21, 26, 31 August, 8 September, King's Theatre
Stravinsky. *The Rake's Progress* (first appearance of Scottish Opera at Edinburgh Festival; with Alexander Young, Elizabeth Robson, Peter van der Bilt, Sona Cervena, Francis Egerton, Johanna Peters, David Kelly and Ronald Morrison)

4, 5, 6, 7, 8, 9 September, Assembly Hall
Stravinsky. *The Soldier's Tale* (Scottish Opera; cast: Gordon Jackson, Nicky Henson, Patrick Wymark and Una Stubbs)

30 August, Usher Hall
Stravinsky. *Ode*
Stravinsky. *Petrushka*
Brahms. *Piano Concerto No 1* (soloist Rafael Orozco)

7 September, Usher Hall
Stravinsky. *Fireworks*
Stravinsky. *Capriccio* (soloist Andre Tchaikovsky)
Mahler. *Symphony No 10* (arr. Cooke)

1968 – Schubert and Britten Year

19, 21, 23, 26 August, King's Theatre
Britten. *Peter Grimes* (Scottish Opera; cast: Phyllis Curtin, Ann Baird, Patricia Hay, Johanna Peters, Elizabeth Bainbridge, Richard Cassilly, William McAlpine, John Robertson, John Shaw, Michael Maurel, Harold Blackburn, John Graham and Dennis Sheridan)

22 August, Usher Hall
Schubert. *Overture in the Italian Style*
Beethoven. *Violin Concerto* (soloist Yehudi Menuhin)
Dvořák. *Symphony No 7*

7 September, Usher Hall (Closing Concert)
Schubert. *Alfonso and Estrella* (concert performance with soloists including Phyllis Curtin, Richard Lewis, and Thomas Hemsley, and Scottish Opera Chorus)

1969

24 August, Usher Hall (Opening Concert)
Britten. *The Building of the House Overture*
Richard Rodney Bennett. *Piano Concerto* (soloist Stephen Bishop)
Berlioz. *Te Deum* (John Mitchinson and Edinburgh Festival Chorus)

12 September, Leith Town Hall
Scottish National Chamber Orchestra
Mozart. *Symphony No 32*
Carissimi. *Domine Deus* (soloist April Cantelo)
Castiglioni. *A Solemn Music* (Cantelo)
Petrassi. *Estri*
Dallapiccola. *Sex Carmina Alacei* (Cantelo)
Haydn. *Symphony No 61*

1970

25, 27, 29 August, King's Theatre
Hans Werner Henze. *Elegy for Young Lovers* (Scottish Opera; cast included: Catherine Gayer, Jill Gomez, Sona Cervena, David Hillman, Lawrence Richard and John Shirley-Quirk)

12 September, Usher Hall (Closing Concert)
(Beethoven Bicentenary Concert)
Beethoven. *Piano Concerto No 5* (soloist Clifford Curzon)
Beethoven. *Symphony No 2*
Beethoven. *Choral Fantasia* (with Curzon and Edinburgh Festival Chorus)

1971

22 August, Usher Hall (Opening Concert)
Stravinsky. *Ave Maria and Pater Noster* (in tribute to the composer, who died in April 1971)
Thomas Wilson. *Te Deum* (with Edinburgh Festival Chorus)
Elgar. *Violin Concerto* (soloist Yehudi Menuhin)
Walton. *Belshazzar's Feast* (John Shirley-Quirk and Edinburgh Festival Chorus)

11 September, Usher Hall (Closing Concert)
Stravinsky. *Ode*
Janáček. *Sinfonietta*
(In the same concert Luciano Berio conducted his Sinfonia)

26, 28, 31 August, King's Theatre
Wagner. *Die Walküre* (Scottish Opera; cast included: Charles Craig, William McCue, David Ward, Leonore Kirschstein, Helga Dernesch and Anna Reynolds)

1972

24, 26 August, 6 September, King's Theatre
Berlioz. *The Trojans* (cast included: Janet Baker, Helga Dernesch, Bernadette Greevy, Patricia Hay, Patricia Purcell, Gregory Dempsey, Delme Bryn-Jones, John Graham, Joseph Rouleau, Norman White, Gordon Sandison and John Robertson)

2 September, Usher Hall
Sebastian Forbes. *Symphony* (Edinburgh Festival commission)
Chopin. *Piano Concerto No 1* (soloist Tamas Vasary)
Penderecki. *Cello Concerto* (soloist Siegfried Palm) (British première)
Sibelius. *Symphony No 5*

9 September, Usher Hall
Lutoslawski. *Poèmes d'Henri Michaux.* (Lutoslawski and Alexander Gibson joint conductors with Edinburgh Festival Chorus)
Walton. *Violin Concerto* (soloist Christian Ferras)
Stravinsky. *Symphony of Psalms* (with Edinburgh Festival Chorus)

1973

19 August, Usher Hall (Opening Concert)
Messiaen. *Hymne au St Sacrament*
Sibelius. *Violin Concerto* (soloist Henryk Szeryng)

Verdi. *Four Sacred Pieces* (with Sheila Armstrong and Edinburgh Festival Chorus)

20 August, Usher Hall
Strauss. *Don Juan*
Bartók. *Piano Concerto No 3* (soloist Annie Fischer)
Brahms. *Symphony No 2*

1974

18 August, Usher Hall (Opening Concert)
Beethoven. *Leonore No 3 Overture*
Mozart. *Piano Concerto in A, K488* (soloist Clifford Curzon) (In the same concert Sir Michael Tippett conducted his *Third Symphony*)

19, 22, 24, 27 August, King's Theatre
Gluck. *Alceste* (Scottish Opera; cast: Julia Varady, Robert Tear, Peter van der Bilt, Delme Bryn-Jones, David Fieldsend, Norman White and Arthur Jackson)

5 September, Usher Hall
Nielsen. *Helios Overture*
Liszt. *Piano Concerto No 2* (soloist John Ogdon)
Sibelius. *Symphony No 2* (In the same concert Thea Musgrave conducted her *Horn Concerto*)

1975

24 August, Usher Hall (Opening Concert)
Robin Orr. *Symphony No 2*
Prokofiev. *Romeo and Juliet Suite*
Beethoven. *Piano Concerto No 5* (soloist Daniel Barenboim)

27, 29 August, King's Theatre
Orr. *Hermiston* (world première) (with Michael Langdon, Lenus Carlson, Nigel Douglas, Patricia Kern, Catherine Gayer and Gordon Sandison)

31 August, Usher Hall
C. P. E. Bach. *Symphony in B flat*
Arias by Monteverdi, Vivaldi, Haydn, and Mozart (soloist Teresa Berganza)
Haydn. *Symphony No 61*
Mozart. *Symphony No 29*

11 September, Usher Hall
A Viennese Evening including Mozart and Johann Strauss (with Gundula Janowitz and SNO Chorus)

1976

23, 26, 28, 30 August, King's Theatre
Verdi. *Macbeth* (Scottish Opera; Galina Vishnevskaya, Norman Bailey, David Ward, David Hillman, Graham Clark, Lola Biagioni and Arthur Jackson)

4 September, Usher Hall
Nielsen. *Helios Overture*
Sibelius. *Violin Concerto* (soloist Miriam Fried)
Elgar. *Symphony No 1*

1977

21 August, Usher Hall (Opening Concert) (Britten Memorial Concert)
Britten. *Sinfonia da Requiem*
Britten. *Phaedra* (soloist Janet Baker)
Walton. *Improvisations on an Impromptu of Benjamin Britten*
Oldham. *Psalms in the Time of War* (Thomas Allen with Edinburgh Festival Chorus)

1978

23, 25, 26 August, King's Theatre
Debussy. *Pelléas et Mélisande* (Scottish Opera; Thomas Allen, Anne Howells, Lenus Carlson, Joseph Rouleau, Gillian Knight and Gillian Ramsden)

9 September, Usher Hall (Closing Concert)
Dvořák. *Te Deum*
Mozart. *Piano Concerto in C, K467* (soloist Clifford Curzon)
Janáček. *Glagolitic Mass* (with Wendy Fine, Anne Collins, Vilem Přibyl, John Shirley-Quirk and John Birch (organ), and Edinburgh Festival Chorus)

1979

21 August, Usher Hall
Weber. *Invitation to the Dance*
Berlioz. *Nuits d'Été* (soloist Jessye Norman)
Rakhmaninov. *Symphony No 2*

5 September, Usher Hall
Debussy. *Jeux*
Brahms. *Symphony No 1* (Lutoslawski also conducted his *Cello Concerto*; soloist: Roman Jablonski)

1, 4, 6, 8 September, King's Theatre

Tchaikovsky. *Eugene Onegin* (Scottish Opera; with Claire Livingstone, Lilian Sukis, Cynthia Buchan, Noreen Berry, Anthony Rolf-Johnson, John Shirley-Quirk, Stafford Dean, Francis Egerton, Norman White and Halcro Johnston)

1980

19 August, Usher Hall

Mozart. *Masonic Funeral Music*

Mozart. *Symphony No 25*

Tippett. *A Child of Our Time* (with Jessye Norman, Alfreda Hodgson, Robert Tear, Norman Bailey and Edinburgh Festival Chorus)

28, 30 August, King's Theatre

Berg. *Wozzeck* (Scottish Opera; Benjamin Luxon, Arley Reece, Gordon Christie, Francis Egerton, Roderick Kennedy, Alexander Oliver, Elise Ross, Norman White, Donald Maxwell and Linda Ormiston)

1981

5 September, Usher Hall (Closing Concert)

Vaughan Williams. *Serenade to Music*

Brahms. *Double Concerto* (soloists Yehudi Menuhin and Franz Schmidt)

Bartók. *Violin Concerto No 1*

Bruckner. *Te Deum* (Felicity Lott, Penelope Walker, John Mitchinson, Marius Rintzler and Edinburgh Festival Chorus)

1982

22, 27, 31 August, King's Theatre

Puccini. *Manon Lescaut* (Scottish Opera; Nelly Miricioiu, Gino Quilico, Peter Lindroos, Raimund Herincz, Gordon Christie, Norman White, Jim Croom, Claire Moll, Paul Strathearn, Alan Oke, John Brackenridge and Brian Bannatyne Scott)

28 August, Usher Hall

Mendelssohn. *Symphony No 4*

Liszt. *Piano Concerto No 2* (soloist Jorge Bolet)

Elgar. *Falstaff*

Verdi. *Force of Destiny Overture*

1983

27 August, Usher Hall
National Youth Orchestra of Scotland
Mendelssohn. *Hebrides Overture*
Webern. *Six Pieces, Op 6*
Ravel. *Sheherazade* (soloist Isobel Buchanan)
Nielsen. *Symphony No 4*

4 September, Usher Hall
Schoenberg. *Gurrelieder* (with Marilyn Zschau, Ann Murray, Jon Frederic
 West, Philip Langridge, Nikolaus Hillébrand and Hans Hotter and
 Edinburgh Festival Chorus)

1991

14 August, Usher Hall
Britten. *War Requiem* (with Galina Simkina, David Rendall and Willard White
 and Edinburgh Festival Chorus)

1992

5 September, Usher Hall (Closing Concert)
Scottish Chamber Orchestra
William Wallace. *The Passing of Beatrice*
Thea Musgrave. *Horn Concerto*
Mackenzie. *Scottish Concerto* (soloist Steven Osborne) Jukka-Pekka Saraste
 conducted James MacMillan's percussion concerto *Veni, Veni Emmanuel*
 with Evelyn Glennie
Whyte. *Donald of the Burthens, finale*

Index